QUALITATIVE CONSUMER& MARKETING RESEARCH

QUALITATIVE CONSUMER & MARKETING RESEARCH

RUSSELL BELK, EILEEN FISCHER
AND ROBERT V. KOZINETS

Los Angeles | London | New Delhi
Singapore | Washington DC

Los Angeles | London | New Delhi
Singapore | Washington DC

SAGE Publications Ltd
1 Oliver's Yard
55 City Road
London EC1Y 1SP

SAGE Publications Inc.
2455 Teller Road
Thousand Oaks, California 91320

SAGE Publications India Pvt Ltd
B 1/I 1 Mohan Cooperative Industrial Area
Mathura Road
New Delhi 110 044

SAGE Publications Asia-Pacific Pte Ltd
3 Church Street
#10-04 Samsung Hub
Singapore 049483

Editor: Katie Metzler
Editorial assistant: Anna Horvai
Production editor: Ian Antcliff
Copyeditor: Rosemary Morlin
Proofreader: Jill Birch
Indexer: Martin Hargreaves
Marketing manager: Alison Borg
Cover design: Jennifer Crisp
Typeset by: C&M Digitals (P) Ltd, Chennai, India
Printed by MPG Books Group, Bodmin, Cornwall

Library of Congress Control Number: 2012939638

British Library Cataloguing in Publication data

A catalogue record for this book is available from the British Library

ISBN 978-0-85702-766-5
ISBN 978-0-85702-767-2 (pbk)

Contents

About the authors

Russell Belk is Kraft Foods Canada Chair in Marketing, Schulich School of Business, York University. He is past president of the International Association of Marketing and Development, and is a fellow, past president, and Film Festival co-founder in the Association for Consumer Research. He also co-initiated the Consumer Behavior Odyssey and the Consumer Culture Theory Conference, two key events in qualitative consumer research. He received the Paul D. Converse Award and the Sheth Foundation/*Journal of Consumer Research* Award for Long Term Contribution to Consumer Research.

Eileen Fischer is Professor of Marketing and the Max and Anne Tanenbaum Chair in Entrepreneurship and Family Enterprise at the Schulich School of Business. She is past chair of the Entrepreneurship Division of the Academy of Management. Her research interests span entrepreneurship and consumer behaviour topics, and she is currently an Associate Editor for both the *Journal of Consumer Research* and *Journal of Business Venturing*.

Robert V. Kozinets is Professor of Marketing and Chair of the Marketing Area, Schulich School of Business, York University. He has authored or co-authored over 80 research publications, including many in the world's top marketing journals, a textbook, and two books. Currently, he is Associate Editor of the *Journal of Marketing* and *Journal of Retailing*. He is the originator of netnography.

1

Introduction

An introductory exercise

Suppose that you wanted to understand the changing meanings of the greeting cards in twenty-first-century London. You are particularly concerned with these meanings and uses among young single adults aged 18–30 who are more likely to be online, socially active, and looking for work or embarking on careers and advanced education. You know that e-cards are increasingly popular, but wonder whether both e-cards and traditional paper cards are likely to be seen as old fashioned by this target group. You also know that Greater London is culturally diverse and composed of many ethnicities and subcultures. And you know that the answer to your question is likely to differ over various card-giving occasions and non-occasions as well as over different types of relationships. How might you go about answering your question? See if you can think of at least one study using each of the following methods:

- survey research administered online;
- focus group discussions;
- observational research;
- individual depth interviews;
- a study of online material in forums, discussion groups, and social media;
- archives of the records of a subscription service offering online greeting cards and gifts.

Try to detail how you would go about conducting the study and what you would observe, ask, or analyse. If you could only use one of these methods, which would you choose? If you could use three of these methods, which three would you use and in what order would you use them? Jot down some notes about how you would conduct and use each of these types of studies, then put your notes in a safe place. After you have completed reading this book or a substantial portion of it, return to these notes and see how you might respond to the exercise at that point. We anticipate that you may well formulate the research differently after reading the chapters that follow and participating in other exercises along the way.

This book has one relatively straightforward goal. We want to help you develop skills in doing qualitative research. Our aim is to provide practical advice that will be valuable to you, whether you are a budding scholar, a budding practitioner, or someone who has been dabbling with qualitative methods (whether in academe or industry) and who wants to get better at using them.

This book also has some slightly more ambitious goals. We want to help promote a wider understanding of the differences, as well as the commonalities, in the ways qualitative research is conducted depending on the purposes for which you are using it (such as to develop a communications strategy for a new product versus to write a journal article for publication). For those doing qualitative corporate research addressing applied business problems, we want to highlight guidelines for what makes effective research. For those who are doing qualitative research and hoping to publish it in academic journals or books, we want to provide some guidance on different traditions that have evolved among scholars studying consumers, markets, and marketing. Depending on which tradition(s) a scholar or corporate researcher works in, they might well collect different types of data and do different kinds of analyses to build theory. The nature of theory itself also differs across contexts. So if this book is to achieve its straightforward goal of helping you do better qualitative research, it needs to pursue these distinctions in the purposes of the research you wish to do.

What makes qualitative research different from quantitative research?

To take the first step toward achieving all our goals, we begin by telling you what we mean by qualitative, versus quantitative, research. First, we point out something they have in common. We believe that *all* research is interpretive, whether that involves interpreting patterns in relationships between quantified observations or in recurring patterns in talk, text, images, or action. Thus we do not consider being interpretive something that distinguishes qualitative from quantitative research. So what *is* different? Table 1.1 summarises the basic differences that we will discuss here. Other, more nuanced differences will become clear in the chapters that follow and are also discussed by Sherry and Kozinets (2001).

Table 1.1 Qualitative versus quantitative research differences

	Qualitative	*Quantitative*
Nature of data	Visual and verbal recordings in rich detail	Responses distilled into numeric scores
Relevance of context	Results are generally assumed to be specific to time, place, people, and culture studied	Results are generally assumed to be generalisable across contexts and cultures
Nature and control of potential causes	Ideally naturalistic with multiple factors shaping the behaviours observed and discussed	Ideally settings are controlled and variables are manipulated or measured to allow simple causal inferences
Key research instrument	The researcher is the instrument and uses skills and rapport to gain insights based on trust	Researcher tries to be invisible and relies on responses to structured measures or choices

Richly detailed data, not quantified data. One rather obvious but salient characteristic of qualitative research that is distinctive is that it entails, primarily, the analysis of data that has not been quantified. This is not to say that qualitative researchers never provide numbers to support some aspect of their analysis; it is perfectly acceptable to include numbers in a supporting role. However, the core contribution of a piece of qualitative research lies not in reducing concepts to scaled or to binary variables that can be compared and contrasted statistically based on the assumption that they provide meaningful measures of the behaviour they seek to understand. Instead, it builds upon detailed and nuanced observation and interpretation of phenomena of interest. Doing so requires a commitment to illustrating concepts richly, whether with words or images or both.

Contextualised rather than decontextualised. A second, related, characteristic distinguishing qualitative research is that it is contextualised: it takes into account the cultural, social, institutional, temporal, and personal or interpersonal characteristics of the context in which the data is collected. While quantitative research may sometimes be contextualised, it is often the case that quantitative data from distinct contexts are gathered and combined, and that interpretations stress that which is assumed to be generalisable across times and places. In qualitative research, data are frequently gathered from a single context or a narrow range of contexts, and immense care is taken to understand how the context matters to the phenomena under consideration. Theoretical claims and managerial insights developed from qualitative data analysis are thus based on characteristics of the context, and it is common for qualitative researchers to circumscribe the domain within which their findings are applicable as a result of the context of the research. For example, a doctoral student in our department, Mandy Earley, is currently doing research on the activists in the Occupy Wall Street movement in New York City. Both the time and place in which this observational and interview data are being gathered constrain attempts to generalise to Occupy movements in other times and places.

Naturalism versus control. A third characteristic is that when qualitative research entails interviews or observations, these are often conducted in settings where people live, work, play, shop or just hang out rather than in settings that are controlled by the researcher, such as laboratories. While exceptions do exist, it is normal for qualitative researchers to try to observe and interact with people in the contexts that shape their everyday behaviours and perceptions. This 'in situ' characteristic of qualitative research contributes to its ability to capture insights that cannot easily be communicated by people who take for granted what is going on in the settings they frequent. And it means that qualitative researchers can often learn things that the people they study may not be able to articulate. For example, one of us (Eileen) is currently observing entrepreneurs' use of Twitter to communicate with stakeholders. She interviewed them first to see what they explicitly state about why and how they communicate. Her analysis thus far shows recurrent patterns in the tweets of some entrepreneurs, such as the use of intensely emotional language. These emotion-laden tweets would not have been anticipated based on interviews alone, and variation in emotional language usage would not likely have been considered for inclusion in a controlled experiment on social media based corporate communication. In this project as in many others, the naturalism of observing actual behaviours affords insights that would otherwise have been missed.

Researcher as instrument versus detached instrumentation. A final point of differentiation between quantitative and qualitative work concerns the researcher's relationship to the data. With quantitative research, care is taken to create instruments (such as questionnaires) that are meant to reduce the impact of the researchers on the data that is collected. In qualitative research, the researcher *is* the primary instrument of data collection. The researcher's skills in building trust as well as in hearing and seeing what is going on in a setting, and in asking questions that could not have been anticipated prior to immersion in the setting, are crucial to the success of a qualitative project. Rather than the hands-off and distant approach of most quantitative research, the qualitative researcher develops a deep connection to the context being investigated and often builds a relationship with those being studied.

Why is qualitative research so valuable?

All three of us have immense respect for the insights that quantitative research can yield. But as people who have spent most of their professional lives using qualitative methods to understand the things that interest us, we are convinced that qualitative research is invaluable because it provides unique insights into *how* consumers, marketers, and markets behave, and into *why* they behave as they do.

Take Christmas gift shopping as an example. In particular, let us try to understand how the Christmas shopping gets done, and why the work of gift shopping tends to get divided rather unevenly in so many families, with women doing the bulk of the work in households that include heterosexual couples (Fischer and Arnold 1990). Quantitative approaches are excellent for measuring variables such as how many gifts each member of a household purchases, how many hours the adults spend shopping, how much money they spend per gift, and how many 'self-gifts' each person buys as they shop for other people. They are also great for looking at patterns of association between social psychological variables (such a gender-role attitudes or gender identity) and specific shopping behaviours.

But qualitative research can help to identify the cultural discourses and market place mythologies that infuse shopping activity with meaning. They can help us understand that Christmas gift shopping has, in North America, been socially constructed as an extension of the feminised work of caring for and perpetuating the ties that matter to families. They can help us, too, to understand the varied experiences recounted by people who enjoy the 'fun' of Christmas shopping in the intensified retail environment that builds to a peak in the weeks leading up to 25 December, compared with those who dread the harried overload of work that Christmas shopping entails, and who attempt to incorporate gift search into their routines throughout the year (Fischer and Arnold 1990). They can also help us understand what consumers mean when they refer to a gift recipient who is 'difficult to buy for' – and to appreciate that consumers feel someone is easy to buy for when they can fulfil certain desirable social roles by shopping for them (Otnes et al. 1993).

As this example illustrates, quantitative approaches are neither inferior nor superior to qualitative ones. Whether you are a marketer trying to help stressed-out women 'cope' with Christmas or a scholar attempting to understand the persistence of patterns of gendered division of labour, when it comes to complex everyday phenomena, quantitative and qualitative methods can be invaluable complements.

Why is it important to learn to do qualitative research now?

We believe that there has never been a time when it has been more important for qualitative marketing researchers, whether they are practitioners or scholars, to develop and refine their skills in doing qualitative research. Why do we make this assertion? There are several reasons.

First, the contexts where qualitative methods can be fruitfully applied are evolving rapidly. In particular, the burgeoning range of online activities in which consumers and marketers are engaging – whether they are networking via social media sites, making exchanges in online markets, or sorting out complaints via company websites – means that there are abundant new contexts where qualitative data can be collected and where new insights into consumption and marketing can be generated. A related factor that is leading to an explosion of new research contexts is the growing appreciation of the need for investigations of contexts outside more economically developed, formerly 'first world', countries. And qualitative methods are well suited to investigating consumer and marketing phenomena within cultural contexts that have previously been overlooked, or across cultural contexts that vary dramatically from one another.

Second, among marketing managers, there is a growing appreciation for the insights that skilled qualitative researchers can bring to bear. The types of qualitative research that managers are commissioning extend well beyond the traditional focus group, encompassing ethnographic interviews, netnographies, pantry studies, shop-alongs, and much more, as we discuss in Chapters 4, 5, and 8. At the same time, the standards by which managers are judging the quality of the research they commission continue to be demanding. Those who provide qualitative research services are required to be able to tailor their approaches and integrate new techniques for data collection on a continual basis. And, regardless of their techniques or data sources, they need to be able to provide inspiring interpretations that facilitate managerial decision-making. In fact, growing competition in most industries and the continual 'scientising' of professional managerial functions in global businesses have led to increased demand for data analysis that cuts across every type and form of data. Business has a bottomless appetite for quality data to inform its decisions. It is these developments, along with a growing sense of the need to get a deeper understanding than numbers alone can provide, that seem to account for the rise of qualitative marketing research methods at a time when scanner panel data, online analytics, and other quantitative measures of consumption and competition are more readily available and abundant than ever before.

Third, for scholars working in the fields of consumer behaviour and marketing, there are many more publication outlets that accept qualitative manuscripts for consideration and that publish a number of qualitative papers each year. Although a small (and decreasing) number of journals cling stubbornly to biases against all qualitative research, the good news is that the majority of so-called top tier publications are now open to publishing qualitative research if reviewers can be satisfied that a manuscript features qualitative data that are rich and relevant, incorporates data analysis that is systematic and thorough, and offers theoretical contributions that are insightful, original and important. The same is true for outlets for videographic consumer and marketing research, as discussed in Chapter 9. Consumer research film festivals, special DVDs and online issues of journals, refereed online video streaming websites, and various broadcast and narrowcast outlets all have a hunger for good quality videographic work.

One challenge – and this is also an opportunity – for scholarly qualitative researchers lies in understanding what any given set of peer reviewers will regard as an insightful form of theoretical contribution. Although there may be considerable consistency in judgments of whether data are rich and relevant, and some consensus on how an analysis can be credibly constructed, there is considerable disparity between communities of qualitative researchers as to what constitutes an insightful theoretical contribution. We will elaborate on this point in Chapters 7 and 8, but here we want to make the point that, if you are going to publish qualitative research, you will be ahead of the game if you start from the premise that there is no one gold standard when it comes to how you should craft a theoretical contribution. Rather, there are diverse sets of practices that you can learn to identify and adapt to depending on where you want to publish. For instance, within some leading journals, the normal way of expressing theoretical contributions is by creating an inventory of propositions; in others, propositional inventories are virtually taboo and findings are expressed in terms of interrelated themes. We believe that the diversity across communities of qualitative scholars is too often glossed over, and that a practical guide such as ours will benefit readers most if we not only tell you about the techniques you may use to gather qualitative data and the approaches you may take to analysing it, but also about the different trajectories of qualitative research practice that have evolved when it comes to crafting contributions.

Qualitative researchers who have a foot in both industry and academe also need to appreciate that the conventions for conveying contributions in these two fields of practice vary considerably. All three authors of this book currently are or have recently been associate editors at top journals in the field. All of us have a wealth of experience as authors and reviewers. In addition, we have also been involved in industry enough to be able to offer perspectives from a range of different and even divergent perspectives. So we are equipped to offer guidance that should help you gain traction in doing qualitative research that will be well received by your intended audiences.

Qualitative research in marketing: a brief history

To appreciate the current practice of qualitative research in marketing today, it is valuable to consider how and when qualitative approaches started to gain currency. In order to do so, we need to distinguish between the fields of academe and industry, since qualitative research of certain types were granted credibility among marketing managers long before it became possible to publish qualitative work in scholarly journals.

The evolution of qualitative market research in industry

Marketing historians identify the 1930s as the decade during which qualitative approaches to applied marketing research first gained recognition (Levy 2006; Kassarjian 1995). In particular, Paul Lazarsfeld, a native of Austria and a leading figure first in European and later in American marketing thought, produced studies through his Institute for Economic Psychology that included systematic analysis of hundreds of interviews conducted with consumers (Fullerton 1990). His approach entailed both probing, detailed questioning of interviewees, and the meticulous collection of survey data. His study 'Shoe Buying in Zurich' is regarded as a classic of market analysis (Fullerton 1990).

Lazarsfeld outlined his meticulous approach to collecting and interpreting consumer data, drawing heavily on the psychological insights of Freud and others, in papers published in the *Harvard Business Review* (Lazarsfeld 1934) and elsewhere. He also popularised his approach by training students, the most (in)famous of whom was Ernest Dichter. Dichter carried out qualitative analyses of such iconic brands as Ivory Soap, and was a leader in the psychoanalytic tradition of qualitative work that came to be known as 'motivational research' (Dichter 1947). Dichter's style was 'free-wheeling' in comparison with that of his mentor Lazarsfeld, but his popularity among executives was unrivalled (Durgee 1991; Levy 2006; Parkin 2004; Stern 2004).

Under the auspices of Social Research Inc. (SRI), which was established in 1946, more qualitative research techniques such as projective methods and ethnographies were adapted for use in analysing meanings in product categories such as greeting cards and radio soap operas. During the 1950s, qualitative studies of consumers' motivations for buying and using beer, cigarettes, soap, detergents, and automobiles were commissioned by *The Chicago Tribune* and publicised widely in presentations to industry leaders. Sydney Levy, who joined SRI in 1948, recounts using interpretive lenses informed by the work of semioticians and psychologists to understand how people 'symbolise their lives in the products and brands they consume, and how they tell each other stories in pursuit of their aims' (Levy 2006, p. 8).

Of all the qualitative methods that gained currency among practitioners, none achieved greater popularity than the focus group, which remains a mainstay of applied market research to this day. Pioneers of the focus group method were Lazarsfeld and his colleague Robert Merton who used them to investigate the impact of media on people's attitudes toward the involvement of the United States in the Second World War (Merton and Kendall 1946). Lazarsfeld and Merton invited groups of people to listen and respond to radio programmes that had been designed to encourage support for the war effort (Merton 1987). Originally, the participants were asked to push buttons to indicate whether their responses were positive or negative. However, this data could shed no light on why participants responded as they did, and in later studies an alternative approach for conducting group interviews was developed to give qualitative voice to participants' views through semi-structured questions that moderators posed to small sets of people gathered around a table (Stewart et al. 2007). While academic researchers have had more interest in individual interviews, commercial market researchers began embracing the focus group method in the 1950s and 1960s. Indeed, so popular is the focus group that the data collection technique has verged on being synonymous with qualitative market research among those who commission such research (Robson and Foster 1989).

Considering the reasons behind the popularity of focus groups, however, helps to shed light on some of the challenges that qualitative research has faced in the practitioner community. Bluntly put, the credibility of qualitative work – including but not limited to focus groups – has been strained in part because it has frequently been regarded as a quick (and therefore cheap) alternative to survey research. Those familiar with the effort required to do good qualitative work will know that thoughtful analysis of qualitative data is rarely fast and is often quite time consuming. When analysis is done quickly, it may well be done superficially. And the superficial quality of much qualitative analysis has long been of concern to proponents of qualitative methods. This problem dates back to at least the 1950s when Lazarsfeld cautioned that expedient approaches to analysing qualitative data were becoming too common, and would lead to a deterioration of the reputation of qualitative research (Catterall 1998).

Although qualitative research continues to grow in terms of market share, its status has often been contested. Catterall (1998) contends that the market research industry thinks of qualitative research as an exploratory complement to its more rigorous and reliable counterpart, quantitative research. Morgan and Krueger (1993, p. 9) note that among market researchers the prevailing myth has been that 'real research' is quantitative.

Catterall (1998) also points out that practitioners of qualitative research bear a partial responsibility for its beleaguered image. For example, she notes that many who make their living via qualitative research have difficulty refusing to comply with a client request for one or two focus groups even when such group interviews may be inappropriate given the client's expressed needs. As another example, she notes that researchers have difficulty refusing client requests to be present during interviews, even though the presence of client observers behind one-way mirrors may have a deleterious effect on the data obtained. Thus, in part due to practised prejudices against qualitative work and in part due to occasionally inappropriate data collection techniques and impoverished analyses that fall short of professional ideals, there remains some variability in the perceived legitimacy of qualitative research among commercial users.

The evolution of qualitative research in marketing academe

It was during the late 1970s and early 1980s that marketing and consumer researchers began to engage in vociferous debates about the sufficiency of logical empiricism, and of the quantitative methods used in theory testing (e.g., Anderson 1983). Influential sociological work published in the 1960s such as Berger and Luckmann's *The Social Construction of Reality* (1966) and Glaser and Strauss's *The Discovery of Grounded Theory* (1967) helped to provide a focus for the discontent that some scholars felt with prevailing quantitative methods. And reflection on the philosophy of science and on the related questions of methodology may well have been further sparked by dynamics in other business disciplines (in particular organisational research) where Burrell and Morgan's 1979 book *Sociological Paradigms and Organisational Analysis* and Van Maanen's 1988 book, *Tales of the Field,* inspired many emerging scholars in management and organisational theory departments to experiment with qualitative methods as a means of generating new theory.

Whatever the sources of inspiration, the mid- to late 1980s saw a proliferation of articles signalling that marketing and consumer research scholars wanted the latitude to pursue alternatives to the dominant survey and experimental methods. Several examples (listed in chronological order by date of publication, and restricted to the 1980s) illustrate the range of forays that were made:

- Bonoma (1985) argued that inductive case research should be considered a valid alternative to typical deductive research approaches.
- Holbrook and Grayson (1986) performed a semiotic analysis of the consumption symbolism in a motion picture.

- Hirschman (1986) advocated 'humanistic inquiry' in marketing research.
- Russ and colleagues including John Sherry and Melanie Wallendorf travelled across the USA in 1986 on a consumer-behaviour 'Odyssey' that entailed both depth interviews and site-specific participant observations leading to papers illuminating, for example, the functioning of swap meets (based on the 1985 pilot study – Belk et al. 1988) and the simultaneously sacred and profane nature of consumption (Belk et al. 1989). The project is summarised in Belk (1991b). See Bradshaw and Brown (2008) for a further, if more speculative, account.
- Wallendorf and Arnould (1988) undertook comparative ethnographic research to explore how object attachment, possessiveness, and social linkage varied across cultures.
- Witkoswski (1989) published a historical analysis of colonial consumers' values and behaviours during the non-importation movement (1764–1776) based on archival data.
- Stern (1989) made the case for performing literary criticism of advertising rhetoric; and
- Thompson et al. (1989) advocated the technique of existential phenomenology.

Lest it seem, however, that the acceptance of qualitative research by marketing academics was seamless, we should note that considerable antipathy was voiced by leading scholars. For example, Calder and Tybout (1987) suggested that qualitative research could yield 'everyday knowledge' but that 'scientific knowledge' relies on quantitative methods that offer 'scientific progress'. And Hunt (e.g., 1990) launched several attacks on those advocating any form of critical relativism that supported qualitative research undertakings.

Overt criticism of qualitative research waned in the early 1990s and the number of qualitative papers accepted for publication in top journals such as the *Journal of Marketing*, the *Journal of Consumer Research*, the *Journal of the Academy of Marketing Science*, and the *Journal of Retailing* has increased steadily. The acceptability of qualitative research in marketing and consumer behaviour outlets is improving, and better than it ever has been, giving us room for considerable optimism.

However, our optimism about the prospects for qualitative research is tempered by the fact that there is, unfortunately, still a subtle but pervasive bias against qualitative research in marketing's academic circles. It would be a mistake to assume that qualitative research methods are uniformly viewed as equally as legitimate as quantitative methods. As one indication of this institutional imbalance, it is instructive to note that one of marketing's most prominent journals (the *Journal of Marketing Research*), though it has published a small number of papers describing various types of qualitative data collection and analysis, has published only one paper based solely on qualitative data that offers a theoretical rather than a methodological contribution (see Workman 1993). As another indication, there are marketing departments in many business schools (among them some of the most prominent schools in the world) that have yet to hire a single qualitative researcher. In addition, those that have more than a single qualitatively-oriented scholar on staff are rare. As a final indication, although it is nearly universal that doctoral students in marketing and consumer research are trained in quantitative methods, most new scholars in the field still graduate without having ever taken a course in qualitative methods.

Qualitative researchers are acting deliberately and decisively to counter these institutional barriers. In the last decade, considerable progress has been made at institution building. The label 'consumer culture theory' (CCT) (Arnould and Thompson 2005, 2007) has been adopted as a brand name by many who do qualitative research. An annual CCT conference designed to feature and foster qualitative research was launched in 2006; it has grown in size and quality in each year since. And senior scholars have taken a strong interest in helping to establish networks to assist students in this area. Training grounds across the world have been established to provide doctoral students and junior scholars with opportunities to learn qualitative methods and to become familiar with theories of particular relevance in CCT research (for example at Bilkent University in Ankara, Turkey, the University of Southern Denmark in Odense, York University's Schulich School of Business in Toronto, and NHH in Bergen, Norway). And there are a number of other leading marketing departments where qualitative research is nurtured and encouraged (for example, the University of Bath, the University of Exeter, Euromed Management in Marseille, the University of Wisconsin-Madison, and the University of Arizona).

These efforts appear to be having the desired effect. For example, publications that take stock of the field, such as McInnis and Folkes (2010), affirm the value and equal status of CCT work and show how it complements and enhances the value of consumer research as a whole. Editorial teams at the *Journal of Marketing* and the *Journal of Consumer Research* have been openly and vocally supportive of quality qualitative research and back up their support with pages of publication. And there are increasingly high quality venues for qualitative work, such as the *Journal of Consumer Culture* and *Consumption, Markets, and Cultures*. We hope that this book not only helps to educate new qualitative researchers but also contributes to the body of work that demonstrates the value and legitimacy of qualitative research. Our cautionary notes should by no means discourage students from using qualitative methods. Rather, they should highlight the payoffs from being well versed in the rationales for qualitative research.

An overview of this volume

This chapter is meant to provide some insight into the current opportunities and challenges facing qualitative researchers. It also gives a sense of the history of qualitative research in marketing that preceded and has helped give rise to the current 'state of the art'.

The second chapter is designed to get you started in undertaking a qualitative research project. It addresses some of the differences that face a researcher commencing an applied project for managerial purposes and those that face someone at the outset of a scholarly project. It covers the key considerations that scholars must take into account when they are choosing research questions, and it looks at the kinds of research questions that can (and cannot) be answered with qualitative research. This chapter also introduces the notion of the varied 'research traditions' that undergird several different types of qualitative research, and identifies the approaches to data collection that fit best with particular traditions.

The next four chapters provide guidance for the process of collecting qualitative data. Chapter 3 discusses the art of the interview. It tells you how to prepare for an interview, and provides guidelines for conducting a depth interview. It also outlines how projective methods, such as word association, sentence completion, and picture drawing can be used to augment the standard interview. It also provides insight into the ZMET technique developed by Zaltman for identifying metaphors that encapsulate consumption experiences.

Chapter 4 addresses the collection of observational data and describes how to engage in ethnographic participant observation. It complements Chapter 3 by discussing how to conduct interviews that are part of an observational study. And it discusses the use of 'aids' to observational research such as pictures, videos, and closed-circuit television. It also discusses some of the observational techniques, such as trend-spotting, that are gaining particular favour among practitioners. Chapter 4 also discusses archives and material artefacts as sources of historical qualitative data for researching consumption of the past.

Chapter 5 details how researchers can employ the techniques of observation, participation, and interviews in the collection of online data. It gives valuable insight into the kinds of online data that exist. It then explores two different methods that practitioners in particular are increasingly using to capture and process such data: data mining and social network analysis. The chapter then turns to discussing the unique characteristics of online ethnography, in particular the specific consumer and marketing research guidelines and procedures developed under the term 'netnography', specifying what it means to observe and to participate in online contexts compared with offline contexts and providing guidance into the conduct of online observation, participation, and interviews.

Chapter 6 concludes the section on data collection by reviewing some aids that can usefully supplement the collection of interview, observational and/or archival data. These aids include audio recording, still photography, audio-video recording, the elicitation of participant-produced data, and other low and high tech data collection aids.

The next section of this volume turns attention toward analysing qualitative data. Chapter 7 outlines approaches to analysing data and building theory for scholarly research. It identifies coding as a central activity in data analysis, and discusses how to begin the 'open coding' process. It also outlines and gives detailed examples of how research questions, the prior literature relevant to the focal phenomenon, and the qualitative research tradition in which you are working can shape the codes that are the backbone of your analysis. It then details approaches to interpretation and theory building that include looking for variation in your data, looking for relationships between categories of codes, and drawing on pre-existing theoretical perspectives.

Chapter 8 explores how to analyse and interpret qualitative data for purposes of managerial decision-making. It emphasises that analysis undertaken for managerial applications must be focused on addressing or informing the relevant marketing decision, and identifies some of the major types of such decisions. It outlines a stepwise process for managerially focused data analysis, and provides 12 focusing tactics that can help enhance the quality of the managerial insight that is generated. It concludes with some suggestions for creating managerially useful interpretations.

Chapter 9 addresses the opportunities and challenges of presenting, disseminating and sharing qualitative research. It shows how different goals ranging from moving the audience emotionally and behaviourally to creating understanding, should shape the nature of the presentation of qualitative results. It considers how prior research and theory should affect research, especially that which is intended for academic publication. It also addresses a fundamental issue affecting the publishability of the research: how to be interesting and how to judge the interestingness of others' research. The chapter addresses questions of what should be presented in research reports and several different options for how your research might be laid out. Finally it goes through the process of submitting research for potential publication and how to handle reviews and prepare revisions. As with the rest of the book, exercises offer help in practising these aspects of the qualitative research process.

Chapter 10 provides some concluding thoughts, warnings, encouragement, and suggestions. These are both overall insights not emphasised in the preceding chapters and a reminder of a few points that we think deserve additional emphasis. It offers some further reflections on the importance and impact of qualitative consumer and market research. And it urges an adaptive outlook as evolving ingenuity and technology open new types of qualitative research in the future.

It is not necessary to read the chapters in order. Some (especially 2 and 7) are more geared to academic research and others (especially parts of 5 and all of 8) are more geared to managerial research. This balance as well as discussions of

how different research traditions and targeted publication or presentation opportunities should affect your research is unique in qualitative research treatments.
The same is true of our emphasis on new technologies and contexts for research
including netnography, videography, data mining, surveillance cameras, social
media, and metaphor elicitation. Although these developments are new as we
write this, qualitative consumer and market research is a rapidly developing set
of methods and approaches and there are certain to be new techniques and new
consumption contexts emerging by the time you read this. So we invite you to
keep an open mind as well as open eyes for new possibilities. At the same time,
the basics of qualitative research discussed here should remain sound, regardless
of the new tools and opportunities that emerge. The book is linked to a website
with further exercises and links to new developments in qualitative consumer
and market research.

2

Getting started: how to begin a qualitative research project

You may find that your initial idea for a research project will come from something you have observed, read about, or become curious about. Perhaps it is a phenomenon like using online deals from Groupon or consumer reactions to a technological development like nano technology, 3D television, or household robots. Ideas can also come from theory, popular culture, stories, or any other source of stimulation that initially pricks your interest. From there you need to find a focus, formulate a research question, and think about approaches to data collection. You might do some preliminary reading, observing, and interviewing or you might begin with a formal research proposal. Your research project may very well not unfold in a linear fashion and you may alternate between reading, observing, thinking, discussing, and writing. This chapter deals with the choices you will need to make when you begin a research project in which you gather and analyse primarily qualitative data. We emphasise that initial choices shape the direction of your project as a whole. In this chapter we will largely assume that your research is being conducted with a view to publishing in scholarly journals that require a theoretical contribution and may or may not place emphasis on managerial implications. Chapter 8 examines what will differ if you are pursuing a managerial project and have no desire to publish in academic journals.

Although we may not consciously think about it, whenever we undertake qualitative research projects we must make a set of choices. The sequence in which these choices are made varies, and initial choices are often revisited and revised. But in general, the choices that qualitative researchers make at earlier stages of a particular project include:

- what research questions to answer drawing on what empirical phenomena;
- what qualitative research traditions will underpin the work; and
- what kinds of data to be certain to collect.

These choices are, of course, inter-related; when we make a choice about one of them, it can have implications for all the others. The following sections offer some practical considerations on how to go about making choices related to research questions, research traditions, and data collection. Subsequent chapters deal with other questions in detail that will arise in the course of the research project, in particular:

- how to analyse the data;
- how to draw on theories when interpreting data; and
- how to create theoretical contributions.

Choosing research questions and empirical phenomena

Nothing is more critical to the success of a research project than choosing research questions that reviewers and readers – and you yourself – find to be (1) original, (2) important, and (3) interesting. It is the research question – not the context in which you study it – that is ultimately the most important criterion in determining the academic worth of your project. That is, an interesting site, event, or phenomenon is no guarantee of an interesting and important research project. It is all too common for work to be negatively evaluated or outright rejected because the authors are unable to convincingly argue that their research questions have not been answered before. And even if you can persuade your audience (whether they are reviewers or your thesis committee) that your question is a novel one, you still need to make the case that the insights that will be generated by answering your question are of sufficient magnitude and richness to be worth pursuing.

In principle, there are two basic sources of inspiration for original, important research questions: prior research, and empirical phenomena. By prior research, we mean both theoretical writing and empirical studies. By empirical phenomena, we mean either specific contexts (such as actors and actions in a particular region, community or market) or types of behaviour (such as gift-giving, gardening, or gossiping). Of course, there may be other sources of inspiration such as prior experiences, novels, movies, poems, songs or art (e.g., Belk 1986). In practice, your sources are inextricably interwoven, since the key to a good research question is that you can identify an empirical phenomenon (or some aspect thereof) that is significant, and that really cannot be fully accounted for by prior theory. Do note that if your goal is to do managerially relevant research, a good research question has an additional feature: in answering the question, you must be able to generate actionable implications for people who manage organisations associated with the phenomenon (e.g., brand managers, business owners, or public policy makers).

For novice researchers, who may not be fully immersed in a body of research, the challenge is in knowing when they have found something that is not adequately understood. Let us consider first the case of research inspired initially by empirical phenomena. It is sometimes tempting to assume that because a context or type of behaviour has not previously been studied, it will be worthwhile to investigate it. For example, you might stumble upon a brand community that no one else has studied. But does the fact that no one else has studied that particular community mean it is going to be possible to make an original, important contribution to some stream of research or come up with insights for brands managers if you study it? Not necessarily. There have been numerous studies of brand communities (to get a sense for just how many have been done, see the literature review and the set of studies included in Schau et al. 2009 and in Thomas et al. forthcoming). By now, a wide array of the characteristics and practices of brand communities have already been explored. So, while the brand community you have stumbled upon might have been overlooked, it is not necessarily the case that by studying it you will be able to come up with novel theoretical contributions.

One approach that can help when you consider whether you can address original, important research questions if you study a particular context or set of behaviours is to **look for some characteristic or dynamic that is particularly salient in that context**. For example, if other brand communities studied have all been thriving and growing, and if the brand community you are interested in is losing membership, you might be able to frame a novel and compelling research question about the factors that lead to the demise of a brand community, or about the processes of community decline. Or if there are warring factions within your brand community, you might be able to frame your research question in relation to the influences on or implications of intra-community conflict, assuming that prior work has not addressed conflict directly. One caution here: it might seem desirable to find a context that is utterly unique, having properties that are not found anywhere else. This is not the case! **If you are going to invest in studying a context or set of behaviours, you want to be able to argue that while yours may be an extreme case, the dynamics or properties you are focusing on can indeed be found elsewhere and are therefore worth explaining.**

What about the opposite extreme? Does the fact that a context has already been studied heavily (e.g., Starbucks, McDonald's, Las Vegas) mean that you should reject it as a context for your research? Again, not necessarily. What matters is finding a unique, refined, or alternative research question and research frame that promises an original theoretical contribution. For example, if Santa Claus has been studied primarily from the perspective of Western young children and their parents, what about examining the role of Santa as a focus of immigrant acculturation in the West, or Santa Claus in non-Western cultures, or Santa as a focus of nostalgia for older adults? If Santa has been studied in contemporary cultures, what can historical studies show about how the image of this mythical gift-bringer changed as department stores emerged and promoted buying manufactured goods as gifts? Or what about a study of the meaning of the old man of the Santa Claus myth in terms of cultural expectations for gift-giving in terms of age and gender?

Now let us think about coming up with research questions by a critical reading of the prior literature. One of the first challenges you will face is figuring out what books and articles comprise a 'prior literature'. Drawing the boundaries around a body of work on a topic is never straightforward. Part of the challenge is that relevant articles will not all use the same terminology. If you have got the notion you would like to contribute to the literature on brand community, you will have to read papers that include not only that term but the many related terms, such as brand tribes, subcultures of consumption, and consumption micro-cultures. And you will normally need to search not only the work published in your own field, but also in allied areas (e.g., sociology, strategy, cultural studies). Indeed, it is sometimes in the most distant fields that we find the most unique insights.

The larger the body of prior work you scope out, the more daunting it may seem to find novel, important – and unanswered – research questions. Here are three suggestions for helping you do that. First, **look for concepts or constructs that are 'taken for granted' but that have not been examined systematically**. Russ's paper on desire (see Belk et al. 2003) is an example of work that asked and answered questions about a major construct that had not been explicitly developed. Another suggestion is to **look for assumptions that are routinely made, but not applicable in every setting**. For example, Zeynep Arsel and Craig Thompson recognised that prior literature had routinely conceptualised marketplace myths as identity resources. They observed that such myths could sometimes place an unwelcome imposition on consumers' identity work, and developed research questions regarding the identity practices consumers undertake under such conditions, situating their work in the context of the 'hipster' subculture (Arsel and Thompson 2011). A third suggestion is to **look for processes that have been ignored or incompletely understood.** For example, our colleague Markus Giesler looked at research on markets and found little that explained how they change. He developed research questions relating to the processes by which markets of particular types (creative cultural markets) evolve and how calculations of price and value unfold over time (Giesler 2008).

To recap, excellent research questions may initially be grounded in either a critical reading of earlier work or in exposure to a field site or a set of behaviours that puzzles you in some way. And it is the norm that as research questions are refined, you will iterate back and forth between prior literature and the empirical phenomenon you immerse yourself in. Rob refers to this as the 'meet in the middle' process.

EXERCISE 2.1

1 Working with a peer, select and read two recent papers on the topic of consumer identity that use qualitative data.
2 Identify the research questions that the papers address (recognising that not every paper states an explicit research question, and that terms like research objective or research goal can indicate the research question).
3 Discuss how the specific contexts or sets of behaviours studied are linked to the research questions: specifically, what aspects of the contexts or sets of behaviours studied are drawn upon by the author(s) to come up with a novel, important research question they address?

Situating work within research traditions

There is not one single approach to crafting qualitative research, but rather a multitude of qualitative research traditions. We use the term tradition to refer to a set of philosophical assumptions and associated research practices that cohere with these philosophical assumptions. From the outset, we want to acknowledge that the language associated with traditions can seem arcane and at times confusing. This confusion is compounded because people frequently use different terms to refer to the same tradition. And it is particularly confusing that terms like interpretivism are sometimes used to refer to all qualitative work (e.g., Hudson and Ozanne 1988), and sometimes used to refer to only certain types of qualitative work (e.g., Prasad 2005).

One observation we make before discussing these traditions is that we have restricted our overview to those genres of research that have certain philosophical (i.e., ontological, epistemological and/or axiological) assumptions that influence research questions and research practices. Another way the term tradition has sometimes been used is to refer to a particular set of research practices that can be associated with virtually any (or at least with many different) philosophical assumptions. For example, ethnography is sometime referred to as a tradition (e.g., Marshall and Rossman 2011), but we do not single it out as such.

This is because ethnographies entail a set of practices (observation, participation, and interviewing), but no single set of philosophical assumptions. (In our book, the practices of ethnography will be covered in Chapters 4 and 5.) Similarly, the techniques of grounded theory development, as they have evolved in practice, cannot be uniquely coupled with any single set of philosophical assumptions. (Some key techniques associated with grounded theory development will be covered in Chapter 7.) We have also delimited traditions from particular theories that have frequently been adopted to inform qualitative consumer or marketing research, but encourage interested readers to familiarise themselves with some of these theories such as symbolic interactionism, Bourdieu's praexology, Giddens' structuration theory, and actor–network theory associated with Latour and others. Some of these theories align well with certain research traditions, even if they do not fully resonate with them. In Chapter 7 we will discuss how these different research traditions influence the way you go about analysing and theorising your data, and we shall discuss how theories can inform your data analysis.

After you have been doing qualitative research for a while, you will most likely be comfortable working within one or two traditions and rarely give thought to the assumptions that underpin the approaches you prefer. Indeed, scholars within any established research programme tend to take for granted an inter-related set of aims, 'facts', and methods (Laudan 1984). However, novice researchers can benefit from familiarising themselves with some of the distinctions between major qualitative research traditions, and from thinking about those within which their work will fit. An understanding of the differing traditions that exist, and of those that appeal most to you, will help make for coherence in the questions you ask and in the kinds of contributions you develop. As we discuss selected traditions below, we shall give examples of research questions that are common for each, and point to works that are partially or fully situated in specific traditions. Given the pragmatic goals of this book, we will give only a brief description of those traditions that are most common in the fields of consumer research and marketing, but we shall provide you with suggestions for further reading if you want to learn more. The traditions we will cover are: phenomenological; hermeneutic; postmodern; critical; semiotic; and neo-positivist.

Phenomenology, more specifically **existential phenomenology**, is one tradition that has gained considerable attention among consumer researchers. Craig Thompson and colleagues (Thompson et al. 1989) thoroughly describe the key assumptions of this tradition, notably that the appropriate focus of research is on the life-world of individuals and that the meanings of people's experiences are always situated in their current experiential context and coherently related to their ongoing life projects (pp. 135–137). In other words, when working within this tradition we are not seeking some universal understanding of a phenomenon like consumers' first automobiles, but instead are seeking a deep understanding of what your first automobile means to you, with the 'you' here being a specific focal consumer. **Given these assumptions, the kinds of research questions that are appropriate to the existential phenomenological tradition tend to ask about the nature of people's lived experience.** A typical 'answer' to such a question is a description of thematic patterns (e.g., automobile as freedom; automobile as extended self; automobile as sexual symbol) that relate to one other and to the overall context of the life-world, including interactions, identity, and activities. The perspective offered is initially person-specific and often attempts to eventually aggregate individual perspectives or provide a structured way of understanding differences (e.g., Tian and Belk 2006). For example, working within the existential phenomenological tradition, Craig and his colleagues (Thompson et al. 1990) studied a set of white, upper-middle class, married mothers. Their research goal was to understand the lived experience of married mothers living in a time when traditional women's roles are in flux. In addressing this goal, they inductively identified a set of three interpretive themes that they presented as mutually related aspects of the women's experience. Further they identified dialectical tensions among these themes that provided insights into the contemporary meanings of free choice.

While there continues to be considerable use of phenomenological interview techniques (see Thompson et al. 1989) among consumer and marketing researchers, it is less common for researchers to situate their work completely within the phenomenological tradition. This may be due to the fact that descriptive research questions and findings can be difficult to publish within some of the journals with higher impact ratings (e.g., *Journal of Consumer Research*, *Journal of Marketing*). Yet descriptive contributions should not be overlooked, and are typically a vital component of qualitative research projects.

Hermeneutics is a distinct tradition, albeit one that has some commonalities with phenomenology (Arnold and Fischer 1994). Among the key tenets of this tradition are the following: all understanding is based on language; we, as researchers, belong to a cultural world entailing an accumulation of beliefs, theories, codes, metaphors, myths, practices, institutions, and ideologies; this cultural world shapes our understandings and those of the people or authors of texts that we seek to understand; this zeitgeist is an asset rather than a liability that should be bracketed when analysing data. Given these assumptions, **the kinds of research questions that are appropriate to the hermeneutic tradition ask how cultural notions are shaping specific kinds of experiences and actions**. Typically, theoretical contributions within this tradition entail analyses of cultural elements that are influential in shaping thought or behaviour. For example, Eileen, together with Cele Otnes and Linda Tuncay asked 'How do cultural discourses influence key cognitions about goal striving?', in their study of women who were using assistive reproductive therapies to pursue the goal of parenthood. Their theoretical contribution involved tracing how both life-project framing discourses and culturally pervasive discourses affect the ways in which consumers pursue goals when they are difficult to achieve but highly culturally valorised challenges (Fischer et al. 2007). A considerable amount of contemporary consumer and marketing research can be situated within the hermeneutic tradition, broadly defined.

Postmodernism is a term that is sometimes used, like interpretivism, to refer to all work that includes qualitative data (e.g., Sherry 1991a). In its more restrictive usage (see for example Firat and Venkatesh 1995), a **postmodern** research tradition is distinguished by tenets such as the following: 'meta-narratives' (widely shared cultural accounts that offer explanations for how societies work, such as the notion of the free market and the law of supply and demand) are unwarranted universalisms; these universalisms masquerade as scientific or value-neutral systems of thought and are oversimplifications that need to be unsettled, but not replaced with competing meta-narratives; all knowledge, including our sense of our selves, is a socially constructed product of language and is contestable. Given these assumptions, **the kinds of research questions that are appropriate to the postmodern tradition ask how taken-for-granted understandings of phenomena can be challenged.** Answers to such questions may offer alternative (albeit not authoritative or universal) accounts for the phenomena of interest. For example, Doug Holt (2002), working within this tradition, posed questions about the adequacy of critical theorists' accounts of why brands and the practices of branded goods marketers 'cause trouble' in society. He offers an alternative, dialectical perspective to account for how brands and branding practices affect and shape consumers in contemporary settings.

Insights from postmodern thought are apparent in a significant portion of qualitative research being published today. Indeed, many postmodern assumptions such as fragmentation of identity, decline of universalising narratives, and de-centring of the self, have so influenced our thought that postmodernism might well be thought of more as a semi-formulaic interpretive lens than as a specific tradition. At the same time, the number of papers that are explicitly positioned strictly within this tradition is relatively small. This may be due to the fact that a deep embrace of postmodernist principles entails ironic critiques of established accounts or understandings of things. Such critiques can be thought provoking but ultimately frustrating to those seeking an alternative account that is more authoritative, not equally open to being deconstructed.

Studies in **critical** traditions, like those in postmodern traditions, are committed to critique of that which is taken for granted. One of the key differences between work in these two genres, however, is that work explicitly positioned within a critical tradition is committed to examining taken-for-granted assumptions and practices that sustain the oppression of marginalised groups within society, and also to identifying possibilities for change (see for example Murray and Ozanne 1991). Those working in critical traditions share assumptions such as the following: reality is socially constructed, but once constructed it comes to 'act upon' actors, shaping their assumptions and practices in ways that sustain established patterns of privilege and oppression; analysis should help to identify assumptions and practices that reinforce power and sustain oppression of specific categories of actors; individuals have the potential to become aware of conditions of oppression and to work to change those conditions. Given these assumptions, **those working within critical traditions tend to ask what factors contribute to the oppression or marginalisation of some group of actors and/or how these conditions could be alleviated**. For example, in Rob's ethnography of Burning Man, he framed research questions about the extent of consumer emancipation that can be achieved and the types of social practices that can be used to enable consumers to escape from aspects of contemporary markets they find oppressive. In answering his research question, he identified several communal practices that distance consumption communities from market logics of efficiency and rationality, highlighting that consumer escape from markets by means of such practices is likely to be temporary and local.

Much work that has been influenced by critical traditions (including Rob's Burning Man ethnography) is influenced by other traditions as well, as the demands for theory building that are common in our journals typically require that scholars identify not only emancipatory strategies but also theoretical insights from their work. At the same time, the recent turn toward transformative consumer research may help to legitimise the pursuit and publication of work that is squarely situated within critical traditions (see, for example, Ozanne and Saatcioglu's (2008) description of and advocacy for participatory action research with a critical change agenda).

Another tradition that has gained a foothold in marketing and consumer research is **semiotics** (see for example Mick 1986). Semiotic analyses focus on the structures of meaning-producing events, both verbal and non-verbal, and investigate the sign systems or codes that facilitate the production and interpretation of signs or symbols. They make the assumption that there is an intimate connection between human sense making and language; that signs are arbitrarily associated with the things they signify within any language system; and that different language systems divide conceptual categories in distinct ways. **The kinds of questions raised in semiotic analyses tend to ask how specific words, phrases, gestures, myths, images, products or practices within a symbol system acquire meaning**. For example, Russ and Xin Zhao collaborated in a study of Chinese advertising that was situated in a semiotic tradition (Zhao and Belk 2008). Their research questions asked how advertising in China historically appropriated a dominant anti-consumerist ideology to justify its promotion of consumption, how this advertising adapted signifiers to help bridge tensions between communism and consumerism, and what structural patterns of representation facilitated this ideological transition. In answering these questions, they developed a structural framework of ideological transitions.

The last tradition we elaborate upon is **neopositivism**. It may be a surprise to some that we include neopositivism as a qualitative research tradition, given the tight coupling that is routinely assumed between positivism and quantitative research. Yet the tradition of neopositivist qualitative work (often taking the form of comparative case studies) is a strong one. Some regard this as unfortunate (e.g., Prasad 2005, p. 4). Others, however, are unapologetic advocates (see for example Eisenhardt 1989). Qualitative work within neopositivist traditions is grounded in assumptions such as the following: while mechanistic, causal, predictive accounts of social phenomena are untenable, relational and probabilistic explanations of patterned regularities in social phenomena are possible and desirable; the pursuit of such explanations requires that constructs that help to explain, or that are in need of explanation, be clearly specified; the goal of research will often be to identify both the likely relationships among a set of constructs, and the contingent conditions under which those relationships might occur. Given these kinds of assumptions, **work within this tradition will typically ask questions regarding the factors that help to explain a particular phenomenon, or the consequences that may arise when a particular phenomenon occurs.** For example, Susan Fournier (1998) posed basic questions about how consumers come to form relationships with brands. Her inductive analysis led to the specification of the construct of brand relationship quality and to the identification of relationship factors conducive to brand relationships of higher quality. Though neopositivist traditions of qualitative research are rarely explicitly acknowledged within the fields of consumer research and marketing, their influence can be seen in that many research projects entail efforts to account for patterned regularities in social phenomena.

To finish our discussion of research traditions, we make three observations. First, it is extremely common for work to span two or sometimes even three research traditions, emphasising some but not all elements of each. Second, research traditions are not set in stone. They evolve over time; practices that originated within one tradition may be adapted to suit the purposes of another. Third, the majority of these traditions have historically focused primarily on the spoken or written word – on what people say rather than what they do. Yet observational methods (see Chapter 4) begin with the assumption that what people say is very often discrepant with what they do. And we believe that much of the best qualitative research incorporates observation when possible. We note that some evolution in research traditions to take into account not only insights based on observation of behaviour, but an appreciation of the materiality of objects (see e.g., Zwick and Dholakia 2006) is occurring, and we welcome this. This should make it clear that we are not presenting these research traditions as rigid orthodoxies to be adhered to in some restrictive manner. Rather, we offer this discussion as a guide that will allow novices to appreciate the variety they observe across various examples of qualitative research, and to think about how their own research might be situated in the midst of that variety.

EXERCISE 2.2

1 Read two recently published papers based on the analysis of qualitative data.
2 Identify the research traditions that the papers are situated in.
3 Consider how the research projects might have differed had they been situated in a different research tradition.

Matching data collection plans with research traditions

Qualitative data can be collected via interviews, projective techniques, archival sources, ethnography, netnography, or observations (on- or off-line). And neither research questions nor research traditions strictly prescribe or proscribe the use of particular types of data. However, it is worth briefly noting that the research traditions in which your questions are situated may make it desirable for you to plan to collect certain kinds of data.

In particular, we would suggest that if your work is to be situated in a phenomenological tradition, you should plan to place the bulk of your effort on gathering interview data. Since phenomenology is focused on the life-worlds of individuals, it would be difficult if not impossible to get insight into these without carefully crafted, non-directive interviews. Introspection can also be a source of data for a phenomenological approach (Giorgi 1985). As supplements, diaries or letters might be useful. Observational data, for example, simply cannot provide the kinds of access to reflective thought that is the main target of analysis in phenomenological work, though it can be a useful complement to interviews and introspection: feeding back reflections on what has been observed to informants who are unaware of their own behavioural patterns can stimulate further introspection on their part. But if you are situating work squarely within a phenomenological tradition, observations alone will not be sufficient.

Work situated in a hermeneutic tradition can draw on interviews, texts produced by relevant people or groups, and on ethnography or netnography. Note, however, that the kind of interviews appropriate for work in the hermeneutic tradition are different from those situated in the phenomenological tradition. As Moisander et al. (2009) argue, psychologically oriented interviews are appropriate for phenomenological research, but hermeneutic research requires interviews that do more to explore the cultural categories and discourses that inform people's views and actions.

Observations alone would rarely be sufficient for projects rooted in a hermeneutic tradition since they require access to understandings as articulated by informants. However, observations can be extremely useful supplements to interview data as they can help researchers to appreciate understandings that are taken-for-granted but not articulated by those being studied. Indeed, the contrast of talk and action can be extremely valuable in work of this kind (Arnould and Wallendorf 1994). Since the scholar working in a hermeneutic tradition is drawing on broader cultural understandings (including their own, of which they may be only tacitly aware) it will typically be vital for those working in a hermeneutic tradition to familiarise themselves with historical, sociological and cultural scholarship that helps to situate the empirical phenomenon under investigation in a socio-historical context. Archival materials available online and in mass media may also be useful for tuning in to cultural understandings.

If you are hoping to situate your work specifically within a defined postmodern tradition, it is likely that texts will be a primary source of data. The metanarratives that are the typical target of postmodern analyses will be enshrined in texts of varying kinds, ranging from advertisements to the writings of other scholars. Interview data may be supplementary to textual data, as the things people say are inevitably influenced by metanarratives and taken-for-granted understandings that can be deconstructed in order to reveal these influences and their logics.

Work within critical traditions will often draw upon interview and ethnographic data to help to understand the experiences of marginalisation or powerlessness that people experience, and their efforts to understand and alleviate that which they find objectionable. To understand the factors that shape conditions that empower some and marginalise others, and to understand the possible ways of alleviating those factors, other data are almost inevitably required. Archival data that sheds light on the conditions giving rise to patterns of power and control will often be useful, as will relevant historical, sociological and cultural analyses of the context under consideration.

Those working in semiotic traditions will typically study archival texts (verbal or visual) that have been deliberately created for some communicative purpose, such as advertisements. However, texts that are created in response to questions, such as interview data, have also been deployed within the semiotic tradition (e.g., Grayson and Martinec 2004). It would be unusual to collect observational or ethnographic data for work within a semiotic tradition.

Finally, work within neopositivist traditions may draw on virtually any and every kind of data. It would be rare for work in these traditions to rely on interview data alone, but it is common for interview data to be included in the set of data collected for such a project. Work in these traditions will often seek triangulation across data sources, so comparing insights from one data source (e.g., interviews) with insights from another source (e.g., archival media data) is common.

Again, we offer these observations as suggestions, not as rules. There is always room for innovation and creativity in qualitative research methods. But we believe it is helpful to understand how and why things have typically been done in certain ways. Here's one more exercise that might be helpful to you.

EXERCISE 2.3

1 Identify an author whose work you admire and try to see how that individual has gone about plying his or her craft.
2 Look at the nature of the work they typically cite. What does it have in common?
3 Look at their research questions. What commonalities do you see?
4 Now compare and contrast this individual's approach with that of some other author you are familiar with to get a feel for the differences.

Having suggested you do this exercise, we want to note that what you see in the final draft of a research paper – the literature review, theoretical perspectives, methods, findings, and discussion – is seldom a good reflection of how the research actually took place. Research does not usually unfold in a linear fashion and often involves cycling back and forth between data collection, reading, thinking, and analysis with fits and starts, breakthrough thoughts and dead ends, and ideas considered, refined, discarded, rethought, and embraced. As we will see in Chapter 9, there is considerable room for creativity and ingenuity in putting your paper or other output together. And once your work is submitted to the review process, you will get considerable additional input on how to frame and interpret your results as well as what works and does not work in your initial analysis and conclusions. But we are getting ahead of ourselves. This is still the beginning of your project. We will develop additional stages in the chapters that follow.

Additional readings on research traditions and specific theories

General readings

Anderson, Paul F. (1986) 'Method in Consumer Research: A Critical Relativist Perspective', *Journal of Consumer Research*, 13 (September), 155–173.
Prasad, Pushkala (2005) *Crafting Qualitative Research: Working in the Postpositivist Traditions*, Armonk, NY: M.E. Sharpe

Readings related to phenomenology

Kvale, Steinar (1983) 'The Qualitative Research Interview: A Phenomenological and a Hermeneutical Mode of Understanding', *Journal of Phenomenological Psychology*, 14 (Fall), 171–196.
Valle, Ronald S. and Mark King (1978) 'An Introduction to Existential-phenomenological Thought in Psychology', in Ronald S. Valle and Mark King (eds), *Existential-phenomenological Alternatives for Psychology*, New York: Oxford University Press, pp. 6–17.
Wertz, Frederick J. (1983) 'From Everyday to Psychological Description: Analysing the Moments of a Qualitative Data Analysis', *Journal of Phenomenological Psychology*, 14 (Fall), 197–242.

Readings related to hermeneutics

Hekman, Susan J. (1986) *Hermeneutics and Social Science Knowledge*, Notre Dame, IN: University of Notre Dame Press.
Ricoeur, Paul (1981) *Hermeneutics and the Social Sciences*, Cambridge: Cambridge University Press.
Thompson, Craig J., Howard Pollio, and Willian Locander (1994) 'The Spoken and the Unspoken: A Hermeneutic Approach to Understanding the Cultural Viewponts that Underlie Consumers' Expressed Meanings', *Journal of Consumer Research*, 21 (December), 432–452.

Readings related to postmodernism

Clarke, David B. (2003) *The Consumer Society and the Postmodern City*, New York: Routledge.
Firat, A. Fuat and Alladi Venkatesh (1995) 'Liberatory Postmodernism and the Reenchantment of Consumption', *Journal of Consumer Research*, 22 (December), 239–267.

Readings related to critical theories

Murray, Jeff B. and Julie L. Ozanne (1991) 'The Critical Imagination: Emancipatory Interests in Consumer Research', *Journal of Consumer Research*, 18 (September), 129–144.
Murray Jeff B., Julie L. Ozanne, and Jon M. Shapiro (1994) 'Revitalizing the Critical Imagination: Unleashing the Crouched Tiger', *Journal of Consumer Research*, 21 (December), 559–566.

Readings related to semiotics

Gottdiener, Mark (1995) *Postmodern Semiotics*, Oxford: Blackwell.
Grayson, Kent and Radan Martinec (2004) 'Consumer Perceptions of Iconicity and Indexicality and Their Influence on Assessments of Authentic Market Offerings', *Journal of Consumer Research*, 31 (September), 296–312.

Readings related to actor-network theory

Cheetham, Fiona (forthcoming) 'An Actor-Network-Theory Perspective on Collecting and Collectables', in Sandra Dudley, Amy Barnes, Jennifer Binnie, Julia Petrov, and Jennifer Walklate (eds), *Collecting Stories, Narrating Objects*, London: Routledge.
Latour, Bruno (2005) *Reassembling the Social: An Introduction to Actor-Network-Theory*, Oxford: Oxford University Press.

3

Depth interviews

The depth interview

Depth interviews, along with observations and participant observation, form the core data collection activities of qualitative research. The depth interview seeks an in-depth understanding of a topic that the research informant is able to speak about. It is usually about something that is important in the informant's life and that he or she has a good deal of information and opinions about that they can be encouraged to reveal. Although there are other types of interviews, including casual interviews, group interviews, and self-interviews, the depth interview is a formal and often lengthy interview (normally lasting an hour or longer). Rather than a superficial excavation of the interviewee's knowledge about a topic or behaviour, it tries to go more deeply into the subject as the interview proceeds. It requires a certain amount of intimacy and a fair amount of skill to accomplish this. As with other qualitative research methods, the key is practice, practice, practice. Thus, we strongly suggest that you do the practice interview exercises suggested in this chapter. We assume in what follows that the researcher is also the interviewer. This is almost always best. But in instances where you are hiring and training interviewers it is even more important to do these exercises in order to sensitise yourself to the problems the interviewers will face. It is not always possible to conduct interviews yourself. For example, maybe you are a male and the interviews are to be with covered Muslim women in the Middle East. Russ has faced this situation and it was absolutely imperative that a woman (in this case his colleague Rana Sobh) conduct the interviews. It is also best that you speak the language in which the interviews are being conducted, thus Russ's lack of Arabic was a second major impediment to conducting the interviews himself.

Using a translator to translate questions from language X to Y and then translate answers from Y to X is both awkward and necessarily loses a lot in translation. In that case, it would be better to train interviewers fluent in the informants' language and step out of the interview scene entirely. This, too, is a lesson learnt from painful experience of having done it the other way. Sometimes there is no other way, but translating interviews on the fly is never ideal. So in what follows we assume that you are conducting the interview yourself and it is in a language that is very comfortable for both you and the interviewee.

Preparing for the interview, recruiting informants, and setting the stage

A good depth interview begins before you enter the field. As McCracken (1988) points out, it is often easier to do research in an unfamiliar culture because everything is new and different. When doing research in your own culture, it is necessary to gain some distance from the topic being studied and to forget what you think you know about the topic. Otherwise, you run the very real danger of imposing your own knowledge and assumptions as well as having informants shut down because you appear to already know everything. For example, if the study is about men and their cars and you know a great deal about cars, revealing this can be disastrous because the informant can in effect say 'You know what I mean', and you can both assume that you do when in fact you have quite different implicit understandings of a phenomenon. It can be a virtue to appear naïve or ignorant concerning the subject of interest (although it is acceptable to reveal knowing something about the topic). Positioning yourself as relatively unfamiliar with the phenomenon means the informant has to explain to you more carefully why, in this case, he feels passionate about his car (if in fact he does).

But an open mind need not mean an empty head. Before entering the field, we advise familiarising yourself with relevant literature as well as identifying the focal phenomenon of interest. Otherwise you would be like a Martian anthropologist asking for explanations of breathing, shaking hands, eating, and sitting. Clearly, you need to be able to have some common basis of understanding. Interviewing someone wearing a suit when you are in jeans and a t-shirt or vice versa can be awkward. Too much distance in terms of how you look versus how your inform-ants look implies inequality. Conducting interviews at a field site may also require conformity to group norms. This was the case, for instance when Douglas et al. (1977) studied nude beaches and when Russ and Janeen Costa (Belk and Costa 1998) studied mountain man rendezvous. In both cases it was necessary to dress appropriately, whether that entailed brain-tanned buckskins or nothing at all.

Never lose sight of the fact, though, that the interview is not about you. It is all about the informant. Therefore interjecting your experiences or feelings is not only inappropriate, but can spoil an interview by disclosing your viewpoints and knowledge. It is better to appear to know too little than too much. And normally the interviewer dresses inconspicuously and all attention is focused on the person being interviewed.

Preparing for an interview also includes getting a recorder ready with fresh batteries and spare batteries, if not a spare recorder. Most often this is a digital audio recorder, but sometimes it could be a camcorder if visual aspects of the interaction are important or if a video is one of the outcomes anticipated for the project. In both cases, the informant should give permission not only to be interviewed, but also to be audio and/or video recorded. Because the informant cannot fully anticipate what may transpire during the interview, in the case of a video interview we like to have people agree to the interview and recording at the beginning of the interview and then agree to various possible uses of the recording at the end. These uses range from none (destroy recording), to researchers only, to showing to students and colleagues, to all uses including television or internet presentations. The exact informed consent forms and procedures that you use vary not only with projects (e.g., children require special permission from parents) but also with location in that different institutions and nations have different informed consent requirements. Be sure to learn about local requirements far ahead of time.

If you are shooting video, informed consent requires extra caution. Because video recordings normally allow identification of informants, special care is needed to assure that the person knows the uses to which he or she is agreeing. These uses may be well understood by middle-class consumers, but not to those in a rural village in Bangladesh that lacks electricity. If video recordings are made, it is possible and often desirable to show informants some of their interview so they can better appreciate how they will be seen by others. We also make clear in gaining permission to interview that the informant is free to stop the interview at any time as well as to hit the pause button on the recorder or request that we do this. Because the informant sometimes takes advantage of this invitation to speak 'off the record', because equipment breaks and malfunctions, and because interviews may sometimes take place in the absence of recording equipment, the interviewer should also practise recalling the interview as completely as possible, including verbatim quotes rather than paraphrasing. This requires active listening and practice. In the event that no recording is made, we often duck into a bathroom, our car, or an isolated corner of the venue and jot down or dictate as much as we can remember of such interviews as soon as possible after the interview takes place. Sometimes mentioning key phrases will be enough to bring back details later when a more complete transcription is made: e.g., big party, blue dress, father angry, flat tyre … Just as these notes should be made as soon as possible after the interview, transcriptions should also be done as soon as possible.

Before the interview takes place you should also think about who you would like to interview. Sometimes this involves a formal procedure of first acquiring management permission, as when seeking to conduct interviews in a retail or workplace setting (e.g., Marschan-Piekkari et al. 2004). In other cases, the informants are recruited with posters seeking participants, with ads, through 'snowballing' (asking initial informants to recommend others), through a commercial firm that recruits people according to specified criteria (Russ and Nan Zhou did this in China for a study of how people interpreted advertisements and Russ, Takeshi Matsui, and Yuko Minowa did so in Japan for a study of baby boomer gift-giving practices). If informants are recruited through in situ meetings at a site of interest, the interviews might be conducted on site or later in the informant's home or at a site chosen by the researcher. When conducting interviews with employees of a firm, unless there are private spaces within the company, choosing a neutral site away from the workplace is preferable in order to assure that there is no suspicion that the interview will not be anonymous and could be accessed by management. When Kelly Tian and Russ (Tian and Belk 2005) interviewed employees of a high tech firm, they chose a nearby restaurant. Do be wary of settings that have excess background noise though: a quiet restaurant is great, but a noisy café can mean the audio recording is nearly useless.

Thought should also be given to getting an adequate cross-section of the group to be studied. This may include being certain to talk to both men and women, young and old, or new members and long-time members of a group. This is not formal sampling and if a difference appears, it is worth repeating the difference to see if it holds up with others (e.g., if men and women in couples tend to describe their holidays differently, talk to enough couples to be convinced that the finding is not idiosyncratic). Sometimes it is diversity of affiliations or attitudes that matters more than demographics (e.g., political affiliations if feelings about candidates or legislation are the focus). Choosing informants should not simply be a matter of easy access or a distorted picture may emerge.

It is often desirable to conduct the interview in the informant's home, both because they feel comfortable there and because the interview may focus on objects within the home (e.g., a pantry check to see what brands of food they have on hand). Whether it is on 'their' turf, neutral ground, or 'your' turf, you should do your best to assure that you have privacy and that the space is comfortable for the informant. Normally you would sit facing or diagonal to the informant, but if the interview involves showing visual materials it may be better to sit at a table or side by side. An additional advantage in this arrangement is that if the informant is looking at or showing the visual material while they are responding, they do not have to meet your gaze and will likely feel less self-conscious and may sometimes almost forget that it is an interview. Your casual yet professional attitude can also do much to set them at ease. It is important to establish from the outset that there are no right or wrong answers and that you are interested in their personal views. In securing informed consent, they should be told that they can ask questions, stop the interview, take a break, or say things off the record at any point.

Interviews as conversations

A depth interview is a special type of conversation. Like other conversations it involves turn-taking, an interest in what the other person has to say, and a coherent flow of topics. It differs from survey research which has fixed questions, in a fixed order, with little concern with the flow or logic of the topics. Even if the questionnaire in survey research seeks open-ended answers, it can jump between questions about cars, houses, and possessions with little concern for logic or continuity. Moreover, survey research interviewers are generally not allowed to deviate from the fixed script of questions using specific terms and a specific order of items. We would not tolerate such rigidness in an ordinary conversation and we should not tolerate it in depth interviews. Another way in which a depth interview differs from survey research using a questionnaire is that while a survey uses a questionnaire that is just that – a list of questions – a depth interview instead uses a **protocol** (although see McCracken 1988 for an argument for using fixed questions). A protocol is a list of topics instead of a list of questions. The interviewer generally memorises the protocol, but has no predetermined specific questions or question ordering. This is relatively easy to do in the first few interviews, but care is needed subsequently not to fall into a routine that begins to become more like repeating an invisible questionnaire. You would not have conversations with different friends following the same sequence of questions with each one. Nor should you do this with different interviewees.

But although a depth interview is like a conversation, it is also quite different from an everyday conversation in a number of important ways. Some of these are obvious: the interviewer and the interviewee are likely to be strangers; the interview is likely recorded in some way, and the interviewee agrees orally or on a written form to allow this. At the start of the interview, the interviewer describes what the topic will be, what is expected of the interviewee, and how long the interview is expected to last. Other differences are a bit more subtle. For example, although there is turn-taking, the interviewer is clearly in charge and directing the conversation. The person being interviewed is expected to disclose information about themselves and their family or organisation, while the interviewer is generally not expected to do so. Instead the interviewer's turn in the conversation is filled with a request, a question, a probe, or a simple indication that they understand. Sometimes they may introduce audio-visual materials for the interviewee to respond to or exercises for them to complete. For instance, Russ and Rosa Llamas are conducting a study of the meaning and interpretation of smiles in different cultures. As a part of this project, we show the interviewee a series of photos and drawings and ask them to tell us what they think is going on. The visual material has been selected to depict people of different races and genders with different smiling or non-smiling expressions in different contexts. This is part of a projective exercise intended to get the person being interviewed to project their own feelings onto the people shown in the pictures. We will talk more fully about such projective methods later in this chapter.

During ethnographic research, there will likely be an array of different types of interviews from casual informal conversations hardly justifying the term interview to full-on in depth interviews that are pre-arranged and recorded. There may also be follow-ups, preliminary interviews, multiple-part interviews on different days, member checks when initial reports are checked with informants for accuracy of descriptive information, and so forth. These different interview types vary widely in their depth, specificity, and detail. The interview might also be about the person's business, organisation, or other professional role rather than their personal life. Sometimes a group interview or pair interview (e.g., couple, parent–child) is appropriate, but most often depth interviews will be one-on-one interviewer/interviewee. We address the group interview in discussing focus groups later in this chapter.

Another important way in which a depth interview differs from an ordinary conversation is that the researcher directs the conversation in some ways that might seem rude or inappropriate in a normal conversation. The interview generally begins with a grand tour about the background of the person being interviewed and non-threatening general topics. It might begin by asking to describe their background starting with their childhood. These may be 'throw-away' topics, but they can also provide useful context for understanding more about the person that you may want to refer back to during the interview. For example, if they tell you that their parents were divorced when they were 10 years old this can help to frame a number of topics such as childhood experiences, family situation when growing up, income of their family of origin, and so forth.

After some preliminary 'Grand Tour' questions, if there is sufficient rapport with the informant, the interviewer may ask the person to 'Tell me about … [your vacation, your involvement with Mini-Coopers, your horses, or whatever the general topic of interest is]'. However, if the topic is highly personal or sensitive (e.g., condom use), involves more abstract concepts (e.g., consumer desire), or is one in which it is important not to initially disclose the study's specific focus (e.g., the smile study), a 'tell me about' question would not be appropriate early in the interview. In these cases, beginning with more general questions, more innocuous questions, or projective questions should precede drilling down to a more specifically focused discussion. A flow from general to specific questions is almost always a good idea and may be thought of as the funnel approach – start broad and get narrower. For example, a study on giving children sweet treats might begin with a discussion of general meal habits for different household members, move on to recent meals, discuss snacks and non-meal foods, then discuss the informant's access to snacks when they were growing up, and finally focus on their own children's access to snacks – what, where, when, with whom, etc. Thus, **guideline 1: Funnel questions in a sequence from general to specific**.

Often the researcher conducting a depth interview is not as interested in what, where, when, with whom, or how as they are in why. Ironically 'Why?' is the one question that we advise you to seldom if ever ask of informants. Why not? There are several good reasons. Perhaps the most important reason is that it asks research participants to describe their behaviour in a way that sounds reasonable, prudent, and responsible. They are likely very capable of doing so, but their answer may be based more on sounding like a reasonable, prudent, and responsible person than on explicating the actual reason for their behaviour. Sometimes the person may simply not know why they did something like buying a sweet treat for their children. Sometimes they may know, but be unwilling to tell (e.g., 'It was the only way I could get Suzy to be quiet so I would have a moment of peace'). In general, asking people why puts them on the defensive and makes them feel they need to justify and rationally explain their behaviour, even though it was not rationally motivated. They may also not know why they did something, or may be unwilling or unable to give 'real' reasons, therefore, **guideline 2: Do not ask why**. If it is necessary to ask for reasons, try to do so in a less threatening or indirect way (e.g., How come? Can you tell me more about that? How's that?).

If a depth interview is going well, the informant provides long and detailed answers and the researcher only offers minimal guidance to keep the interview on track. It is usually a sign that the interview is not going well if the questions are as long as or longer than the answers. In this case the fault is usually with the interviewer rather than the interviewee. Examining the questions may reveal that they call for specific answers, especially ones where 'yes' or 'no' answers will suffice: 'Have you ever done X?' 'Was that when you first found out?' 'Is that what you thought?' It is fine to ask such questions, but be ready to follow-up with non-yes/no questions that ask for elaboration and more depth. You might follow up, for example, with 'Can you tell me more about that?' But these are often questions that can be asked instead of the yes/no question rather than in addition to it. Here we suggest **guideline 3: Do not ask yes/no questions**. A further reason not to do so is that in the semi-structured free-form interview, the interviewer needs to reflect on answers and prepare a next question. If the answer being obtained is a simple 'yes' or 'no' (or a number or other equally short answer), the interviewer is left with very little time to prepare the next question in their mind.

Because a depth interview is designed to obtain deep reflections and thick descriptions, it is important to be relaxed and relax the informant. This is so the informant has time and confidence to continue without feeling rushed and so the interviewer does not shut down topics after superficial answers by moving on to the next topic too quickly. One common way to encourage the interviewee to keep talking and to elaborate on their initial answers is to use a **probe**. These are short verbal or non-verbal responses that request more of an answer. One of the most common probes is the repeater probe. In using the repeater probe when the interviewee stops speaking, the interviewer takes his or her turn; but instead of asking a question the interviewer repeats the last phrase or key words from the interviewee, raising their voice at the end to turn it into a question seeking clarification and further detail. So for example, if the interviewee's answer ends with an unelaborated description like '... and so I gave him the gift with the usual ceremony', the interviewer might probe 'The usual ceremony?' Another type of probe is simply a non-verbal nod, or eyebrow raise meant to suggest, 'Ah, that's interesting, please go on', which could also be said verbally, but is slightly more disruptive. Or the interviewer can signal interest by a sort of humming – 'hmmm'. The idea with these latter probes is to indicate you are listening, find what is being said interesting, and want to hear more. The interviewer can also respond 'Ah', 'OK', or 'I see', but needs to be certain that this is not meant to reinforce a particular type of answer. The idea is to reinforce the talking and elaborating, but not the specific answer. The interviewer should be accepting of whatever is said, but not evaluative, as if to say 'That's what I want to hear' or 'That's good'.

Depending on how it is going, the researcher can also ask for more specific elaboration: 'When was the first time you can remember that happening?' 'How did that make you feel?' 'What happened after that'. Sometimes another type of probe can also be used: silence. Silence is uncomfortable and eventually (it may be a few seconds, but can feel much longer) the interviewee adds more detail. This would be relatively rude in a normal conversation, but once again, a depth interview is not a normal conversation. Generally speaking, if there is a lull in the response it may be a good time to probe. If the informant keeps going, there is no need for a probe unless the conversation is going in an unproductive direction and you want to bring it back on track (but see below). In that case you might say, 'A minute ago you mentioned Christmas gifts when your family was poor. Can you tell me a little more about that?' If instead the informant had gone on from a description of Christmas gifts when the family was poor to talk about something that is productive for answering the research question (e.g., Christmas gifts now that they are no longer poor), it is better not to interrupt the flow of their answer and to simply remember to come back later to the topic of when they were poor. So in general, **guideline 4: use probes judiciously and strategically to elicit elaboration without interrupting the flow of an answer that is going well on its own.** Probing is perhaps the most critical element in getting depth in a depth interview. Unpractised interviewers are often too uncomfortable with silence and too quick to move on to the next topic. Doing this reinforces superficial answers and fails to let all of what an informant has to say come out.

Circling back to topics of interest mentioned earlier in the interview also gives the researcher a chance to think about the logically related topics that may or may not have already been covered. So the researcher might say 'So those are some of the Christmas gifts that you gave to your children in the past ...' As the researcher is saying this, he or she should be also be thinking about what is missing (e.g., Christmas gifts that the informant received when he or she was a child, Christmas gifts to his or her children now, non-Christmas gifts to children in the past – as for birthdays for example, everyday giving to children in the past when there was no special occasion). Time, generation, and occasion are just a few of the pairings or continua that the researcher might think about exploring. Others in this context might be extremes of emotions (happy, sad), idealism (idea, actual), family role (child, parent), and gift role (giver, recipient). So circling back not only seeks greater depth on topics mentioned too briefly, but also provides a chance to see what is missing in covering the substantive or emotional domain. We therefore suggest, **guideline 5: try to circle back to earlier topics for greater depth and as a lead-in to missing areas of the discussion.**

While going from general to specific, circling back, strategic probing, and logically linking from one topic to the next can give some structure to a depth interview as well as help assure deep and thick descriptions rather than superficial answers, the interviewer needs to keep the interview flowing and productive. Still, we do not know what we will discover. If we did, there would be no point in conducting a depth interview. This means that the interview needs to be flexible and willing to deviate away from the interview protocol in order to explore emergent topics of interest and relevance. Having told the informant the general purpose of the research, we have specified a destination: this is where we want this interview to go. While keeping this destination in mind, we also need to be willing to take side trips that the informant wishes to take us on in answering our questions. In some cases, these sidetrips will stray too far from the destination and as interviewer you will need to guide the informant back to the main road. But in other cases, the side road may turn out to be more interesting and informative than the main road that the interview was previously travelling. For example, suppose in the previous example of a study of gift-giving the person being interviewed starts talking about her Japanese heritage and how important wrapping is in Japanese culture. Even though the initial focus of the study was about the gifts themselves, you begin to realise that the wrapping and the rituals of gift giving can also be considered to be a part of the gift that is being given. In this case, the side road to talk about gift wrapping should be thoroughly explored in this and subsequent interviews. The side road has turned out to be as informative and helpful as the main road, maybe even more so. In other cases, the side road will turn out to be a dead end. This might be the case if the interviewee begins to tell long stories about the gift recipient. This is always a judgment call, and if you err, err on the side of going too far afield rather than sticking to the straight and narrow main road. Thus, **guideline 6: be willing to explore tangential topics that the interviewee brings up, but use good judgment about when to guide the interview back on-topic.** This may also depend upon the research stage and how far along the analysis is; analysis should begin in the field as we will see in Chapters 7 and 8. During early stages of the research, the interviews may be more exploratory and going farther afield can be more fruitful.

━━━━━━━━━━━━━━━━━ EXERCISE 3.1 ━━━━━━━━━━━━━━━━━

Choose a partner, ideally one who is also practising how to conduct a better depth interview. Interview them using a recorder to capture the interview. Learn as much as you can about a hobby or special interest of this person, using the guidelines above and your best interviewing skills. Be sure to structure the interview starting with grand tour questions. Use a funnel approach and probe. Try to get a good and natural flow in the interview, remembering details that you want to come back to when the flow stops.

When you have completed a 15-minute interview, switch places and have the other person interview you. You should both also jot down some fieldnotes about what you learnt non-verbally. Play back the recording and listen to what went well or not so well, getting comments from your partner as well. Pay attention to not only how good the substantive information you elicited was but also how comfortable both you and your partner felt in these two roles. What lessons can you derive about improving the process and outcomes of depth interviews?

Focus groups

Paradoxically, while focus groups remain the most commonly used qualitative method in business, they are the least commonly used qualitative method in academia. The reasons for the popularity of focus groups in industry include being relatively quick, easy, and inexpensive to conduct as well as able to give managers (often behind one-way glass mirrors) a first-hand glimpse of their potential customers (Stewart 2010). The main reasons for the lack of popularity of focus groups in academic research are that they are complicated by group dynamics, they generally lack the depth of one-on-one interviews, and some people may be more reluctant to express their feelings and behaviour in a group setting, even though the focus group is generally composed of strangers. Group dynamics include dominant or persuasive focus group members leading the group in a type of group-think. There may also be a tendency to take more risky stances in a focus group due to the 'risky shift' that can arise due to the diffusion of responsibility in a group (Catterall and Maclaren 2006). But in a well-conducted focus group, group dynamics can also result in a free-form sharing of opinions if the moderator is able to nurture a creative environment in which participants are accepting, there are no wrong answers, and diversity of opinion is healthy. Let us look at some of the guidelines for conducting good focus group interviews before examining their merit in greater detail.

Recruiting focus group members

General advice for the number of participants for a focus group is 6–12 people, with 8 being a common target (Catterall and Maclaran 2006; Stewart et al. 2007). At least, this is the advice commonly given based on the assumption that the group is convened in a single location for a face-to-face interview. When it is to be a virtual focus group conducted online, it is best to use a smaller number of people with 5 being a good maximum (Kozinets 2010a). For face-to-face focus groups, participants should generally be relatively homogeneous with respect to age, gender, and degree of expertise in the area of interest (e.g., cooking, car repair, gardening). Age and gender homogeneity are less important in virtual focus groups unless a synchronous visual form of communication is used. However, asynchronous virtual focus groups, like those conducted on closed membership forums, offer greater conversational ease (if less group spontaneity) for participants (Fox et al. 2007; Kozinets 2010a). Although focus groups for any given project are generally too few and too small to worry about representativeness, having appropriate heterogeneity across groups can give some feel for differences in key consumer variables like income and education. Market research firms offer focus group recruitment to client specifications, but there is sometimes a danger of getting 'professional' focus group participants. They are often motivated by money (common for focus groups where participants must come to a central location) and participate in many focus groups such that over time they become atypical consumers. Generally speaking, focus groups work on the principle of anonymity, so that strangers are better recruits than friends (Catterall and Maclaren 2006). An exception might be when naturally occurring interactions are of interest, such as when studying the group phenomena involved in everyday texting and social media. Where participants are difficult to recruit, such as doctors or CEOs, greater incentives as well as creativity may be required. For example Stewart et al. (2007) describe a research project in which CEOs were invited to an all-expense paid weekend cruise with their partners in order to gain access to a floating focus group with these executives.

Preparing for and running a focus group

While many of the techniques for individual interviews like preparing a proto-col, funnelling, probes, and use of projectives also apply to focus groups, there are some additional considerations. Participants should be given name tents or name tags with their first names on them so that they can begin to address each other rather than the interviewer over the course of a typically one- to two-hour group interview. They are often provided with water, soft drinks, and light refreshments. Sometimes stimuli like products, packaging, or advertising are used during the interview to direct attention to a focus of researcher inter-est. The moderator also needs to provide a safe comfortable environment in which focus group members feel free to express themselves. When some par-ticipants start to dominate, the moderator may want to stimulate others by calling on the shy or asking for what others think. When group-think seems to be emerging, the moderator might specifically ask for other opinions or points of view. Projective methods (discussed below) can also be useful in getting more diverse opinions. Protocols should be pretested as well to see what works best. Sometimes the group dynamics can be of interest themselves to observe processes of conflict resolution, consensus building, and coalition formation (Gaskell 2000; Mariampolski 2006).

When to use and not use focus groups

As Catterall and Maclaren (2006) emphasise, focus groups are especially good when the researcher wants to examine shared meanings and shared terminol-ogy. For example, if the researcher wanted to gain some familiarity with hip hop culture in the Netherlands or uses of summer roller skiing among those who compete in cross-country ski races in the winter, before attempting participant observation focus groups with appropriately screened participants might pro-vide a good introduction. They may also work well for taste and smell tests or reactions to package design, although group dynamics can still be a concern. As noted above, focus groups are also a good way to investigate certain types of group dynamics (Gaskell 2000), such as how males versus females (or mixed sex groups) reach consensus. At the same time, there are many topics where focus groups are not the best approach, including those in which the intent is to elicit long narratives and those in which the intent is to gauge attitudes (Barbour 2008). In general, focus groups are probably best used for exploratory research. It is important to bear in mind that, despite the moderator's best efforts, they may suffer from group-think and are not representative in any case. They may serve to tease out answers to concrete managerial issues like a change in customer service policies, but it is extremely rare that an academic journal will accept a paper based solely on focus group data.

Analysis of focus group data

Often times the moderator of a focus group is asked, especially in managerial studies, to present a report on the focus group not long after it has taken place. But it is important not to rush to judgment based on recollections and re-examining audio or video recordings of focus groups. Like depth interviews, these group interviews should be carefully transcribed. Given the group dynamics at play, it is even more important to capture non-verbal information in these transcripts. Chapter 6 has more to say about the mechanics of recording fieldwork and interviews. A further difficulty with focus groups is attributing who said what. Even if the moderator manages to get the participants not to talk over one another, an audio recording is often difficult to transcribe with proper attributions. Video recordings are better in this regard, but if an oval table has been used (as is often recommended), a two camera setup is needed to capture conversations on both sides of the table. Boundary area microphones can also assure good recording of voices all around the table. Once transcripts have been made, analysis can proceed with the sorts of coding and data reduction described in Chapters 7 and 8.

▓▓▓▓▓▓▓▓▓▓▓▓▓▓▓▓▓▓▓ **EXERCISE 3.2** ▓▓▓▓▓▓▓▓▓▓▓▓▓▓▓▓▓▓▓

Assemble a team of 6–8 co-workers or fellow students. Either act as moderator or choose a moderator from the group. Take some time to prepare a topical protocol for a focus group on a topic from current popular culture (e.g., contemporary music, automobiles, organic food). Run the group for 30 minutes using good moderator techniques. When the discussion is complete or time has run out, conduct a post-mortem with the group. Were the opinions that came up the true opinions of the group? Did everyone with something to say on the topic participate? What dissuaded some from participating fully? How could the moderator have done a better job?

Projective methods

Projective methods derive from psychotherapy. The idea is that people are more readily able to project their feelings onto others (or animals or cartoons) than they are to attribute these feelings to themselves. In addition, the use of metaphors in which a thought or characterisation is made using an 'inappropriate' vocabulary (e.g., If brand X were an animal it would be ...) can be revealing beyond the words people would use in a more straightforward question about brand image. Furthermore, projective exercises often are a light-hearted break for both participants and researchers, helping to alter the pace of the interview and allow everyone to relax (Gordon and Langmaid 1988). While the interviewer should always make clear that there are no right or wrong answers to depth interview questions, it is self-evident that this is the case when we show a cartoon and ask what the person portrayed might be thinking.

There are several additional reasons for using projective methods in interviewing and more use should be made of such methods. As Moisander et al. (2009) emphasise, consumers are not vessels of truthful answers about their lived experiences. Projective methods help informants to say things indirectly that are difficult to say directly. For sensitive topics or those with socially desirable responses, projective methods are less threatening and less apparently self-revealing. Many realms of consumption imagery are inherently fanciful, and projective methods can do a good job of tapping into consumer fantasies. And projective methods are often fun and break-up the routine of giving 'serious' answers to questions. Dennis Rook (2006) groups projective methods into three categories, depending upon the amount of information they generate. The smallest amount of information is generated by word association, sentence completion, cartoon tests, and symbol matching. A moderate amount of information is elicited by object personification, shopping list analysis, and picture drawing. And the greatest amount of information is revealed by collage construction, thematic stories, dream exercises, psychodrama, and autodriving. The research objectives should drive the choice among these methods. More information is not necessarily better.

Gordon and Langmaid (1988) trace the earliest use of **word association** to Sir Francis Galton in 1879. The idea is to give participants a series of unrelated words one at a time and have them respond with the first thing that comes into their mind. For example if one of the words is 'beer' the association might be a brand name or a characterisation like 'sloppy'. Such top-of-the-mind unguarded associations can provide insights into how the product category is thought of by consumers. By presenting the words on a computer screen, it is also possible to measure the participant's response latency as an indication of how familiar and comfortable the person is with this association. For example if you were testing potential brand names for a children's cereal using word association, and the name Quax generated associations like duck, doctor, and hacks, both the frequency of elicitation and the brevity of response latency might suggest that the association is an easy one to make. One way of quickly grasping what associations have been obtained is by depicting them as a word cloud. Danes et al. (2010) studied word associations for two fast food chains. Figure 3.1 shows the word cloud they obtained for In-N-Out Burger (top) versus McDonald's (bottom). How would you interpret these results?

Sentence completion is also intended to get unguarded top-of-mind associations, but provides more of a stimulus than a single word. For example, Russ

Figure 3.1 Word associations for In-N-Out Burger (top) and McDonald's (bottom)

Source: Jeffrey E. Danes, Jeffrey S. Hess, John W. Story, and Jonathan L. York (2010) 'Brand Image Associations for Large Virtual Groups', *Qualitative Market Research*, 13 (3), 309–323

(Belk 1985) used sentence fragments including the following in validating a measure of materialism:

Christmas is a time when …

Owning a house with a yard …

The one thing that would make me happiest at this point in my life …

Results were then categorised as materialistic or non-materialistic and instances of each type of association were compared to scores on materialism scales.

Whereas word association and sentence completion elicit only a few words, **cartoon tests** present a simple drawing of a situation and ask participants to describe what they think is going on. These stories may then reveal assumptions and attitudes. For instance, the cartoons in Figures 3.2A and 3.2B depict an angry male customer with a female clerk and an angry female customer with a male clerk in order to learn something about the role of gender in retail service encounters. Sometimes thought or speech bubbles are used for presenting people in cartoon tests. For example in Figure 3.3 we might elicit thoughts about purchasing shoes versus choosing which ones to wear. Something similar to this was used in a study of gift-giving by McGrath et al. (1993) to study buying for self versus buying as a gift for others.

In **symbol matching**, we can get a quick visual metaphor for a person, brand, company, or other object of interest. For instance, we might present an array of cups from dainty and delicate tea cups to hardy large mugs and ask which one represented a company better. Or we might use an array of animals like those in Figure 3.4 and ask, for instance 'If Oprah Winfrey were one of these animals, which one would she be?' We could do the same thing with various breeds of dogs that seem to represent different human traits: the fast Greyhound,

A   B

Figure 3.2 A & B

Source: Figures 3.2A and 3.2B courtesy of Tian, Vane-Ing, Chinese University of Hong Kong

A   B

Figure 3.3 A & B

the hardy Siberian Husky, the elegant Poodle, the homely cute Pug, the hard-working Collie, the rather slow-witted Bloodhound, and so forth. Or we could do the same things asking people to match people, brands, or companies with different automobiles, abstract designs, decorated rooms, shapes, colours, foot-wear, clothes, hats, houses, or other expressive symbols. One study with children examined children's consumption stereotypes by reversing the stimulus and the symbol and asking which of several cars (shown in pictures) and which of several houses (also shown in pictures) different types of people would own – e.g., a grandfather, someone who has lots of friends, a doctor, a postman, etc. (Belk et al. 1982). Cars were chosen that were small versus large, new versus old, and sporty versus non-sporty, while houses were new versus old and large versus small. By examining how much agreement there was among students of differ-ent ages, the study was able to determine how strong consumption stereotypes are at different ages.

Some of these symbol matching tasks are quite similar to **object personification** projectives, except that these are usually non-visual. In object personification, we might ask 'If this brand were a television star or movie star, who would it be?' Or we might use more anthropomorphic representations such as animals or cars. For instance, in a study with loyal Apple computer enthusiasts we ask what kind of car a Macintosh computer would be and what kind of car a Windows operating system computer would be (Belk and Tumbat 2005). We were consistently told that the Apple would be a Volkswagen 'beetle' or van (and in one case Buckminster Fuller's Dymaxion car), while the PC would be a non-descript Chevrolet that was falling apart. These descriptions suggest several things. The Mac was seen as the 'little man' or underdog to the mainstream PC (at the time). There was also an associa-tion of the Mac with the hippie era and the Volkswagen van that was a part of that culture (Vanden Bergh 1992). And the PC was seen as stylistically bland and unreliable in comparison to the Mac.

Figure 3.4

One of the oldest marketing studies using projective methods is a **shopping list** study by Mason Haire (1950). Housewives in the 1950s resisted buying instant coffee despite its convenience. So Haire showed women one of two nearly identical shopping lists, each containing a can of Rumford's Baking Powder, a bunch of carrots, two loaves of Wonder Bread, one-and-a-half pounds of hamburgers, two cans of Del Monte peaches, and five pounds of potatoes. However one list also included a one-pound can of Maxwell House Coffee (drip ground), while the other listed Nescafé instant coffee. The women were asked to describe the personality and character of the shopper who had constructed the list they saw. Results showed the pattern of results shown in Table 3.1. While there was a tendency to

Table 3.1 Mason Haire study of shopper descriptions

Description	Nescafé	Maxwell House
Lazy	48%	4%
Fails to plan household purchases/schedule well	48%	12%
Thrifty	4%	16%
Spendthrift	12%	0%
Not a good wife	16%	0%
A good wife	4%	16%

see the instant coffee buyer as a spendthrift, the most striking results were that this shopper was seen as lazy, a poor planner, and a poor wife. Clearly, instant coffee was seen as too easy a way out of the 'proper' housewife role of brewing coffee. While replications have found that these perceptions have largely disappeared, the use of this shopping list study uncovered results that very likely would not have emerged in more direct questioning. Similar methods have been used to study impression formation based on the consumption evident from the contents of a wallet or purse (Belk 1978) as well as to the contents and neatness of a person's room (Gosling 2008).

Picture drawing is a technique derived from child psychology. For example, the Machover Draw-a-Person test asks a child to draw a boy or a girl and makes inferences about the child's intelligence and personality based on the pictures (e.g., Goodenough 1926; Levy 1950). For example, Chan (2006) had Hong Kong children draw 'a child with a lot of new and expensive toys' and 'a child without many toys'. Sample drawings are shown in Figures 3.5A and 3.5B. She found that younger children (ages 6–8) were more likely to show differences in happiness, friendships, and feeling good, while older children (ages 11–12) were more likely to depict having many new and expensive toys as being wasteful. Clark (1995) had children draw pictures of Santa Claus, the Easter Bunny, and the Tooth Fairy in order to investigate children's understandings of these mythical figures. Among other findings, she learnt that children were likely to depict the Easter Bunny as more like rabbits in nature, while adults were more likely to personify and anthropomorphise the character. The drawings also proved to be a useful way to focus interviews with the children who were then able to elaborate on the drawings and amplify what was going on. The use of drawings in consumer and marketing research is not confined to children, and drawings can be requested for a variety of things of interest. With visual construction techniques in consumer research it is always a good idea to follow up the visual with an interview rather than let the drawing or other visual representation stand on its

This child has a lot of new and expensive toys.   This child does not have a lot of toys.

A

This child has a lot of new and expensive toys.   This child does not have a lot of toys.

B

Figure 3.5 A & B

Source: Kara Chan (2006), 'Exploring Children's Perceptions of Material Possessions: A Drawing Study', *Qualitative Market Research*, 9 (4), 352–366.

own. Gordon and Langmaid (1988) suggest working out interpretations jointly with participants for all projective tasks.

The advice to have participants co-construct interpretations also holds for **collage construction**. With collages, participants are traditionally given scissors, glue sticks, magazines, and a poster board and are asked to do a collage that expresses a theme of interest such as desire (Belk et al. 2003), dream (or nightmare) honeymoon (Leonard 2005), or nostalgia (Havlena and Holak 1996). Figure 3.6 shows several of the collages from the first two of these studies. Although we would not advise trying to interpret these collages without the narratives of their creators, in this case you may be able to guess which one of each pair of collages was by a male and which one is by a female. You may also be able to surmise which of the desire collages is from Mediterranean Turkey and which one is from the USA. When Russ was part of a team teaching European PhD students about qualitative methods, participants formed groups to construct collages of financial security. Inadvertently, one group was composed of Northern Europeans and the other of Mediterranean Europeans. The first group arranged their images carefully with equal spacing between them and relatively conventional content. The Southern Europeans by contrast has all sorts of colourful and sexy images splashed on the page with angles and little blank space. Clearly beyond the images of financial security we accidentally learnt a great deal about cultural differences. Magazines as well as other print material like photographs can be supplied to participants or they can be asked to collect their own. We anticipate that in the future the cutting and pasting will be done on a computer instead of using scissors and glue sticks. This is the case with the collages that are a part of the **Zaltman Metaphor Elicitation Technique** (ZMET). Computer collages also allow presenting a standard set of images to participants.

The ZMET includes collage construction as one of the steps in a multi-step research method that seeks to uncover basic metaphors that express how consumers think and feel about a focal topic (Venkatesh et al. 2010; Zaltman 2003; Zaltman and Zaltman 2008). Metaphors can be a powerful way of understanding these thoughts and feelings. For example, Durgee and Manli (2006) derived the following metaphors for bathing and showering experiences that led to different new product ideas: car wash, waterproof control panel in a speedboat, sauna, water aerobics, and tropical island. Coulter (2006) provides the example in Table 3.2 of the six steps in the ZMET technique where the focus is on the experience of going to Broadway plays. The informant in this case is asked to bring in images that represent the Broadway experience in their mind. The overall metaphor that emerged for one informant was 'Broadway brings balance to everyday life', as visually depicted in the digital collage shown in Figure 3.7.

Thematic stories usually involve giving participants a drawing or photograph and having them tell a story about it. This can be considered a variation of

(A) Desire collage

(B) Desire collage

(C) Two nightmare honeymoon collages

Figure 3.6 A, B & C

Source: Courtesy of Güliz Ger, Bilkent University
Russell W. Belk
Courtesy of Hillary Leonard, University of Rhode Island

the Thematic Apperception Test (TAT) methodology developed in psychology and used along with scoring manuals to measure traits such as achievement motivation (Morgan and Murray 1935). But while the TAT was designed to produce reliable quantitative scores from qualitative data, storytelling in qualitative research is usually interpreted qualitatively (Rook 1988). Nevertheless, the same

Table 3.2   ZMET steps: the Broadway experience

Storytelling. The informant describes how each image represents his thoughts and feelings about the Broadway experience. *Interviewer probe:* 'Please tell me how this image relates to your thoughts and feelings about your Broadway experience.'

Missed images. The informant is asked if there were important ideas he wanted to express but for which he could not find relevant images. *Interviewer probe:* 'Were there any thoughts and feelings for which you were unable to find an image? Please describe the thought or feeling, and tell me about an image that you would use to represent the thought or feeling.'

Metaphor probe/expand the frame. The informant is asked to widen the frame of a selected picture and describe what else might enter the picture to better understand his thoughts and feelings. *Interviewer probe:* 'If you could widen the frame of this picture in all directions, what else would I see that would help me better understand your thoughts and feelings about Broadway theatre productions and the role they play in your life?'

Sensory metaphors. The informant is asked to express his ideas using various sensory images – colour, taste, smell, touch, sound, and emotion. *Example of interviewer probe:* 'What sound could I hear that would represent your thoughts and feelings about Broadway theatre productions and the role they play in your life?'

Vignette. The informant is asked to create a story about the Broadway experience. *Interviewer probe:* 'I would like you to use your imagination to create a short story. The story should express your thoughts and feelings about Broadway theatre productions and the role they play in your life. Please include at least these characters: 1) you, 2) Broadway theatre productions, and 3) a similar form of entertainment you might enjoy.'

Digital image. The informant, with the skilled assistance of a computer graphics imager, creates a summary collage using his images and supplemental images from a database, as needed.

Figure 3.7   Digital ZMET collage, 'Broadway brings balance to everyday life'

Source: Courtesy of Robin Coulter, University of Connecticut

directions normally given in TAT research can be given to participants in interpretive research. For each photo or drawing, the directions ask the participant to take 10 minutes and tell a story that answers the following questions:

1 What is happening? Who are the people?
2 What has led up to this situation? That is, what has happened in the past?
3 What is being thought? What is wanted? By whom?
4 What will happen? What will be done?

Rook (1988) suggests using at least three pictures and selecting those that ask questions and challenge the viewer to solve a puzzle. Pretesting to find good evocative pictures is recommended. The pictures should vary in terms of their degree of ambiguity and show things (e.g., product contexts, brands, people with different characteristics) that are of theoretical and practical interest. The idea is to tap into consumer fantasies – a rich source of ideas for advertising, brand imagery, packaging and other fantasy-laden elements of consumption and marketing.

In **dream exercises**, the researcher takes advantage of the fact that dreams are a fantasy realm where a wide variety of things are possible. Someone might be instructed to describe a (hypothetical) dream about a BMW or about a man in an automobile showroom. The power of eliciting stories in this manner is illustrated in a study by McCann-Erickson (1988). The advertising agency was interested in why women were not buying a product called the Black Flag Roach Motel which was a yellow plastic structure that attracted roaches inside, where they died. They elicited dreams about roaches from women and also had them draw scenes from their dreams. The analysis of the stories and drawings led to the conclusion that women commonly associated roaches with the men who had done them wrong and therefore took great pleasure in watching the roaches squirm and die when they were sprayed with ordinary roach killer. But this fantasy could not be played out with the roach motel where the insects simply disappeared from view.

Psychodrama is another technique borrowed from psychotherapy (e.g., Yablonsky 1976). In this case, the informant is asked to act out a particular role in a situation. She might be asked, for instance, to take on the role of a customer whose car is being serviced and who is told that it is not ready as promised and is going to cost twice as much to be repaired as they had been led to believe. In some cases, the researcher or a hired actor plays the role of the service manager and may specifically introduce certain features into the scenario like the availability of a loaner car or facilities for the consumer to wait and snack, read, or watch television while they wait. If this were being done for therapeutic purposes, there might also be a role-reversal exercise in which the informant plays the service manager, but this is less likely in the consumer research context.

Autodriving or **visual elicitation** is a depth interviewing method that uses visual stimuli to derive interpretations and stories from the informant (Heisley and Levy 1991; Sayre 2006). Often times these stimuli are photos or videos depicting the informant in an earlier context. For example, if you were observing someone bargaining at a swap meet, it would be too disruptive to stop their negotiations to ask them questions about it. But by photographing or video-recording the behaviour, these pictures and videos can be shown to the informant after the negotiation has been completed in order to find out what was really going on in their minds as they insisted that a certain price point was their limit. The method also works using people's own family photos as stimuli (Chalfen 1987). With smart phones the researcher could even call an informant, ask them to use their phone to photograph their setting at that moment, and have them e-mail the photo to the researcher for auto-driving then or later. It is also possible to use historic photos to prompt memories from informants and compare changes that have taken place (e.g., Page 2001).

Summary: depth interviews and projective methods

There are a variety of techniques and issues in depth interviews and the use of projective methods. We have only presented a sample of the more common and basic topics and types in this chapter. We have not touched upon topics like the role of gender among researcher and informant pairings (e.g., Warren 1988). We have also been unable to include other research techniques like regressing informants back to childhood (Rapaile 2006), diary research (Patterson 2005), oral histories (Elliott and Davies 2006), creative interviewing (Douglas 1986), narrative elicitation (Elliott 2005; Hopkinson and Hogg 2006), giving the 'natives' the cameras/camcorders to tell their own stories (Sunderland and Denny 2007), or introspection and auto-ethnography (Brown 2006a; Gould 1995, 2006). Other related methods like netnography, online interviewing, videography, and ethnography will be covered in Chapters 4, 5, and 6. Nor have we emphasised topics like the interpretation of non-verbal informant behaviour (Gordon and Langmaid 1988; Mariampolski 2006), which will also be brought into Chapters 4 and 5.

We conclude this chapter with the reminder that the only way to really learn qualitative methods is to practise them. Therefore, we offer two final exercises that we strongly encourage you to try. And we offer one last word on projective techniques drawing on a story from anthropologist consumer researcher John Sherry. When John was on the faculty of Northwestern University, he had his master's students go out and conduct interviews about dog food. The students, logically enough, conducted depth interviews with dog owners. When they returned from the field, John asked where the data was from dogs themselves. The students were initially shocked at the suggestion, but dutifully went out to interview dogs. As they bent down with their microphones to ask the dogs what they thought of their dog food, the nearby owners would often verbalise something like 'I ruv my Kibbles and Bits'. They found that live dogs were excellent projective stimuli to tease out psychodramatic role playing by their owners.

EXERCISE 3.3

Choose one of the projective exercises outlined above as well as a topic like the brand images of different prominent mobile phone companies, computer operating systems, or clothing brands. Find a partner to serve as an informant and complete the projective exercise. When you are through, switch roles and have the former informant utilise a different projective method for a different product category. Interpret your results for each other. Given these insights what might be a useful next stage in pursuing this line of research?

EXERCISE 3.4

Select one of the projective techniques not covered in this chapter from those referenced in the first paragraph of the summary section above. Look up the studies or reference works cited and learn what you can about this method. Unless you have chosen introspection/auto-ethnography, proceed to try out this technique with a partner. Once again switch roles and compare your results at the end of the exercise.

4

Ethnography and observational methods

The principles of observation

This chapter considers and explains the use of different forms of systematic observation as practices or techniques within the context of social scientific research data collection. Because, in consumer and marketing research, we tend to approach observational studies as revelatory of particular external realities, which will be generalised to greater or lesser extents to other contexts, we often consider that their so-called 'external validity' is particularly strong. However, we must also always consider the crucial situation of the researcher in observational studies. If the researcher is indeed instrumentalised as the 'instrument' or filter through which data in some sense flows, observational research in marketing and consumer research perhaps provides more and almost constant opportunities for the exercise of researcher judgment. Rather than simply setting up some sort of instrument to record data or observations, the observational consumer researcher is instead engaged in a nearly endless series of acts of decision-making about where to focus her attention, what to overlook, what to respond to, how to respond to it, what to record, and how to record it. As such, it can be quite easily seen that all observation is active. As perceptual science teaches us, there are a vast number of conscious and unconscious decisions and acts that contribute to the ostensibly passive act of observation.

Because of this, observational research places particular demands upon the researcher that require her or him to, in some sense, become increasingly aware of unconscious and subconscious processes in the act of conducting research.

The observational researcher cannot merely see the world through her or his own eyes as if through a transparent lens, but must increasingly open those eyes and interrogate not only what is seen and why it is seen, but also *how it is seen*. Observation is not merely external; it is inherently and unavoidably internal. The rigorous method of observation requires an observation, then, of the very act of observation. Understanding the social world of consumers demands that the researcher understand the act of research and the acts of the researcher.

On the surface, observation seemingly allows us to encounter the external world and the social world as events transpire, to catch the 'capta,' and to maintain 'information in context, as a gift, rather less invasively excising it for examination out of context, as a fact' (Sherry and Kozinets 2001, p. 166). Seemingly, observational methods can be as straightforward as pointing a camera and simply recording what is there, what 'actually' happens. But the wise social scientist realises that there are layers of deception wrapped up in the act of capturing capta and re-representing them as data. First, there are all of the native biases, motivations, values, and embedded interests of the contemporary researcher, not to mention the variously and partially bracketed and unbracketed theories and hypotheses that she or he carries along into the field. Why, after all, did you point your camera at *this and not that*? Why release the shutter *now and not then*? Next, and interrelating with many of the psychological and social filters that this embrace-of-bias perspective affects, are the simple physical limitations of the researcher, who may have limitations in vision, hearing, smelling, and so on, or who may have limited access to a site, or a limited range of movement within it. In a recent study of people's in-home consumption for a corporate client, Rob was accompanied by a colleague whose much finer sense of smell led to research realisations that would not have occurred without her assistance. The limitation can be social as well as physical in many cases; certain doors may simply be closed and meant to stay that way. For a literal example, some of the bedroom doors to the sanctum sanctorum of Arab homes remained closed or were only opened to Russ and Rana Sobh after considerable time in the field (Sobh and Belk 2011b, 2012). Finally, although observational techniques assume that people do not always do what they say, we must also question whether people will act as they normally act in the presence of a researcher and/or her or his various recording devices.

As we extensively discuss elsewhere in this book (see Chapters 7 and 8), direct quotations and the other products of researcher–consumer interviews are useful and relevant co-constructed narratives that reveal how consumers envision their thinking about particular topics and then represent them to researchers in particular research contexts. They are highly constructed manifestations of a confluence of overlapping social forces, including social desirability, financial or other compensation, status and social class, time of day, mood, recency of events, effects of social networks, and other effects. Yet we must not forget that the same effects are also in play during observational work, in addition to many kinds of observer effects. Still, as with Winston Churchill's oft-repeated quip that 'Democracy is the worst form of government, except for all those other forms that have been tried from time to time', we might consider that, despite their challenges and limitations, observational techniques are the worst way to gather data about the lived experiences of consumers, except for all the other forms of gathering data.

Observation methods grew out of the long anthropological tradition that dates back at least to Herodotus, an ancient Greek historian who lived circa 484–425 BCE and who recorded detailed cultural data around the time of the Greco-Persian wars. Marco Polo's systematic observations of different people and their customs in the thirteenth century earned him the title of 'the father of modern anthropology' (Rowe 1965). Thus, by the time that anthropologists were working in the field in the 1920s and 1930s in the so-called 'Chicago school tradition' (e.g., Whyte 1955), defined by extended periods of observation in real life social fields (Schwandt 2001, p. 179), we can say that observational and ethnographic approaches were already at least 2,300 years old.

The fundamental ethnography: learning ethnographic fundamentals at home

The focal point of the shrine is a box or chest which is built into the wall. In this chest are kept the many charms and magical potions without which no native believes he could live. These preparations are secured from a variety of specialised practitioners. The most powerful of these are the medicine men, whose assistance must be rewarded with substantial gifts. However, the medicine men do not provide the curative potions for their clients, but decide what the ingredients should be and then write them down in an ancient and secret language. This writing is understood only by the medicine men and by the herbalists who, for another gift, provide the required charm. (Miner 1956, p. 504)

In his classic article on the strange practices of the 'Nacerima' tribe, Horace Miner makes the point that observational ethnography has at its core the defamiliarising of the familiar until it seems strange. Only when something as ostensibly commonplace as a medicine cabinet filled with prescription medicine can be described as a household shrine filled with potions from the local medicine man can we begin to understand just how constructed and contingent are all of our naturalised social practices. Morris Holbrook (1998) offers a more elaborated version about the Kroywen – the inhabitants of Manhattan island – using auto-ethnography and stereoscopic photography.

(Continued)

(Continued)

In this one-week warm-up exercise in assuming a participant observational stance, you will perform fieldwork on your own life as if you were entering it as a stranger. Not only is this an excellent preparation for ethnographic and observational work in general, but also may serve as an interesting new source of research ideas from your own life that you can speak about with authority, as in the semi-autobiographical ethnographic sub-field of auto-ethnography (see Ellis 2004; or in consumer research see Holbrook 2005 and Gould 1990).

1 For one week, keep elaborate and detailed field notes on your life as a member of your current culture(s). You can focus on some particular elements of your culture (such as food, work, socialising, entertainment, internet use, hygiene habits, etc.). In your fieldnotes, focus on sensory experiences that go beyond the obvious. Notice sights, colours, sounds, smells, tastes, touches, and emotions, as well as events, words, and social interactions.
2 Collect 'artefacts' from your own life and habits. When you go places, collect the various items, business cards, and brochures. Keep them with your fieldnotes and build on them, annotate them and analyse them.
3 Shoot photographs of events that would normally be too mundane for you to analyse. You might also make video recordings. Dwell upon what you would normally dismiss as too 'normal' to be of interest. See Holbrook (1998) and Ziller (1990) for examples.
4 After three days of this research, decide upon a particular area that you will focus on. Conduct at least three interviews of at least 30 minutes each with people who know about this focal area. The focus should no longer be about you, but is instead expanded to an aspect of culture that you have observed in your life. For example, if you were studying food you might focus on food preparation or food shopping, or left-overs, or desserts. If it was left-overs, you might interview three friends in their own kitchens and have them talk about left-overs and go through their refrigerators and shelves with you. If you have observed details like the sharpness of knives in food preparation or the size and colour of packages in shopping or rituals of the order in which foods are eaten, try to engage those you interview in topics relating to these elements.
5 After the week is over, transcribe the interviews and keep this data as well as your observational fieldnotes somewhere you can readily retrieve them. You may use this data for your analysis in one of the future sections of this book (e.g., see Chapters 7–8).

In general, observational research methods are qualitative techniques in which the researcher systematically seeks to capture and record in some way the manifest acts of a particular group of people and then to rigorously analyse them for some scientific purpose. Observational methods must involve the direct first-hand eye-witness accounts of social activities such as 'practices,' a research practice which has been elevated and developed in the recent rise of the 'practice theory' orientation (see Schatzki 1996; Reckwitz 2005). In these recent schools, strong attention to the actual physical elements of social action is the focus of research. In addition, these schools of thought are influenced by actor-network theories which direct attention to the role and even agency of non-human physical objects (their ability to affect or influence people; for an excellent example of how a table affects family life see Epp and Price 2010).

Observational methods differ from other marketing research methods such as interviews, focus groups, and surveys in that they include more of the social context and interactions surrounding a consumer's behaviour and setting, rather than relying largely or exclusively upon what consumers say about such matters, as when they tell us what they do. Needless to say, observational methods are naturalistic. That is, they demand that data be collected within a field site, the location where and when the consumer behaviour of interest occurs.

Observational research methods are popular within both academic and practitioner-oriented consumer and marketing research (Lofland and Lofland 1995). In marketing and consumer research, observational methods can be defined as *qualitative consumer and marketing research methods in which the researchers view, record, and then analyse the manifest actions of consumers as they engage in some market-related activity*. We can consider many such activities that we might observe. Observational methods cover many sorts of consumer and marketing research. They would include the sort of detailed cultural observation that transpires when researchers join subcultures such as Harley-Davidson riders in order to understand their structure, values, and wider social significance (Schouten and McAlexander 1995), when they observe brand communities in a small city (Muñiz and O'Guinn 2001), or when they spend time with modern Mountain Men in contemporary Rendezvous gatherings (Belk and Costa 1998). Observation also includes the collection and analysis of recordings of large groups of anonymous people, as with positioned stationary cameras and CCTV apparatus set up in public city spaces and private retail spaces. These methods also encompass placing cameras in people's homes as part of an agreed upon research period of study (e.g., Jayasinghe and Ritson forthcoming).

When used as a method for generating data about human experience, observation traditionally has tended to be characterised by the following elements (Schwandt 2001, p. 179):

- Social acts, events, and practices are viewed from the perspective of the people being studied.
- Attention to detail is prioritised.
- Events, practices, and actions have been understood by situating them in a particular social and historical context.
- Social acts are regarded as dynamic and processual rather than as discrete events or sets of events.

- Some general theoretical framework shapes the initial contact and construction of the observational framing; however,
- The premature imposition of theoretical notions on participant perspectives is avoided, presumably by some effort of will of the researcher in which she or he brackets preconceptions and attempts to overcome her or his own inherent biases and tendencies.

We can certainly add an enhanced attention to social practices (Reckwitz 2005) and to the influence and agency of non-human objects (Epp and Price 2010; Latour 2005) to the list. In order to deepen our understanding of observational techniques, it will be instructive to develop our understanding of their role in ethnographic methods. We proceed from a look at ancient history to discuss some of the more modern and futuristic variations of observational methods that collect data using CCTV and also those that use videography as a research and representational technique. Moving to a more archaeological and artefactual approach, we then talk about historical methods of observation that involve the collection and analysis of artefacts. Each section will build upon the fundamental understanding of the principles of observation gained through a more in-depth examination at the foundational principles of the ethnographic approach.

About ethnography

Ethnos is a Greek term denoting a people, a race or a cultural group. Combined with the suffix graphic (writing or representing) to form 'ethnographic,' the term refers to a subdiscipline known as descriptive anthropology – in general terms, the social scientific pursuit devoted to describing and, to a greater or lesser extent explaining, humanity's different ways of life. Ethnography has been defined as 'the social scientific description of a people and the cultural basis of their peoplehood' (Vidich and Lyman 1994, p. 25). Ethnography is the premier scientific method for writing about the study of cultures in many fields of inquiry, and has been so, as mentioned earlier, for millennia.

In the consumer research field, ethnographic descriptions of cultures of consumption are only the most recent manifestation of consumer behaviour's interest in using ethnography to research the cultural foundations of consumer behaviour. The first and still probably the most influential presentation of ethnography in consumer behaviour studies are Hirschman (1986), Belk et al. (1988), and Wallendorf and Belk (1989) who explicated the 'humanistic inquiry' methodology of Lincoln and Guba (1985), and adapted it to marketing and consumer research, as well as Belk et al. (1989), which described the sacred versus profane aspects of consumer behaviour through participant-observation of buyer and seller behaviour at swap meets.

It should also be noted and acknowledged that there is a long tradition of qualitative research within marketing and consumer research, particularly in the form of focus groups, open-ended surveys and interviews. For example, Sidney Levy (1981) examined the meaning of food consumption, which built on the theories of the anthropologist Claude Lévi-Strauss to suggest how different types of tastes for food were class-based in their origins. The differences between focus groups and interviews, on the one hand, and ethnographies, on the other, lie in the ethnographic fieldwork emphasis on researcher immersion, prolonged exposure and participation-observation in a naturalistic setting (Arnould and Wallendorf 1994).

Since 1988, published accounts of ethnographic investigations of cultures and consumption practices have regularly contributed to the consumer research literature. McCracken (1988) studied 'Lois Roget' who sought to preserve family stories by inculcating in her children the histories of the family heirlooms in her home. Arnould (1989), also a pioneer in marketing ethnography, explored the geopolitical and theoretical ramifications of consumption in the cultures of Zinder Province, in the Niger Republic. Hill and Stamey (1990) and Hill (1991) explored the consumption world of homeless persons. Workman (1993) contributed to marketing research with an ethnography that explored the culture of marketing practitioners in a high-tech firm. Arnould and Price (1993) interpreted the service relationships of the river-rafting experience. Peñaloza (1994) examined the consumption acculturation of Mexican immigrants to the United States. Holt (1995) sat in the bleachers in Chicago's Wrigley Field in order to arrive at a consumption experience typology. Schouten and McAlexander (1995) explored the 'subculture of consumption' existing among rich urban bikers in Harley-Davidson riding clubs and at rallies. These important studies and the many others that have been published since 1995 have introduced and developed powerful, innovative and useful new terms and concepts to the field of consumer and marketing research such as consumer acculturation, brand community, brand relationships, and the transfer of meaning. They have yielded new frameworks for testing and have stimulated philosophical and methodological thought.

Aside from informing scholarship, marketing ethnographies may also contain practical marketing insights. Several of the research projects cited above have resulted in, or been part of, studies specifically designed to answer industry questions and inform industry strategy. Often marketing managers – especially those in service industries – are interested in accounting for the incredible success of one outstanding product in their field. What lies behind the incredible marketing success of Marlboro cigarettes? Why do multiple generations of people become Grateful Deadheads, Beatles worshippers, or Disney fans? What makes for the 'star appeal' of any outstanding product or service? These types of questions suggest the need for ethnography – a researcher entering, indulging, and becoming a fully-participating member of a culture of consumption, what Arnould and Wallendorf (1994, pp. 500–501) term a mode of 'thick inscription' in 'marketing-oriented ethnography' that results 'when the ethnographer becomes an intimate insider in a consumption context or culture'.

Beginning a scientific publication-oriented ethnographic inquiry

Let us consider an ethnographic research project whose purpose is to develop scientific knowledge about consumer and marketing research that could be published in a major academic journal such as the *Journal of Consumer Research*. Chapter 2 provided ideas of how to begin conceptually. Now consider how to begin in terms of fieldwork.

- How would you initiate the fieldwork for such a project? What would you do? Would you start with a fieldsite? Or would you start with an idea for a topic, and then try to find a fieldsite in which to investigate it?
- Once you identify and locate a few possible fieldsites, how would you judge which sites to investigate?
- Upon arrival at your fieldsite, what kinds of observations will be helpful? What will you look for? What sort of people will you interview? What will you ask in your interviews? What information and observational material will you be seeking?
- Might you use other research methods in coordination with this method of observation?

The example is intended to get you started in building an understanding of how to think about deploying specific ethnographic methods. The aim is to bring the lived reality of consumers into marketing and consumer research in a way that builds upon a body of scholarly literature and contributes to ongoing research conversations. For more specific advice about how to conduct research-oriented ethnographies, and for the answers to the questions we pose in this exercise, please see the chapter section entitled 'Doing ethnography'.

Thorough analysis often depends upon a negotiated understanding of the perspectives of the embedded and culturally-familiar informant with the researcher's own knowledge, customs, and agenda. Participant observation, a combination of the two perspectives that emerges from immersion in the field for a prolonged time, is the hallmark of ethnography. Alternately intrusive and unobtrusive, ethnographers attempt to apprehend through direct experience, using as many sensory channels as required, the cultural worlds that consumers live within. In a way, the ethnographer seeks to be re-acculturated and resocialised through the ethnographic encounter. Intimacy and engagement are the goals; rapport and trust are the means. When successful, ethnographies provide a vivid window into the world of others, a chance to bridge an intersubjective boundary and gain a more profound understanding. As Walsh (2000, p. 237) notes, ethnography 'opens out the possibility of an understanding of reality which no other method can realise'.

Mariampolski (2006, pp. 8–9) usefully elaborates the key characteristics of ethnography as including some or all of the following: engagement, context, subject-centredness, improvisation and flexibility, triangulation, and a holistic perspective. At its core, ethnography is about the conduct of naturalistic research with a cultural focus. Unlike laboratory experiments, focus groups, or questionnaire-based surveys, ethnography involves a 'going out' of a researcher into a socially pre-existing setting or event rather than a 'taking in' of a research 'subject', 'informant', 'member', or 'participant' into a constructed research setting. The latter techniques were known in early anthropology as front porch ethnography, in which the subjects were made to come to the researcher in something resembling a master–servant relationship. This is no longer done today except in behavioural experiments. Flexibility and adaptability have enabled ethnography to be used for over a century to represent and understand the behaviours of people belonging to almost every race, nationality, religion, culture and age group on the planet.

Ethnographic research enables consumer and marketing researchers to gain a detailed and nuanced understanding of a consumption or marketplace phenomenon, and then to capture and convey it with full attention to its cultural qualities. Ethnographies can provide a strong sense of the lived experience of culture members. As with case studies, ethnographies build on related fields of knowledge and are grounded in context; they become infused with local knowledge. The hallmark of ethnography, then, is in 'fieldwork', where fieldwork 'means living with and living like those who are studied' (Van Maanen 1988, p. 2). The history of ethnography places an extremely high standard on what, traditionally, has counted as fieldwork: the full-time and lengthy involvement and engagement of a researcher with the human members of a culture upon their home turf.

Fortunately for many consumer and marketing researchers, the basic methods for conducting ethnography are now well established in our field, although the standards and definitions have been shifting for decades and continue to change. As sociologists began to adapt the techniques to the study of nearby street corners and subcultures, and as new variants of these cultural studies were spawned, the urban cultural focus meant that researchers did not have to leave home in order to ethnographically study the Other. In fact, the Other could be situated right in the researcher's own backyard. By the second half of the twentieth century, ethnography's methodological advantages had been recognised (although still not widely) by industry research buyers, by marketing and marketing research communities, and by dozens of specialised firms and practitioners who applied their training, education, and unique observational skills to study the habits and habitats of the wild, untamed consumer (Angrosino 2007).

Professional marketing researchers and applied anthropologists Patty Sunderland and Rita Denny (2007) consider it sufficient for a study to be called ethnographic if its insights are gathered from 'in the field' observations of people as they go about their daily lives. Ethnography in its contemporary academic and marketing research form is thus a specialised, imperfect (for purists), but useful adaptation of the observational (and, less often, the participative) techniques developed by anthropologists for the study of so-called 'primitives'. So, rather than, say, having to understand female teenage shoe consumers' habits by participatively living with and living like teenage shoe consumers, modern marketing research ethnographers attempt instead to study and understand them, their lives, their consumption habits, their meanings and lifestyles in a naturalistic setting, like a shoe store, a teenager's bedroom and closet, shopping mall, or online forum about fashion or shoes. This data can, and often should, be enhanced with first person perspectives obtained from interviews as well as self-generated data such as written or video journals.

Ethnography is also an inherently open-ended practice. It combines with multiple other research practices, such as interviews, discourse analysis, literary analysis, semiotics, still photography, and videography. Any given ethnography will already deploy multiple methods. Increasingly, as we will discuss in this chapter, other adjuncts such as photography, videography and audio recording are incorporated into research acts of participant observation (see also Chapter 6).

Although it places demands upon the researcher, and the research participant, getting close to the consumer through ethnography is a source of valuable intelligence about how consumers actually behave in certain situations. Because ethnographers are focused on the subtleties of cultural members living in natural contexts, no two ethnographies and no two ethnographers employ exactly the same approach. Ethnography relies on what consumer anthropologist John Sherry (1991a, p. 572) calls 'the acuity of the researcher-as-instrument'. The rough outline of several of the elements of this acuity has been sketched in sections above, but it must be built upon a foundation of self-awareness. That acuity is also in constant flux, based upon adaptation and bricolage, and is incredibly dynamic, continually being renewed, reinvented, and refashioned to suit particular fields of scholarship, research questions, research sites, times, other contexts, researcher preferences, skill sets, methodological innovations, and cultural phenomena.

Developing the procedures for a
management-oriented ethnographic inquiry

Let us examine a managerially-oriented ethnographic research project. Consider the needs of a hypothetical fast food company seeking marketing research about consumers' changing tastes in fast food. Let us call this company Annie's Donuts. The decision that managers are interested in researching concerns which menu items they should offer to consumers at their donut store locations.

- How would you develop an ethnographic project to inform this managerial decision?
- What would you need to know? What kind of observations would be helpful? What would you look for? Where would you conduct your observations? Who would you observe?
- Would you need to interview anyone? Why? What questions would you ask them in the interviews?
- Could you use other methods in coordination with this method of observation?

The example is intended to have you start to build an understanding about how ethnographic methods can be a very valuable way to bring the lived reality of consumers into marketing decision-making. For more advice on how to think about theory development and data collection in managerially oriented projects, see Chapter 8 in this book. For more detailed examples and advice, we recommend two excellent books on the topic: Mariampolski (2006), and Sunderland and Denny (2007). McCracken (2009) is a related and inspiring book about the need for more cultural understanding in the world of management and marketing.

Doing ethnography

Observational research in general does not necessarily involve participation captured in fieldnotes. However, in ethnography, it almost always does. Observational research in general can be very close, or it can occur at a distance, such as with the placement of CCTV cameras. In ethnography, observations are always close. Ethnographies tend to define people by their groupings or gatherings, as well as by the way they identify their culture. Observations have no such obligations to cluster people by particular identities or cultural groupings. Therefore, all ethnographies involve observation, not all observational research is ethnographic.

Thus far, this chapter has only described ethnography without providing practical, hands-on, how-to guidelines for the conduct of ethnography. The reason for this is partly that ethnography, unlike interviewing or focus groups, *is not in itself a method.* Ethnography is instead *an approach to doing research that draws primarily from its participant-observational stance.*

As Brewer (2000, p. 59) notes 'Ethnography is not a particular method of data collection but a style of research that is distinguished by its objectives, which are to understand the social meanings and activities of people in a given 'field' or setting, and an approach, which involves close association with, and often participation in, this setting' (Brewer 2000: 59). Goffman (1989, p. 125) insists that field research involves 'subjecting yourself, your own body and your own personality, and your own social situation, to the set of contingencies that play upon a set of individuals, so that you can physically and ecologically penetrate their circle of response to their social situation, or their work situation, or their ethnic situation'.

Many ethnographic methodologies build upon a philosophical base of phenomenology or social phenomenology (Schutz 1962; Berger and Luckmann 1966). As noted in Chapter 2, phenomenology and ethnomethodology interpret and explain human action and thought utilising descriptions that refer to their basis in taken-for-granted (or 'doxic') reality. Because the sense of doxic reality seems self-evident to social members who share it (Bourdieu 1977; Garfinkel 1967), social phenomenologists focus their research on everyday subjective meanings and experiences, communications and content (Holstein and Gubrium 1994, pp. 262–264). For example, Goulding et al. (2009) performed an ethnographic study of UK club cultures and paid close attention to interpreting the illicit pursuit of pleasure in these venues, often through recreational drug use. In emphasising the shared, or 'intersubjective', quality of the construction of pleasure in these places, Goulding et al. (2009) applied a phenomenological foundation to inform their ethnographic perspective.

An illustrative case

For illustration purposes, let us consider one example of an academic ethnography in some depth. Through this illustration, we will briefly consider a number of fundamental principles of ethnography such as how to pick a field site, how to gain familiarity with the culture, how to assume a role in the research setting, what sorts of research actions to take once there, what to consider when taking field notes, how to write field notes, how to collect other observations, what actions to avoid when doing research there, and how to build connections with groups. Unfortunately, in this short summary we will be unable to go into very significant depth on these vital topics. However, we will refer to some excellent fundamental texts on ethnography that can be used to further guide the interested reader.

The example will be Rob's PhD dissertation research on the *Star Trek* media fan community and culture. For the initial research study, Rob booted up with a non-specific interest in media fan communities and *Star Trek* culture in particular that was largely guided by Baudrillard's notions of hyperreality and also driven by the then-current cultural success of one of the *Star Trek* television series' syndicated franchises. In order to investigate the phenomenon, Rob needed to localise the aspects of it that were of interest and from there proceed to identify specific groups of people who might be accessible and amenable to the ethnographic intrusion. Those cultural gatherings consisted of groups of people who were united around the consumption practices, meanings, and symbolic systems of that particular media franchise and manifested through local fan clubs, through regional and national fan conventions, and over the internet. Thus the ethnographic research project transpired across these sites, and included fieldwork at: a dedicated local *Star Trek* fan club; *Star Trek* and *Star Trek*-related conventions; and on *Star Trek* and science fiction fan-community-related forums on the internet.

In order to prepare for this research, Rob sought to engage with and understand as much as possible about the community and the materials that mattered to it. This included viewing and re-viewing the television series shows and seven movies as well as reading a variety of professionally produced and fan produced *Star Trek* information. In addition, it meant that he needed to pay careful attention to 'what matter matters and what matters matter' to the members of these communities and this culture. Understanding the world of objects, practices, values, meanings, and understandings, required careful observation, conversation, and related research and reading about the products and practices of the fan community.

Engagement, immersion, and participation

In marketing, full participation in ethnographic inquiries has been inconstantly applied. Wallendorf and Arnould (1991) did experience their own Thanksgiving rituals, Arnould and Price (1993) did go on river-rafting expeditions, and Schouten and McAlexander (1995) did taste life as bikers. Overall, however, many marketing ethnographies have adopted an experience-distant stance that emphasises the observational element of participant-observation at the expense of the participative element. Methodologically, the work on *Star Trek* fan communities sought to re-emphasise the crucial role of participation in consumer behaviour ethnography, as did related work on Mountain Men rendezvous (Belk and Costa 1998) and on the Burning Man project (Kozinets 2002b). In general, and following anthropological practice, we believe that this type of profound engagement should be highly valued in marketing and consumer research ethnographies.

Although many ethnographers recommend an 'ethnographic year' of 13 months, there is no de facto set time span for a high-quality ethnography. The guideline, as with grounded research, is to reach theoretical saturation. Rob's fieldwork took place through participating in four *Star Trek* conventions and also through becoming an active member of a Canadian *Star Trek* fan club. Participation unfolded in an organic manner, with attendance at a regional convention leading to conversations with local fans and with members of the recruitment commit-tees of local fan clubs. After learning about these clubs, one was selected, and Rob paid his dues (literally) and became a member. With full disclosure of his identity as a PhD student and aspiring researcher, he volunteered for the Command Crew executive of the club. He held the position of Marketing Director and served on one committee before volunteering as recording Secretary for the fan club's execu-tive committee, a position that allowed him to take notes naturally as a part of his fan-related role. When participating in the community, he completely assumed the fan role while also being open about his stance as a researcher. This illustrates a strategy commonly used by ethnographers to volunteer in various positions in order to learn about as well as partake in a particular community or culture as an insider. The secretary position is also a common and useful vantage point.

Ethnographic research is based upon immersion in a field phenomenon for an amount of time sufficient to develop a deep understanding of a phenomenon, group or culture. This longer-term aspect of ethnography has been called 'pro-longed engagement'. Wallendorf and Belk (1989, p. 71) ask 'how prolonged is prolonged?' The particular amount of time required to gain a sufficiently deep understanding of the phenomenon under study obviously varies by project. The amount of time spent in the field, and the way it is reported, varies widely. In the consumer behaviour field, Hill and Stamey (1990, p. 306) spent 'more than 1,000 hours in the field', continuously from early 1985 to the middle of 1989. Arnould and Price (1993, p. 30) went on five river-rafting trips. Schouten and McAlexander gradually deepened their involvement in the Harley Davidson cul-ture over a period of three and a half years. Data collection for the *Star Trek* pro-ject took place over 20 months of fieldwork, a period that was sufficient to obtain a detailed understanding of the specific topic under study. The research focused upon the meanings acquired through the collective (e.g., in the fan club or at a convention) and collectively-influenced consumption (e.g., at-home collection of memorabilia) of goods in the *Star Trek* culture of consumption, rather than, for example, a general study of the entire *Star Trek* fan phenomenon itself.

Inscribing fieldnotes

Whatever the length or level of engagement, it must result in a data record. Thus, one of the most important elements of ethnographic fieldwork is in the research act of producing fieldnotes, which is where data is generated. 'Fieldnotes are accounts *describing* experiences and observations the researcher has made while participating in an intense and involved manner' (Emerson et al. 1995, pp. 4–5; italics in original). Fieldnotes are intended to record every aspect of the field-worker's sensory, social and communicative experiences, including and ranging from what the researcher thought, to what they felt, to what they saw, heard, smelt, touched, and tasted. Through fieldnotes, researchers seek to capture every element of the ethnographer's experience in the field, as vividly and with as much attention to both detail and emotion as possible. They also should be captured as close to the experience as possible. With some training, considerable detail and large amounts of information are capable of being held in memory and recalled until being developed and written into fieldnotes.

Some methodologists counsel keeping a separate 'reflexive journal' (e.g., Wallendorf and Belk 1989), a type of personal diary in which the researcher offers reflections, tentative interpretations, and planning regarding the data collected and the data collection process. Although the process of fieldnote creation is still largely a black art untaught in books and courses (Emerson et al. 1995; Wolfinger 2002), most methodologists counsel keeping short, point form or shorthand 'jot-tings' while in the field, and then expanding or 'annotating' these jottings into full and detailed text as soon after exiting the field as possible. Chapter 6 discusses various aids like smart phones that can facilitate these processes.

Through processes such as these, the ethnographer is expected to produce field-notes and related written 'journal' materials, which will accumulate throughout the continuous exposure process of fieldwork. Since 'most contemporary field researchers rely heavily upon both fieldnotes and recordings' (Emerson et al. 1995, p. 218), mechanical recordings of field experiences such as photographs and audiotapes are often used to supplement the extensive fieldnotes and inter-view transcriptions. Contemporary fieldwork manuals regularly emphasise the use of mechanical recording equipment (e.g., Ellen 1984; Jackson 1987; Wilson 1986). However, these recordings can never substitute for the process of inscrib-ing fieldnotes because cultural understanding emerges through the process of inscription. Writing fieldnotes is thus not simply a way to record data. 'To view the writing of descriptions simply as a matter of producing texts that *correspond* accurately to what has been observed is to assume that there is but one 'best' description of any particular event' (Emerson et al. 1995, p. 5; italics in original). In fact, inscribing fieldnotes is instead a part of the very conduct of fieldwork itself (see Joy et al. 2006).

Geertz (1973) has been one of the pre-eminent anthropologists noting, devel-oping, and exemplifying the idea that writing is the cornerstone of ethnography, and fieldnotes have traditionally been viewed as the foundation of that writing. However, considerable obscurity exists about the required content and process of creating fieldnotes. Van Maanen (1988, p. 223) rather dismissively critically covers the topic:

> To put it bluntly, fieldnotes are gnomic, shorthand reconstructions of events, observations, and conversations that took place in the field. They are composed well after the fact as inexact notes to oneself and represent simply one of many levels of textualisation set off by experience. To disentangle the interpretive procedures at work as one moves across levels is problematic to say the least.

In Rob's *Star Trek* research, the 'levels of textualisation set off by experiences' initially took shape through his tape recorded notes (and, yes, it was on actual mini-cassette tapes) and with hastily scribbled 'jottings' in a small journal or on small scraps of paper created while he was still immersed in field settings like fan club meetings or conventions. These notes were subsequently developed into full, detailed, dated and numbered entries that were typed into a laptop computer and saved as individual files for later organisation in a QDA or qualitative data analysis program. During fieldwork in public places such as conventions, a still camera was used to take photographs of activities of interest. Throughout all of this activity, the notes that returned were 'messy' texts in Marcus's (1998) sense of the term. That is, the fieldnotes contained gaps, contradictions, ruptures, and fluidity, and were situated openly within particular interests and subject positions. For example, consider how observation is messily merged with personal reflective experience in this fieldnote excerpt recorded directly after the Toronto Trek IX convention in Toronto, Canada:

> I went into the trade room or the dealer's room where they had all kinds of Star Trek merchandise. It is just such a rich collection of consumption information I can't even begin to describe it all. There were all sorts of things, I'll just give some quick impressions. There was one guy standing there with a microphone showing a new piece of software that he had which used the security system of the Deep Space 9 TV show and had voice identification so it was a computer and it said you had to identify yourself so you said 'Odo, let me in', – Odo's the security chief on DS9, and either he lets you in and the gates open and you're into your Windows-based program or else he says 'Stop playing with my computer' or some other off-putting type of comment. There were people at the back selling scripts, original scripts from the series, as well as writers' guidelines. . . . There was a real strong pressure that I felt – this is a subjective datum, but I consider it to be a valid one – to buy fan-related things. Spending a hundred dollars for a signed picture, or spending a hundred dollars for a page of fan artwork of your favorite character from the show, seemed not to be a very big deal. And in fact I felt a very strong pressure in myself to want to indulge in these sorts of things. I think one of the reasons for that, the reason that I came up with after reflecting on it the next morning, today, is that it's kind of like being on vacation, in that you want a memento of this place that you really had a good time. There's very much that same carnival-escape type atmosphere as in a vacation spot.

This fieldnote excerpt seeks to record and reveal some of the subjective reality Rob felt while participating in the *Star Trek* convention. It is the data of direct experience, full of emotion, desire, humour, even lust for possession. The in situ observations from the convention have clearly been expanded based upon subsequent after-exposure reflection, yet they seem to contain some of the rawer, reactive, more immediate emotions that were felt when Rob was physically and avariciously present in the dealer's room. As a typical fieldnote, this is not the simple, transparent transmission of factual data, but the contextualised writing of a very personal experience. 'The ethnographic task is not merely to record the indigenous view of a shared life-world, but to reveal the subject's and ethnographer's interactive assessment of, and response to, it' (Page 1988, p. 165). To reflect this interactive dance of interpretation, Rob later expanded upon some of his ethnographic experiences as a Star Trek fan researcher in a research-inspired poem entitled 'me/My Research/ Avatar' (Kozinets 2011, p. 479). The following is a short quote from the poem that uses fieldnote excerpts to reveal some of the ethnographically-exposed emotions

red screens that cascade, careen and
scream like doubling buck shot soap bubbles bursting towards a
consumption of presents.
a consuming presence. a consuming of presence in the dark gloom of
consumer envy.

(Kozinets 2011, p. 479)

Field-workers place themselves in the field, into the context of experience, in order to permit the reflexive process of interpretation, understanding, and sense-making to be known first-hand. The point is not that an ethnographer can live the lives of Cultural Others in any sort of complete manner, but that she can live them close enough to begin to understand how their worlds have been constructed. Fieldwork of an ethnographic kind is authentic to the degree it approximates the stranger stepping into a culturally alien community to become, for a time and in an unpredictable way, an active and embodied part of the face-to-face relationships in that community.

In summary, this short section of our chapter on observational research has sought to provide some guidance about the conduct of ethnography. Using a brief overview of the ethnographic work from an unpublished PhD dissertation that examined *Star Trek* fan culture, the section illustrates concerns about choosing a topic; linking it to a site of cultural activity; engaging in participation, immersion, and engagement; capturing data; and inscribing ethnographic fieldnotes. For further guidance, please consult a recent and more detailed methodological text such as Fetterman (2010), Murchison (2010), or Wolcott (2008). For further details on the articles that resulted from the study described, see Kozinets (2001, 2007).

What's the difference? Ethnographies for theory and practice

If you have been following along and completing the exercise in this chapter, you have now planned two ethnographies. If you have not been following the exercises and thus learning by doing, then you are missing out on a major opportunity afforded to you by this book! Consider completing these two exercises, and then finish reading this box.

You have now (we hope) completed two exercises, one that has directed you to develop an ethnographic project for a consumer research or marketing a scholarly journal article, and the other for a marketing research project to inform the practice of marketers.

Now, consider this question. Is an ethnography performed for marketing research in industry purposes different from one performed for scientific consumer research intended for publication in a journal such as the *Journal of Consumer Research*?

If you think that the two forms of ethnography are indeed different, have a look at what you wrote for your exercise and then write down some of the main differences you have found before reading on.

We believe that, although the basic approach is the same, the two kinds of ethnographies differ in, at least, the following five ways:

1 **Focus**: an academic ethnography is expected to contribute to theory by examining focal constructs in a natural context; practitioner ethnography is expected to contribute to marketing strategy or tactics by revealing consumer wants, desires, attitudes, or behaviours.
2 **Immersion and time**: academic ethnographies typically require long-standing immersion in a culture of community, often on the order of an ethnographic year (13 months, by convention); practitioner ethnographies tend to be more time-sensitive, often taking place over approximately an 8-week period.
3 **Contexts**: academic ethnographies tend to observe more social interaction between culture members; practitioner ethnographies are often more concerned with the ways that individuals act and express themselves in a context. In addition, practitioner ethnographies may be more attuned to how consumers interact with particular objects in use, in order to suggest improvements to packaging or design.
4 **Methodological explication**: academic ethnographies tend to spend considerable time thinking about, refining, and explaining method; practitioner ethnographies do not tend to focus as much on method or its explanation.
5 **Representing results**: Ethnography actually means 'writing about culture' and its form of representation has been held to be extremely important in the conduct of cultural anthropology. Academic ethnographies consider as their final output a written text formatted like a conventional journal article, which will likely have gone through several rounds of peer scientific review. Practitioner ethnographies tend to use PowerPoint slides and, increasingly often, videography, to present their findings to managers.

From their purpose to their final execution, then academic consumer research and practitioner marketing research ethnographies turn out to have many important differences. There are more details on these differences, in general and in some specific instances, in Chapters 8 and 9 of this book.

Observational interviewing

Observations of behaviours during interviews are yet another valuable source of data for marketing and consumer researchers. Although observation can certainly happen in artificial settings such as software usability labs, or during focus groups when consumers are presented with packages, prototypes, or other objects of interest, observational interviews do not usually occur in front of other consumers or behind one-way glass.

Observational interviews are also frequently called 'in-home interviews' or 'ethnographic interviews'. The key aspect of these interviews is that they take place in a naturalistic setting, namely in a setting that is familiar to the consumer. Ethnographic research leads us to the conclusion that observations of product use as well as consumer interviews are more valuable when they take place in locations where the product is usually shopped for, examined, purchased and, especially, consumed. In those naturalistic settings such as consumers' homes, consumers' favourite stores, in front of consumers' computers, and even in consumers' workplaces, the consumer tends to relax and generally finds it much easier to recall their recent actions, thoughts, and opinions (Sunderland and Denny 2007).

In terms of how to conduct the interview, Abrams (2000) insists that it is very important to maintain a laid back, easy going, and highly relaxed attitude. In depth interviews as well as casual ethnographic interviews, it is imperative that the researcher gain the trust of the consumer during the interview. The interviewer should maintain a sense of quiet interest in what the consumer is doing, but not exert any sort of pressure or reflect any sort of judgment. Simultaneously, the interviewer will employ a refined, revised, and precise observation and interview guide in order to ensure that all of the relevant questions are being asked and that the informant is given an opportunity to thoroughly answer.

The observational interview will usually be recorded, often with a digital audio recorder. It is also often useful to help the interview along by using various projective techniques (see Chapters 3 and 6 for additional details). One method, which was used by Coupland (2005) in her study of household brand usage, was to use everyday household objects as the projectives for observational consumer interviews. So in a study of car washing behaviours, consumers might be asked to hold a chamois and to talk about the chamois and about car cleaning, and perhaps cleaning and cleanliness in general. Depending on the participant, the interview style, and the overall mood of the interaction, this sort of projective usage could lead to nostalgic reminiscences of 'Mom's insistence on a clean floor everywhere' or 'the first time I ever cleaned a car with my Dad', to a discussion of the natural versus artificial chamois materials, the price of chamois, where to find the best retail selections of chamois, or to many other interesting culturally-inflected consumption paths.

Sometimes, following the axiom that six eyes are better than two, it is useful to conduct observational research with a small team of researchers. It is not uncommon for a small number of marketing and research practitioners to enter the homes of research participants. There should not be too many researchers relative to participants so as not to outnumber the actual participants in your cultural site. During the conduct of the observational work, the members of the research team will carefully observe, inspect, interview, film, record, and take notes after their close encounters with consumers in their natural habitat. Often, they will build their understanding from observations of individuals, smaller groupings, and/or the entire family proceeding with their usual consumption and shopping behaviours. After the study, the team will regroup and debrief together at an offsite location. They will review their notes and plan for future sessions. After they complete their rounds of observational interviews, the team will write up their findings and present their recommendations (Abrams 2000).

The 'mystery shopper' method is another very common observation method used to audit and research retailers. With the mystery shopping method, a researcher or small group of researchers will enter a retail environment and pose as ordinary consumers. Acting out the role of the shopper, these observational researchers (who can be quite amateur, recruited on the internet, paid per report), gather specific information about the various factors of the retail experience. How long until you were approached by a salesperson? Was the store well lit? Was Product X on display? Where in the store was Product X? How long did you need to wait before you were checked out? What did the salesperson say to you as you paid? Questions will tend to assess the quality of the retail service as well as specific elements of product choice and display. Mystery shoppers will report their findings either to other researchers who then will aggregate the data or they can also report directly to the final client.

For a view of consumers shopping, another commonly used technique is shop-alongs (Lowrey et al. 1998; Otnes and McGrath 2001). In this technique, the researcher accompanies a shopper or a natural group of shoppers like a family as they go through one or more stores performing their normal shopping activity. It is important to establish rapport first, so a shop-along might be undertaken after one or more depth interviews are conducted earlier with the same consumers. The researcher not only observes, but casually converses with the shopper(s), sometimes getting them to amplify their thoughts in accepting or rejecting certain goods as well as their overall experience shopping on that occasion.

In the presence of a skilled researcher, consumers will usually begin to relax, act naturally, and to disclose interesting consumption information within a period as short as a few minutes. One general indicator of their veracity is that researchers can rapidly become confidantes to private knowledge. Research participants can quickly disclose things that might not be socially acceptable. For example, husbands might reveal that they have a deep-seated need for their wives' approval. Parents' might reveal their deep-seated need for their children's approval. We might even learn some consumers' 'dirty little secrets' – that they don't floss, brush, comb, or clean as often as they feel they should or that their house is always 'a mess' (Belk et al. 2007). All of this disclosure of socially negative behaviour is an indicator, but far from an ironclad guarantee, that the researchers are building trust and rapport with informants, and that consumers are not behaving in a significantly different way in their homes when the researcher is present than they would if the researcher were not present. However, it is important to note that every social act is a construction. So it is likely that consumers are used to performing these acts differently with different people. In other words, we act differently when eating alone than we do when we are eating with a spouse, with our parents, with a group of friends, with guests we barely know, and so on. The more contextually delicate the research, the more the ethnographer can tap into these various social contexts for theoretically useful and industrially applicable details.

Using videography, cameras, and CCTV in observational research

Over the last two decades, the technique of 'videography' has gained significant acceptance and even popularity both within the professional and academic areas of marketing and consumer research (Belk and Kozinets 2005; Kozinets and Belk 2006). In consumer research, videography involves the use of audiovisual recorders to capture the naturalistic observational and interview data generated by and about consumers and consumption, and then the subsequent use of edited audiovisual material to represent these findings as useful knowledge. So, just as an ethnography refers both to the act of doing naturalistically embedded research and also the written or textual product of this research, so too does a videography describe both the use of audiovisual recordings for data collection and for research representation.

As noted elsewhere (e.g., Belk and Kozinets 2005), one of the key drivers of the growth of videographic methods lies in its increased accessibility. The expenses that accompany the production and distribution of high quality video material have fallen drastically over the past decade due to the rapid economies of scale in the manufacturing of digital technology – both hardware (such as prosumer cameras) and software (such as video editing suites, e.g., Adobe Premiere, Final Cut Pro). Where filmmaking once was prohibitively expensive, and only the domain of broadcast professionals, now marketing research for both academics and practitioners can easily enter this realm with excellent results.

The videotaped individual or group interview constitutes the single most common, and perhaps most unimaginative, use of videography (Belk and Kozinets 2005). These interviews can be conducted in a research facility or, preferably and more in sync with the naturalistic principles of ethnographic and observational research, in a field setting. Compared to audio recordings of interviews, e-mail interviews, phone interviews, or surveys, videotaped interviews offer major advantages in that they allow the capture of body language, facial expression, gestures, and other temporal and spatial dimensions of human behaviour and social meaning.

The second most common use of video is to employ the video camera to record naturalistic observations. These sorts of observational methods can also involve the installation of cameras, or the usage of existing cameras. In many cases, locations already have closed-circuit television cameras (or CCTV) installed, as they do in many retailer stores and in the public spaces of many metropolitan areas (see Exercise 6.4 regarding the ethical issues involved). It is even possible to call up live footage from thousands of remote CCTV cameras on personal computers and smart phones with readily available apps. For example you can get reasonably good quality footage of restaurants, bars, beaches, and ski resorts around the world. Sometimes the researcher can even pan, tilt, and zoom these cameras remotely.

In industry, but not in academia, using installed cameras has become an increasingly popular method for consumer research. In one popular use, marketing researchers choose consumer homes and approach the consumers about installing cameras in areas of interest. The consumers are financially compensated for installing a camera in a particular living area. Jayashinghe and Ritson (forthcoming) report a study in which a camera was able to record people watching television in order to see how people actually engage with or ignore advertising in situ. Popular rooms to videotape in the home include the kitchen, living room or family room, and bathrooms. These are all sites of interest because they are where the consumption of product such as toiletries and cosmetics, television and snack foods, and meals and snacks take place. Once it is in position, the camera can either stay on, or be motion sensor-activated to record all of the events that take place in the room. Once the data is collected, it can be analysed for patterns in behaviour. There are even programs that assist researchers in their coding and analysis of the video data by allowing them to examine, categorise, and remark upon individual frames and sequences of film (see Chapter 9).

Unobtrusive observations caught on video recording devices such as CCTV utilise concealed video equipment. This is a practice that must be used with caution, as it can be unethical and even illegal (see Chapter 6). In certain situations like tourist venues, the use of camcorders is ubiquitous and likely to go unnoticed, although standard informed consent procedures still apply (Belk and Yeh 2011). Like all observation and qualitative research, videographic data analysis follows the basic principles of interpretive analysis, from coding, to grounded theory construction, comparative case analysis, and hermeneutic circling.

Observational research film techniques originate from a school of film known as cinéma vérité that was developed in the 1950s by documentary filmmakers in the United States and France. In cinéma vérité, the filmmakers are tasked with becoming as unobtrusive as possible so as not to disturb the natural flow of social action. Often times, in its practical application as a form of data collection for consumer research, the interpretation of cinéma vérité entails having a researcher who can fit into a particular social situation, and who offers a prolonged engagement whereby research participants become accustomed to his or her presence (Belk 2011b). The Toronto ethnographer and videographer Bruno Moynie is an excellent example of a videographer who has mastered the art of living with people and gaining their trust so that the videorecording so produced evokes a naturalistic flow of everyday events (see http://vimeo.com/13910332). As a videographer like Bruno Moynie begins blending into the lived everyday context of the consumer, he or she can start to capture surprising revelations as well as the no-less-interesting truly familiar and genuinely mundane aspects of consumers' everyday existence.

There are many interesting and useful variants on the use of videography. Sunderland and Denny (2007) have given video cameras to consumers in a 'video diary' method and asked them to directly capture on videotape various aspects of their lives. Although they offer a wealth of background for understanding and employing the method, these techniques reveal an insight into the 'social context that frames respondents' lives . . . how exasperated a mother becomes with her toddler right before she turns off the camera. A boy videotaping his mother's commentary turns the camera on himself to playfully contradict what his mother just said' (Sunderland and Denny 2007, p. 256). In addition, the video diarist reveals him or herself in the conventions that they use to construct the diaries, such as 'setting the diary to self-produced music, creating titles, inserting credits at the end' (ibid.) and even making the researchers sign a form to protect the consumer's own copyright over potential reuse in public, all tell the researchers much about the lives, roles, and relevant social contexts of their consumer participants in the age of YouTube and other social media. This video diary technique thus can be said to possess some distinct advantages compared to researcher-conducted video observation. It is less intrusive and is also less directed by the researcher's own motives and needs. It may therefore allow new and unrealised (by the researcher) insights to come to light in the research process (Kozinets and Belk 2006; Sunderland and Denny 2007).

The advent of the smartphone means that the researcher need never be without a device for recording audio, photographs, and videos when in the field. It can even be a device for taking rough fieldnotes that can be fleshed out after observations when the researcher is back at a computer. This, too, could be done on a smartphone, but a tablet or laptop computer offers faster input. Examine the following note as we consider what to observe and how to analyse it. It is a note recorded by a participant observer into a cell phone during a shop-along expedition:

> HMV, only for sale really. Football songs. Best of brit pop, Oasis, Stone Roses, Indie. Dad gets music and films. Football manager v. championship manager. ... Films James Bond, Rocky Bond. His brother into fashion. Topman. Knows the layout of the shop. Wants to get smart for the future. Polo shirts. No pink. Blue. No adventures. Cheap. Shoes no slippers. Mum and shopping underwear. Next, only with mum. Before that Madhouse. Umbro. In Next, too golfy. A sports shop. Just looking. Point out Adidas jacket, Oasis style. Too expensive. Then to the magic place. Never buy full price. Shorts with a team. Passing by pink lady shoes. Laughing. First sport, world sport. Outside the Yas shops. Price sensitive, but not for tickets. Connection with the club. Mobile phone, tourist shops on Princes St. James and music. Not a recreational thing, shopping. What with people judging others on their looks. Watching the ladies. Tesco for deo, toilet, also clothes. Matalan, some designer stuff [excerpt from notes taken during shopping go-along]. (Hen and O'Donohoe 2011)

Videography is a compelling observational method with many advantages, which is why it has become an increasingly frequent, and often-demanded accompaniment to traditional marketing research interviews and ethnography. We live in a video and internet age, an era where YouTube is the second-most popular search engine in the world. We are used to getting our information fix videographically. Videography thus is an amazingly useful tool for capturing the cultural moment and the interactive event, freezing them and opening them up to cultural analysis, making them transferable and share-able, and building them into future educational experiences such as presentations, training, and education. With videographic research, consumer and marketing researchers are able to capture more of the subtle temporal, social, and spatial dimensions of consumer culture. The results can be emotional, vibrant, and humanising in a way that PowerPoint and written documents simply cannot be (Belk and Kozinets 2005; Kozinets and Belk 2006; Sunderland and Denny 2007). Chapter 6 expands further upon videographic methods.

Online observational and trendspotting techniques

As it is currently practised across academia and in the world of industry, qualitative research is a set of socially constructed practices with differing taken-for-granted understandings of what is 'good' or 'acceptable'. That is, these understandings vary across different researcher communities. The rapidly developing worlds of online observational techniques provide a wonderful example through which to discuss some of these differences.

Currently, and mainly in the world of industry, there is a new generation of observational research at hand, one driven by the pioneering efforts of internet and information communications researchers. Information monitoring services such as those offered by Nielsen Online and TiVo have developed observational technologies that can unobtrusively measure people's media viewing habits across a range of media and then combine them. Consumers' online viewing habits are now tracked and shared by the Neilson Online measurement systems. The system now reveals, for example, the most popular streamed television shows and websites, and it is even capable of breaking this information down by location and demographic characteristics of viewers, making it comparable with similar data collected for television, print, and radio advertising and programming.

TiVo, the company that invented and successfully marketed the first personal video recording device, and its related offline and online services, has also been a pioneer in digital television data collection. In 2004, TiVo was the primary source of information about how many people actually saved or rewound the image of Janet Jackson's exposed breast during SuperBowl XXXVIII. Although TiVo does not store the viewing records of individuals, and individual viewers are able to opt out of having their own personal data collected, TiVo receives a vast, steady stream of consumer television data from its viewers, and it has marketed this information.

In 2011, Nielsen Online developed new offerings that combine viewers' data with their API (Application Programming Interface), Internet protocol, cookies, and Facebook information to attach reliable demographic profiles to online clickstream and viewership data. The goal is to provide verifiable measurements of important online behaviour such as internet advertising campaign viewership and responses. A number of social media savvy companies, such as Google, Amazon, and Facebook have also benefited from the powerful ability created by the internet to track consumers' online actions. Some of these data collection efforts have raised ethical questions regarding privacy, but thus far opposition has been sporadic and scattered (e.g., Humphreys 2006; Singh and Lyon forthcoming). Wherever companies collect data on the various consumption habits of consumers, including their consumption of different media, as well as traditional and social media, this information has value. Furthermore, turning that data into information and intelligence is a skilled research process that also has value.

Researchers can now monitor and measure what people watch, comment upon, read, interact with, and actually buy online. Further, by combining this information with data that reveals their identity – in a sophisticated double-blind procedure that does not directly violate privacy laws – research companies are able to link television, print and radio viewing habits, as well as scanner panel data, credit card data, panel data, and other information about offline purchases with online viewing, commenting, and clicking behaviours. In the next few years, we will see an incredible amount of data coming on-stream that will enable consumer and marketing researchers to learn more than ever before about how consumers use traditional media, new media, social media and purchase behaviours, with all of these being interrelated. Trendspotting and trend-watching companies are employing technological innovations of many sorts to gain more rapid feedback on the latest changing trends. For instance, a Toronto-based company called Hotspex uses social media methods to develop panels of consumers who help companies brainstorm innovative new product and service ideas. The billions of conversations flowing through the internet have become a very important source of consumer and marketing research data for technologically-enabled observation methods like data mining, opinion mining, and netnography. In Chapter 5, we treat all of these methods in more detail.

Although these online observational methods offer many unique advantages for understanding consumers' manifest behaviours, they do have several very important drawbacks. In the first place, they offer researchers a rather distant view of consumer's behaviour. In this way, they are dramatically opposed to 'experience-close' or 'consumer-close' methods such as ethnography or face-to-face interviews and observation. The commercially aggregated types of data offer far less context, trust, or intimacy, but rather they favour precision and anonymity. Because of this, these methods may be excellent for observing personal acts that consumers might rather keep confidential. The methods may be far less likely to pass the stringent standards that institutional review boards and other research ethics committees require of academic researchers.

However, the more experience-distant online observational methods might be usefully combined with experience-close methods such as ethnography. The precision, verifiability, quantification and accuracy of these online methods can complement the more subjective, tightly sampled, and contingent nature of ethnographic observation. Moving from broader to closer views, the distance and decontextualisation of these observational methods can be compensated for by the close observational, contextualising, deep understanding and rich data provided by the ethnographic engagement.

In another example of a technologically-mediated use of observational methods, a number of different online companies have built invitation-only online communities in which they recruit and deputise people – usually young people – to act as amateur trend-spotters and observers. Each of these consumers is required to submit a constant stream of market-based information to the company by various means, such as sending photos, video, and SMS messages. Community members are also assigned to events such as parties, concerts, and sporting events and given the means and motivation to record and share it with the companies that hire them. Trend-spotting firms such as Boston-based BzzAgent also share product opinions, seeking to induce word-of-mouth among influential consumers and their social networks. Online research community creators such as Boston's Communispace have built similar communities that they use for ongoing panel discussions. (For a more critical take on the ethics of these practices, see Quart 2003.)

There is an online universe of qualitative social media data for us to explore. With allegedly almost one billion active Facebook users and one half billion Twitter users as of June 2012, massive amounts of qualitative, public, conversational, consumption-related WOM (word-of-mouth), and C2C (consumer-to-consumer) interactive data already exist and are created daily on the internet. The hundreds of millions of YouTube videos offer another natural archive of consumer behaviour (see Belk 2011b). The explosion in social media and social media marketing has led consumer and marketing researchers to seek tools and techniques to collect, analyse, interpret and make sense of this data. Considering that consumer-to-consumer conversations occur naturally on the internet, each of these technologically-mediated aided observational techniques offers naturalistic and unobtrusive data. Companies like NetBase, Radian6, Sysomos, and MotiveQuest have pioneered sophisticated data mining, NLP (natural language processing), coding, and analysis tools to analyse these online conversations and present them in manager-friendly, actionable forms such as marketing 'dashboards' (the reader is advised to search Google images for 'marketing dashboard' to see plentiful recent examples).

Another observational method developed over the last fifteen years as a direct adaptation of ethnography to the dynamic technological realities of the internet is called 'netnography' (Kozinets 2002a, 2010a). In Chapter 5, we discuss and explain netnography in greater detail, paying particular attention to practical data collection techniques. Netnography gives consumer and marketing researchers a window into naturally occurring behaviours, such as social media discussions of brands, lifestyle concerns, or particular events. However, unlike content mining, netnography adopts a cultural approach that requires interpretive sophistication. Compared to traditional, in-person observational methods such as in-home research, interviews, and ethnography, netnography can require less time and money spent on recruitment, personal meetings, travelling, recording observations, and conducting and transcribing personal interviews. However, it can still provide very rich data and include the opinions of large numbers of different consumers, and it benefits from highly interactive unelicited data in which consumers converse with one another about topics that matter to them. In this rapidly evolving area of qualitative consumer and marketing research, there is little doubt that these technologies will change significantly and continuously in the near future. Although this means that some of our descriptions may be out of date even before they are printed, we hope that our readers share our enthusiasm for the evergreen potential that these rapid transformations in research technologies herald.

Historical archival, archaeological and artefactual forms of observational research

Besides looking forward to changing consumer digital practices in the future we can also use observation to look backward at consumer practices in the past. Consider the notion that texts are, in the final analysis, always artefacts. Similarly, all artefacts are a kind of very rich text that have the potential to tell us meaningful stories about times, places, and people, thus revealing culture. So, if we consider all human-made objects to be representative of human culture, we can benefit from ways of studying and understanding culture through them. As we consider the nature of observational data collection, it is now useful to introduce a general discussion of historical, archaeological, and artefactual observational data and its use in consumer and marketing research. In this category, we can include such diverse sources as ancient artefacts like Greek pottery, paintings, and consumer research conducted using adapted archaeological methods, such as garbology and the analysis of historical consumption artefacts such as ceramics.

If pictures can be said to be worth a thousand words, physical objects must be worth entire volumes. Physical artefacts can be analysed in order to find insights about particular places, practices, and times. From the careful analysis of a set of material objects, an understanding and narrative of a historical era emerges, even if it must be constructed based on some good guesses. This is the only source of observational data for archaeologists unless they are dealing with a recent historical period. Even prehistoric data based on observing artefacts and excavating ruins can (and must) be analysed in this fashion.

An example of analysing very old consumer artefacts is John Pfeiffer's (1982) analysis of the artwork and percussion instruments found in 10,000 to 30,000 year old Cro-Magnon caves of the Pyrenees. He found that the magnificent artwork was inevitably in a large cathedral-like room of the cave that could only be reached by a labyrinthine passageway. Together with the spectacular acoustics of the rooms and the 'Venus' statuettes found in the area, he speculates that ceremonies:

must have happened in the rotunda on a number of occasions 10,000 to 15,000 years ago, an event designed deliberately to evoke a feeling of displacement, an unreal dreamlike setting, a shock of surprise. The entire experience, the … features along the route, was dedicated to the achievement of this instant illusion. Under such conditions, probably intensified by other effects, people formed powerful associations and remembered for a lifetime what they heard and saw. (p. 133)

In other words, Pfeiffer speculates from the evidence that these tunnels and paintings were used in initiations into what may have been one of the world's earliest religious ceremonies.

In another application of clever forensic consumer research, Morris et al. (1979) studied the Greek origin of non-verbal gestures in Southern Italy by comparing photographs of people in contemporary Italy and Greece to depictions of certain gestures in ancient Greek literature. They found that a head-tossing gesture called an *ananeuo* and meaning 'no' could be traced to Homer's *Iliad*. Today it is found in Greece and in those parts of Southern Italy visited by Greek sailors, but not further inland. Verbal traces of the sailors had largely disappeared, but non-verbal traces have persisted for more than 2,000 years. Collett (1984) reports similar gestures in Naples that can be traced to ancient Greek Pottery.

In other work, Belk and Ger (1995, 2005) examined the rise of consumer culture at two overlapping periods of time in late Ming China and Golden Age Dutch cultures based on artwork of the two periods and places. They found similar explosions of interest in collecting art among the nouveaux riches of both cultures, but also found considerable cultural differences in the sorts of art created in these cultures. Dutch art revelled in realistic sumptuous still-life paintings of the riches of natural treasures, foods, and flowers from the New World, while Chinese art paid tribute to nature through paintings and poems that reflected a much less domineering and possessive relationship with the natural world. Although the Dutch painting genre called *vanitas* art expressed some religious uneasiness with the new-found wealth of the period, their way of expressing their affluence was a much more conspicuous standing out in comparison to the Chinese emphasis on fitting in.

Another interesting use of the qualitative richness of historical texts to understand the past of a culture is in the analytic use of different forms of imagery, such as radio and television archives. O'Connor (1988) notes that historical analysts have much to learn from the analysis of photographs, some of which now go back over 170 years, the analysis of motion pictures, which now goes back over 120 years, and the analysis of television, which now stretches back over 70 years. Documentary films are nearly as old as film itself and form a different sort of historical archive compared to fictional treatments (Belk 2011b). Archives of corporate public relations films from the twentieth century can tell us a great deal about how companies sought to portray their employees, dealers, and customers (Prelinger 1996, 2010). Many of these films are now available on YouTube which provides a vast archive hosting more than 150 million films as of this writing.

In the field of consumer research, we have had some very interesting explorations of cultural meanings that analyse motion picture and television shows for their cultural meanings. For examples, pioneering consumer anthropologist John Sherry's (1995b) 'telethnography' of coffee culture resulted from an *Association for Consumer Research* Special Session on the topic. In that research, Sherry uses 'an anthropological perspective to explore the dimensions of "coffeeworld" as it is depicted on prime time network television programming' (Sherry 1995b, p. 351). Rather than examining advertisements, as might be customary, the analysis focused on the programming context of top-rated programmes which are held to employ 'the stuff of everyday life, albeit in extraordinary circumstances, to create verisimilitude' (Sherry 1995b, p. 353). We can see related interpretations of consumption meanings from Holbrook's hermeneutic analysis of the films *Gremlins* (Holbrook 1988) and *Out of Africa* (Holbrook and Grayson 1986), as well as from Hirschman's (1988) interpretive analysis of *Dallas* and *Dynasty* television shows for their meanings about the ideology of consumption and the class based motivations for consumption (see Holbrook and Hirschman 1993 for a compendium of this work as well as other literature and poetry).

Spencer-Wood (1987) considers the consumer goods acquired during the eighteenth and nineteenth centuries in America using archaeological methods. The data in some of these studies included: shards of ceramics deposited in various refuse cites; the presence of old fish remains such as bones and bone fragments in a trash site; personal property records; and the crumbling masonry piles of old furnace sites. The framework employed by the contributors to Spencer-Wood's volume relates this archaeological data to a range of behavioural variables, including socioeconomic status, market access, ownership of the means of production, foodways functions, ethnicity, household size and composition, and political status (Spencer-Wood 1987, p. 11).

There are certainly special considerations involved with the selective record of such sources as probate inventories of possessions, historic diaries, and media (Belk 1992, 1994; Karababa and Ger 2011). Once we move back a century or two in the historical record, the presence of lower-class materials becomes virtually non-existent, as only the wealthy have significant possessions to be included in such inventories, which were incomplete and often used for taxation purposes. Paper, unfortunately, does not stand the challenges of time well, and we have relatively few mundane records preserved. In the Museum of Anatolian Civilisations in Ankara, Turkey, however, we do have remarkable examples of ancient documents written in tiny cuneiform letters on clay. Incredibly, these delicate items have withstood millennia, and they tell us that consumers have been using bills of sale, and inventorying their possessions in order to pass them on to their heirs, for thousands of years. Furthermore, the same museum also preserves what appear to be early brand symbols, many of which use animals as totemic and identifiable figures that date back 3,000 years or more (for early branding analyses see Eckhardt and Bengtsson 2010; Hamilton and Lai 1989; Moore and Reid 2008).

Another interesting and useful form of artefactual analysis examines and classifies household garbage or waste in contemporary times, rather than only historically. The anthropological technique of 'garbology' has been in ongoing development at least since 1970 and is based upon the use of specially marked plastic garbage bags to conduct a form of unobtrusive investigation of consumers' garbage (e.g., Rathje and Murphy 1992). Sorters record the contents of household trash using various qualitative and quantitative categories and link them to census locations of households. Cote et al. (1985) usefully employed the method of garbology to study the disparity between stated consumption intention and actual consumption behaviour for 15 common consumer food and beverage products. Wallendorf and Reilly (1983) examined garbage by census tracts in Tucson, Arizona and detected a phenomenon of 'over-assimilation' in which Hispanic census tracts consumed more white bread and Anglo census tracts consumed more tortillas. Reportedly some of the first marketing research conducted, before survey research, panel diaries, and scanner data were available, was by Charles Parlin in Philadelphia. Hired by Campbell's Soup to find what types of consumers were buying their ready-made instant soup, he looked for cans in the garbage of different neighbourhoods of the city and related this to affluence and other characteristics available by observation of people, their houses, and carriages in each area.

Other examples of clever unobtrusive or non-reactive observational records of consumption are discussed by Webb et al. (1966) and Lee (2000). The originally planned title of the former book was 'The Bullfighter's Beard', because it had been observed that anxiety produced more rapid growth of facial hair among male bullfighters, such that stubble was a good predictor of the likelihood of a fighter being gored. A range of unobtrusive data types exist, including erosion records (e.g., floor wear in front of exhibits at the Chicago Museum of science and industry), archival records (e.g., municipal water flow rates when people flush their toilets during half-time of the Superbowl), accretion records (e.g., number and height of noseprints on display window glass), simple or contrived observational measures (e.g., what incidence of horn honking occurs when a Fiat versus a Mercedes is 'stalled' in traffic), and other physical trace records (e.g., the history of URLs visited by shoppers on demo computers), all of which might be employed by the resourceful researcher. The possibilities are limited only by your creative imagination and ethical concerns for privacy.

Once someone has collected such interesting objects as ancient cuneiform tablets, broken ceramics from refuse or construction sites, or garbage from people's homes, how does he or she analyse the data? In terms of analysis of such historical items and artefacts, it should come as no surprise that the full battery of qualitative consumer and marketing research methods can be deployed to assess, code, categorise, and interpret this data. For instance, a researcher can utilise content analytic, semiotic, and/or archaeological methods in order to code and analyse a huge variety of historical and artefactual data. Yes, as the above-mentioned example clearly indicates, even garbage – fresh or ancient – can be analysed this way. Situating such analysis in research traditions is discussed in greater depth in Chapters 7 and 8 of this book. At this point, after a concluding exercise, we turn instead to a summary of this chapter's lessons that expands upon the advantages and limitations of these observational methods.

━━━━━ **EXERCISE 4.1** ━━━━━

Eww! Yuck!! Aha!!

In this chapter, we have detailed some of the many observational methods, including garbology. Although it may seem a little bit disgusting, we can return to the lit(t)eral roots of our field of consumption studies by lit(t)erally studying what we have consumed. Because you may find it patently sickening to study someone else's garbage, we have designed a brief exercise for you to conduct using your own garbage.

1 Choose a bag of garbage from your own home. If you are in a home with recycling and or composting, then choose a bag each from all of the categories you collect.
2 In an open space (such as a backyard), open the garbage bag(s) and spread out the contents.
3 Sort the contents into logical piles based on any classification scheme that makes sense. Name the piles. Write down the names. Photograph them.
4 Look at the relative amounts of waste in each pile. Analyse this as data.
5 Look at the types of items in each pile. How can you describe them, their condition, their relationship to each other?
6 What sorts of conclusions about the 'types' of consumers and the 'types' of consumption can you make about the members of this household through an analysis of their garbage?

Please do not be too put off by the nature of this research. If you perform it, the results may truly surprise you.

The strengths and limitations of observation methods: a brief overview

Following our encounters with the past, present, and future of observational research methods, it is useful to turn our analytic lens to a consideration of some of the key strengths and limitations of observational research methods.

As with many qualitative consumer and marketing research methods, one so-called 'limitation' of observational methods such as ethnography is that it tends to draw from and represent a relatively small number of research participants (Lofland and Lofland 1995). As we have emphasised throughout this book, however, it is critical for the researcher to always remember that this is inductive research based upon the (usually) detailed analysis of a (usually) small group of people. The reason that this statement about qualitative research is qualified is that, in some cases such as online observations or CCTV (this chapter), or netnography or data mining (see Chapter 5), considerably larger samples may be used, and the data may be handled through some sort of filter or sorting mechanism, most often a software algorithm.

With small samples, it is useful for marketers and consumer and marketing researchers to test their initial insights further to determine to what extent they are idiosyncratic and unique, bounded by contexts, prevail only under certain conditions, or are broad and generalisable. If the appropriate means are employed to interpret the findings of observational, ethnographic, archaeological, unobtrusive, and archival research, then their conclusions can be carefully verified. However, also as noted elsewhere in this book (Chapter 10), some studies are valuable for revealing particular contexts or uncovering unique insights. Consider the theory generation possibilities of ethnography of the Brazilian 2016 Olympics audience. Assume that consumption of the multi-screen experience of the Olympics, which encompasses mobile broadcasts, television, and internet coverage simultaneously, is studied in context across 10 Midwestern American homes. If the findings reveal interesting and unprecedented coordination of consumption across all three screens (including tablets such as the iPad), can this result then be used to discuss changing viewership habits around the world? It depends upon the type of theorising that is being developed. If, for instance, the ethnography introduces and develops a new type of viewership that has not been described and seen in the literature previously, then the sample size is largely irrelevant. This is a finding analogous to finding a 'Black Swan'. All prior swans seen have been white, but the one discovered is not. However, it would be inaccurate to argue that this change is happening in all households, or to try to argue that it is gaining popularity. There is simply no data to support any sort of quantitative assessment of the adoption of these multi-screen behaviours of the Olympics or, indeed, of any other broadcast material.

If, for instance, you are interested in exploring the consumption practices of a particular new subculture, let us say a group of female senior-citizen hipster wakeboarders called the Glam Grams, then observational research that involves a 'deep hanging out' with this new subculture can be sufficient in and of itself. However, if a cosmetics company wishes to generalise the findings of that study to develop a new anti-ageing product advertising campaign intended to appeal to all female senior citizens, then it is advisable to test the core conclusions (e.g., the appeal of the 'gray wakeboarder' image) among a wider population of female senior citizens who represent the target for the product and its accompanying campaign. As the example indicates, investments in verifying results from smaller samples should be undertaken before costly other investments in production and marketing are made. When the objectives of the research are instead academic, the degree to which possible generalisability may or may not be an issue likely depends on the particular journal or other outlet. In general, more managerially oriented journals may be more insistent on evidence of generalisability, although this is not always the case.

Another limitation to some observational methods is their cost. Because observational research methods such as ethnography tend to be time-intensive, and to demand significant researcher skill, these studies can be relatively expensive to conduct. It is partially for this reason that newer technological forms of observation such as data mining and CCTV observation have been developed. Because observational methods now are quite diverse, there are alternatives to ethnographic interviews. Observational research no longer only means sending research teams out to investigate consumers' homes to conduct weeks of gruelling in-home interviews. Combining and choosing from the menu of observational methods discussed in this chapter, researchers can tailor an observational research plan to the specific needs of the project.

A further limitation of observation, if used by itself, is that while we can see (or hear, smell, etc.) what consumers do, we cannot observe why they do it. In the example of Glam Gram wakeboarding, we might like to know whether the group previously all knew one another, whether they first came together online, or whether they were drawn by a programme at the local senior citizen's council; we might like to know whether they wakeboard for the exercise, because it is fun, because they see it as a way to meet friendly old surfers, or for some other reason; and we might like to know whether this is a one-off activity in a series of adventures by the group or whether it is their passion and will be pursued for some time to come. Obviously the way to answer such motivational questions is to do more than simply observe. Participant observation combined with prolonged engagement, depth interviews, netnography, and the perusal of local media archives for news stories about the group are just some of the ways we might follow-up.

The goal of observational methods should be to provide in situ, contextualised, meso-level data rather than simply counts of numbers of people coming and going, or clicks on a webpage. Because of this, observational methods must take seriously the patient, skilled, immersive approach of anthropologists and others who practise ethnography. In fact, it is exactly this impetus to reach a more profound analysis that leads us to combine participation – however it may be constructed to be relevant in the particular research situation – with observation.

Rushed data collection, or what is sometimes called 'blitzkrieg ethnography', is going to result in weaker data, no matter whether the method used is an in-home 'depth' interview or a survey. The training and skill of the researcher is exposed by observational and interactive methods such as ethnography. Some researchers might walk into a teenager's bedroom filled with dirty clothes and empty cans of energy drinks and see nothing but a lack of adequate parenting. Others might theorise about the ever-increasing need to process large amounts of information, and the relationship of stimulant consumption to teenagers' information-and-media rich lifestyle. Others might see an opportunity to develop a new soft drink brand that builds on a portrait of chaos, freedom, and an untamed creative ethos. And still others might see the teenager's bedroom as an ideal methodological site for revealing the teen's personality, lifestyle, anxieties, hopes, and aspirations (e.g., contrast the approaches of Arbitron nd; Brown et al. 1994; Gosling 2008; Gregson, 2007; Lincoln 2004, 2005; Miller 2008; Odom et al. 2011; Salinger 1995; Spaarman 2007; and Steele and Brown 1995). Observational data is uniquely valuable. With all its elusiveness and limitations, it is still the only data that can promise authentic consumption and marketing data about what is currently occurring in the world.

5

Online observation and netnography

The internet is a social space. Like an ocean teeming with life, the online environment offers researchers an incredibly varied and vibrant pool of rich qualitative 'data' consisting of conversations, messages, photographs, music clips, videos, drawings, avatars, comments, discussions, and much more. The internet contains billions of interconnected files of various sorts authored by hundreds of millions, if not billions, of people worldwide. It has forever altered how we communicate, entertain ourselves, find partners, get directions, gain a sense of community, and ask and answer questions about a massive variety of different topics. Many of those questions, it turns out, are marketing and consumption related. In addition, many consumers use the internet to make purchases, to bid in auctions, to view advertising, to gamble, to download coupons, to watch and share – legally and illegally – licensed material, to write reviews, to offer recommendations, and much more. The variety and intensity of consumer and marketing experiences possible and present through online media increase every year.

In this chapter we will overview and explore the major techniques that qualitative consumer and marketing researchers use to explore and analyse this rich and increasingly important environment for consumer and marketing research. What is the nature of online qualitative consumer and marketing research? In particular, what kinds of data exist and how can they be collected in a rigorous manner by researchers? We will first briefly explore two different methods for working with online qualitative data: data mining and social network analysis. Next, we will detail netnography, the practice of online ethnography. Finally, and related to this, we will discuss the techniques of online interviewing which often accompany netnography.

Prior to our discussion of techniques that deal with large amounts of online data, we note that you might wonder if ostensibly decontextualised data such as that produced by data mining and social network analysis techniques can appropriately be considered to be qualitative. However, in this book, we do not consider the distinction between qualitative and quantitative data to be obvious or hard and fast; qualitative and quantitative are not polar extremes of data, nor are they mutually exclusive ways of looking at the world. Rather, we view these labels for data as somewhat arbitrary points along a continuum that takes richly contextualised real world observations ('capta' as anthropologist John Sherry puts it; see Sherry and Kozinets 2001) and codes them for particular elements of content and context, consequently and inevitably stripping them of other elements of content and context. Some of this coding can involve assigning a quantitative code to qualitative data, such as counting the number of words in an online posting, or rating Twitter messages for their use of emotional language. The same is true, for example, when researchers code the qualitative stories of thematic apperception tests (TATs) to derive scores on various psychological traits (see Chapter 3).

Because data mining and social network analysis collect large amounts of data that can fall toward the qualitative end of the spectrum, we choose to discuss them in this text on qualitative research, while recognising that the data that these techniques yield can also be aggregated in a quantitative fashion. If we are to consider the conversations, connections, and reflections of other lived social experiences to be, in some sense, a type of 'content' that can be said to exist apart from its context, we can regard the data that such techniques produce as useful for purposes of qualitative research.

Data mining

Data mining techniques have a long history of being used in marketing and consumer research primarily to yield quantitative data (see Kassarjian 1977; Iacobucci 1996). There are rare instances of qualitative academic researchers applying these useful methods. However, in the last decade, data mining has frequently been applied to online conversations and connections by 'mining' or 'scraping' text and relational data from their original source, collecting it in certain ad hoc or predetermined ways, and then analysing or sorting it en masse using various types of automated, semi-automated, computerised, or software-driven processes. An increasing number of researchers are beginning to deploy these techniques with online data in order to enhance, develop, guide, and validate the findings from more contextualising methods such as netnography (see Jayanthi and Singh 2010; Füller et al. 2006).

For the contemporary qualitative researcher interested in using data obtained from the internet, finding tools for dealing with the collection and analysis of a large amount of data is an advantage and, increasingly, a necessity. The field of data mining has grown up in institutional settings where enterprises have found it beneficial to collect and analyse often overwhelming amounts of data. For example, hospitals have used data mining techniques in order to spot disease- and treatment-related trends in patient records. Government agencies have used data mining on their records and census data in order to understand better and cope with the need for public services. Environmental agencies must deal with massive amounts of data in order to help withstand seasonal and manmade fluctuations in weather patterns and in environmental toxicity. The techniques they use to collect and analyse data are all related.

For consumer and marketing researchers, a variety of topics are of interest that can be approached using data mining techniques. For example, a marketing researcher might be interested in the total number of mentions per hour of a particular brand, such as McDonald's, on a social networking site such as Facebook. What time of day do such mentions peak? What type of person mentions McDonald's the most? Moving into a more qualitative type of analysis, what do those mentions say about McDonald's? Are they positive or negative? What topics are mentioned the most? What competitors are mentioned? What products are mentioned? Answering these practical questions can help to illuminate the mass consciousness and popular opinions surrounding a brand, a product or service category, or almost any type of consumption imaginable (even, for instance, travel to a specific city, support for a certain non-profit cause, or voting for a political candidate or party). A scholarly researcher interested in market dynamics might need to follow the website, Facebook, and Twitter updates of rivals competing for market share. She, too, will find data mining techniques invaluable.

Storage media for such large amounts of data are already inexpensive. A one terabyte drive can be now commonly bought for less than US$50, and prices are still dropping. Data sensors and automated programs for data collection are also becoming more common and less expensive. And cloud storage offers even larger and less expensive possibilities. The collection and storage of large amounts of data are easier than ever before.

However, the biggest issues in data mining that remain involve how to analyse the data. As our concern is with qualitative data and their analysis, this chapter will not detail the most sophisticated quantitative and mathematical bases of data and content mining, but, for the interested reader, will reference several excellent books that do so. However, it is important that the chapter provide a basic understanding of some of the principles of data mining so that they might be built into basic internet data collection procedures.

What is data mining?

Data mining is the process of discovering useful patterns or knowledge from sources of data such as databases, websites, text files, images, or videos (Liu 2008, p. 6). According to Cios et al. (2007, p. 3) we can also define data mining as the attempt to 'make sense of large amounts of mostly unsupervised data, in some domain'. An essential part of this definition is that we are dealing both with 'large amounts' of data (often in hundreds of megabytes, or possibly gigabytes; some large organisations, such as NASA or Wal-Mart may deal with terabytes). Second, the term unsupervised indicates that this is naturalistic data, data for which the analyst has no predefined classes or categories; as well as data whose generation was not carefully managed or cultivated. Finally, we see data mining as a part of a process of sense making or knowledge creation, in which operations on vast amounts of qualitative data should render it understandable, valid, novel, and useful. The emphasis therefore should be on an understanding of the data and on aiming toward the eventual deployment or use of results.

Data mining seeks to discover useful information or knowledge from the information available in a particular database, whether that database exists in a company's private backroom servers, on a person's desktop, or on the internet. Content mining is a variety of data mining that treats data more widely, often including visual images, audio-visual files, and sound files. Web mining is another subset of data mining that 'aims to discover useful information or knowledge from Web hyperlinks, page contents, and usage logs' (Liu 2008, p. vii). In data collection, information can be extracted from the content of web pages, user access patterns determined from usage logs, and the structure of various technical and social relationships determined from various types of linkages, such as hyperlinks, mail direction, or message responses.

The most important distinguishing characteristic of data mining is that, rather than beginning with a particular model and then fitting data to it, as with structural equation models and their goodness of fit indices, data mining attempts to begin with the data. In short, although its methods are usually mathematical, the approach is inductive; it is data driven. Data mining begins with large datasets and tries to build a data model that is parsimonious and not overly complex, but which still describes the data well. In other words, the rule of Occam's razor is followed. In this inductive characteristic, and in its 'knowledge discovery' or 'knowledge creation' approach, data mining intersects with qualitative methods that seek to find patterns of meaning from complex naturalistic situations.

Data mining: the Netflix prize

In October, 2006, the American online rating and DVD rental company Netflix launched an open competition to find a better way to predict consumers' ratings, and therefore their apparent liking, of motion pictures. Netflix challenged people to improve the algorithm it used to predict consumer tastes by at least 10 per cent. The winner would receive a cheque for US$ 1 million. In order to do so, competitors in the contest needed to use sophisticated techniques of data mining and analysis (see Baker 2009).

Netflix provided over 50,000 competitors with a staged series of large datasets. These were:

- a 'Training set' of 99,072,112 ratings
- a 'Probe set' of 1,408,395 ratings
- a 'Qualifying set' of 2,817,131 ratings

The title and year of release of each motion picture were provided in a separate dataset, and no information was provided about users. In fact, Netflix changed some details of the data in order to attempt to protect the privacy of customers. In the training set for example, the average movie was rated by over 5,000 Netflix consumers. There was also wide variance in the data. Some films had as few as three ratings, while one Netflix consumer rated over 17,000 movies.

At this point, the task facing the data mining competitors was to understand the influence of a large number of factors. Even the massive number-crunching abilities of computers were challenged to account for scores of different factors. Things like the time of day, the type of film, consumer demographics, the mood of the consumer (i.e., whether she had previously rated other movies negatively or positively), and the time since the movie was viewed were all found to have effects. According to reports, the winning team had to account for a possible 19 trillion variables and find ways to reduce that complexity.

After many rounds were used to refine and test the power of particular algorithms to the consumer film rating dataset, each team applied its model against the dataset in order to predict the scores. The winning formula, devised by a team composed of a collaboration of seven computer scientists and researchers from the USA, Israel, Austria, and Canada, had hundreds of algorithms, all of them derived from carefully applying the principles of data mining to large consumer datasets derived from online rating responses. For companies such as Netflix, using data mining is well worth the 1 million dollar investment, because the predictions it enables are worth far more to their business.

Source: Baker, Stephen (2009), 'Netflix Isn't Done Mining Consumer Data, Company's Goal is to "Predict People Earlier" – When they First get to Site', *Business Week*, 22 September, accessed online at http://www.msnbc.msn.com/id/32969539/ns/business-us_business/t/netflix-isnt-done-mining-consumer-data/#.T0pybUret1A.

How does data mining work?

The basic approach used in data mining is the same as that used in text mining, web mining, content mining, or any of the other forms of data mining that can be imagined. The text box in the chapter entitled 'The Netflix Prize' provides an actual, and high profile, example showing how data mining is used to understand and predict consumer behaviours in the real world (see Baker 2009).

- The data analyst, or data miner, identifies suitable data sources and target forms of data.
  - These data sources are usually driven by curiosity about a phenomenon or a question, such as 'what are young people in Brazil saying about Coca-Cola this week?'
  - It could also be driven by a general interest in or curiosity about a particular site or source, such as 'What is going on in the Kraft Recipe website?'
- Raw data is 'pre-processed' or cleaned in order to remove noise and/or abnormalities.
  - This usually involves specifying what is to be excluded. Sometimes subsets of the data are altered so they can be treated in a way that is consistent with the way other parts of the data are being processed. Boolean logic and simple programming can be useful for this procedure.
  - The dataset may also be too large, so it may require reduction. It could have too many irrelevant attributes, so a new dataset differing on particular attributes might need to be chosen.
- The pre-processed data is then processed further by a data mining algorithm that tries to recognise or represent patterns in the data.
- Because not all discovered patterns are useful, understandable, valid, and/or novel, the next step involves the identification of patterns that are useful for intended applications, and the rejection of those that are not. Different evaluation and visualisation techniques are deployed in order to make those assessments.
- The entire data mining process is usually iterative, taking multiple rounds to achieve results.

Data can be aggregated in a process also known as 'unsupervised learning'. In unsupervised learning, data have no pre-determined or pre-arranged categories assigned to them. A computational algorithm must find the hidden commonalities and regularities in the data (Liu 2008). A key method is clustering, in which data are organised into groups or clustered based on their similarities or their differences. So, for example, we might cluster online mentions of the mouthwash Listerine by whether they mention its taste, its colour, or its price.

Supervised learning is probably the most frequently used data mining technique in practice. Supervised learning is a form of classification in which a category or classifier function is learnt from data that has previously been labelled with similar pre-defined classes or categories. That classifier is then applied to place other, new but similar data, into those classes. Because the existing classification supervises the process, it is known as supervised learning.

Database methods can be applied that combine supervised and unsupervised learning, a process known as partially supervised learning. In addition, other techniques such as association rules and data cubes are used. More recently, advanced methods that require considerable mathematical sophistication have been developed to help approach the challenges of data mining. Some of these methods include SVD/PCA, the use of wavelets, and support vector machines (Han et al. 2011). One of the more useful, complex, and interesting forms of data mining is called opinion mining, which we describe in our next section.

Opinion mining

Opinion mining works with the large amounts of naturally occurring or 'unstructured' text present on the web. Usually opinion mining operates only on the text of user generated content or user generated media, because the processing of images, video, music graphics, and sound files is still far too complex for our current computational algorithms to handle (but not too complex, however, for netnography, which we consider in the next section).

Opinion mining is useful because it attempts to measure online word of mouth. However, it is still technically very challenging because it needs to use *natural language processing* (often abbreviated as NLP), a type of information processing that recognises the information in naturally occurring language. In software functions, NLP programs must match actual language with predefined categories of sentiment. For example, 'excellent' would be coded as a stronger sentiment than 'great' and 'great' would be coded as a stronger sentiment than 'good'. Ultimately, it is the goal of NLP to have software 'understand' the meaning of phrases such as 'ridiculously outrageously awesome' by being able to recognise as much of its context as possible and to classify it correctly and automatically. In practice, however, the task is extremely difficult given the vast number of permutations and conventions in human language and expression. For example, while a human being will almost instantly understand irony, sarcasm, and idiosyncratic spelling, these modes of representation are very likely to confound software programs. Although computers make excellent chess players and calculators at our current stage of technological development, human beings are still far more sophisticated information processors than even the smartest computers when it comes to understanding the incredible complexity of natural written, spoken, or represented language.

There are three key elements to opinion mining.

- First is sentiment classification. Like text classification, the data mining system or algorithm needs to determine whether a particular text expresses either a positive or a negative sentiment.
- Second is feature-based opinion mining. At this level the system would move to the level of sentences or statement to discover details about which attributes or aspects of a product, service, or candidate people were communicating about. For example, in the comment 'the screen of this tablet computer is too small' the sentiment is negative and the comment concerns screen size.
- Next is comparative mining, in which one object is compared against one or more similar objects. For example, comparison is explicit in the sentence 'The brightness of the HP tablet screen is much better than the brightness of the iPad'.
- Finally, the strength or passion of particular opinions can be assessed. In this case, the recognition of adjective and adverbs can be extremely important to the appropriate processing of the comment or review. For example, 'The form factor of the new Samsung tablet is ridiculously outrageously awesome!!!' Recognising the meaning of this sort of a statement will require natural language processing.

There are many different ways to approach data mining, and interested researchers should not be deterred by believing that it is overly difficult. In fact, we all use a form of data mining software whenever we perform a search on Google. From a universe of possibilities we narrow our choices using search terms and keywords, finally settling on a particular site or set of sites to inform our search. There are many basic programs available to help researchers with this type of search. Companies such as NetBase with its ConsumerBase engines, Visible Technologies, Sysomos, and Radian6, among many others, produce web mining and classification software products that are user friendly and that easily produce customisable, attractive research reports. These types of search engines will crawl the web and mine any areas that they can. The mine-able areas usually include pages on the World Wide Web, such as different product or company forums, different blogs, archives of Twitter feeds, and other locations. Chat rooms and social networking sites such as Facebook are generally not mine-able. With some of these programs, opinion scores can be rated for influence. For example, opinions appearing on top-rated and highly visited blogs might be weighted in indices more heavily than opinions appearing on new blogs with few followers. Opinions also have a temporal dimension that can reveal trends over time. So, for example, we could chart the opinions towards President

Obama from his campaign years through various events in his presidency and through his re-election campaign. Opinions can also be presented in a variety of different visual forms and using a variety of different infographics. Although pie charts and bar charts are still very popular for presenting the features or attributes found in feature-based mining, there are many creative ways to visually present this data, such as scatter diagrams, adjustable diagrams, and word clouds, one of which is shown in Figure 3.1.

Finally, one important consideration in opinion mining is how the program will treat spam and other noisy aspects of the naturalistic opinion data available on the internet. Companies often post press releases that tout and praise their own products online. Newspaper articles and blog articles can be sponsored, and posted and reposted online. There are numerous companies and public relations agencies that pay people to post positive reviews of their product and services online, and sometimes to produce and post negative reviews of competitor's product and services. Often these conflicts of interest are unreported or invisible (despite US Federal Trade Commission and related global regulations stipulating that such practices are illegal). In addition, high quality original content is valuable and rare on the internet. Many posters will simply cut and paste, or point with hyperlinks, to other reviews or content. Thus the amount of duplicate information about products and services can be very considerable. Because of such tendencies in posting, high quality spam detection in software programs is a very important filter before data mining is initiated. This sort of detection will look for content similarity, detect rating and content outliers, look for unusual reviewer/poster behaviour, and detect suspicious spikes in ratings. In these cases, the algorithm will attempt to flag, minimise and often automatically eliminate the influence of suspicious or repeat opinion data.

Considering a data mining research project

As an example, consider that a business would like to find out what people are saying about a particular product category, such as potato chips.

Think about a research or industry-related question that could be answered using a data mining approach. For example, what cultural meanings do potato chips involve?

One free online software program that will perform data mining is called social mention and is available at http://socialmention.com. Turning to social mention or another of the available software and online services that can help to collect and sort online data, think about performing your search.

Which online sites and areas will you focus upon? List them. We performed our test research on potato chips and cultural meanings using social mention and used the very basic search term 'potato chips'.

Collect the data. Clean and preprocess it. On the front page of social mention, we found that the top ten keywords related to potato chips were: Lays, food, chip, good, sweet, Doritos, factory, work, smart, and price. Social mention also told us that potato chips were mentioned online at a rate of about 1 minute per mention, that the strength of mentions was about 15 per cent, that the passion index was 25 per cent, and that the sentiments regarding potato chips were balanced 5 to 1 in favour of positive mentions.

Interpret your results. What did you find?

We decided to look at the qualitative mentions that social mention gathered from online space, rather than to focus on the more general classifications that the program offered. Reading through some of the most recent entries, most of them on Twitter, we found a number of mentions of addiction and overload, particularly in relation to people talking about how they had eaten an entire bag or half a bag of potato chips. Taking these findings to another level of qualitative interpretation, we might suggest that this level of guilt and confession suggests that potato chips are seen as a guilt-inducing sin food with questionable health value, but high conversation potential. Potato chips seem to be popular topics when they are the subject of food-related confessions.

Try different forms of output. Which are the more useful forms of visualisation?

How difficult is interpretation? What sorts of skills are involved?

Can you reach some general conclusions from this exercise? For what sorts of questions is a data mining project useful? What does the approach lack? What kinds of questions cannot be answered with the data mining approach? What kinds are more difficult?

A short data mining project example

In the corporate world, understanding how consumers view and talk about your brand is critical information. A number of search companies have developed natural language processing algorithms to try to accurately code and assess the emotional content of social media data such as conversations about brands and products. The ways that this information can be analysed and then represented are almost infinite.

Figure 5.1 is a 'Brand passion index' created for a report by NetBase using their ConsumerBase search engine. The data for this diagram came from a web-crawling engine that analyses a huge variety of online discussions from forums, blog posts, Twitter feeds, and other textual sources. The software then uses a set of rules to

(Continued)

(Continued)

distinguish between positive and negative emotional stages and also to classify the strength of those emotions.

In this diagram, which NetBase provided around Father's Day, they analyse discussions about wristwatches, a popular Father's day gift in North America. In the plotting of this information, the size of the circles indicates the amount of online data, i.e., the relative amount of discussion.

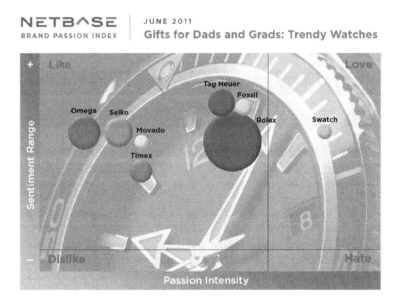

Figure 5.1

Diagram © 2011 NetBase Inc. Used with permission of NetBase Inc.

As we can see from the diagram, most watches are about equivalent in terms of how much they are liked. Omega, Seiko, Rolex and Swatch all appear to be liked approximately the same amount, with Tag Heuer and Fossil liked a bit more, and only Timex liked significantly less. In terms of intensity of emotions, however, Swatch turns out to be the brand inspiring the most intense passion, while Omega and Seiko brands are liked with much less passion. In terms of mentions, Rolex clearly dominates the discussion, even though that brand is not as intensely loved as the Swatch brand.

The benefits of such information can be quite powerful to brand managers. What improvements would you make to these software products and their output? Would you want more details about the kinds of emotions expressed? Would you want more context about the conversation than merely the size of the bubble? Would you want more targeted information? For example, would you only want to include

QUALITATIVE CONSUMER AND MARKETING RESEARCH

conversations about gifts, or by men, or by children of men aged 50–65? What other information do you think is important and should be included?

An entire new generation of software programs such as this one is constantly being devised. Today's researchers will certainly benefit from being a part of that developing conversation.

Social network analysis

Another research method that marketing and consumer researchers have found to be valuable for analysing online qualitative data is social network analysis. For examples of what might be done with such analysis see Baym (2010) and Papacharissi (2011). Social network analysis, or SNA, is a technique that looks at social relationships as networks, and considers both the structure and the patterns of their linkages (Berkowitz 1982; Wellman 1988). In a social network, we can consider that there are two main elements: the social actors themselves (termed 'nodes' in SNA) and the relationships between them (termed a 'tie').

Because we are dealing with actual relationships and contexts online, the nature of actors and of their ties is a highly flexible matter. For example, on a marketing oriented website, the 'actors' can be corporate marketing managers, consumers, public relationship people, brands, or products, or even messages, images, or video files. The nature of their ties or relationships could involve requesting information, economic transactions, responding to messages, posting new messages, or some other actions. Social network analysis considers these sorts of relationship interesting because they possess recurring patterns. These patterns are relevant to an understanding of the online social space because, in such key marketing matters as word-of-mouth (also termed 'word of mouse' online) and the diffusion of new products, we are interested both in the influence of individuals within a social network and in the patterns of the spread of influence and adoption. So, for example, the social structure of an online brand community devoted to sharing men's shaving tips might be of interest to brand managers at the Procter & Gamble brand Gillette. Of more general interest to marketing and consumer researchers might be the process of the pattern of influence depicting how a posted consumer-generated video about Imperial margarine spreads (no pun intended) across the internet and thus 'goes viral'.

Ties belong to the dyad formed between any two actors in the network and they refer to resources that are exchanged through the tie. These relations can be characterised by their content, their direction, and their strength. Strong ties tend to indicate friendships or close relationships, revealing kinship, intimacy, and frequent contact. Weak ties tend to be about people one barely knows but with whom they might come in contact sporadically, such as two people who belong to the L'Oréal community Facebook group, but do not message each other. As this example indicates, from Facebook to Twitter to all the forms of social media, the internet has become an excellent way to create the sort of casual exposures that a social network analyst would recognise as weak ties.

Internet scholar Caroline Haythornthwaite (2005) has noted how social media and the networks they build help weak ties grow into strong ties, as people in these networks build new types of connections. Although they still have a very long way to go before they have mastered the intricacies of social media marketing, marketers over the last few years have become increasingly savvy about using social media and their social networks and ties to create increased brand loyalty and spur not only word-of-mouth, but actual purchases. We should note that although the approach discussed here in the context of data mining is a 'top-down' approach beginning with a large pool of data, an alternative 'bottom-up' approach to network analysis begins with a small number of users who are examined individually. Miller (2011) provides an example of this approach in the context of Trinidadian social networking online.

Collecting data for social network analysis

Although the data used in social network analysis has traditionally been gathered through questionnaires and interviews, in the age of the internet it has increasingly come to be gathered by methods directly related to data mining. There are a growing number of social network analysis software packages available to assist marketing and consumer researchers interested in analysing the online social space. A relatively easy starter application is NodeXL, which exists as a free plug-in for Microsoft Excel. NodeXL offers good documentation and is good at producing visual graphs of network information. Statnet, a fully functional network analysis application, is considerably more sophisticated. There are also a number of other packaged applications, such as Visone, Pajek, Pnet, Tnet, and UCINET. All of these programs are either available free as open source software or freeware, or offer free trial versions.

For consumer and marketing researchers interested in word-of-mouth, influence, and the diffusion of products, communications, and ideas on the internet, SNA can be a valuable approach. It is able to use current online data and its orientation to analysing the structure of online relationships is suitable for many contemporary marketing concerns. For applied marketers, SNA can be extremely useful for informing segmentation, targeting, and positioning decisions, as well as in directing tactical efforts.

Learning about social network analysis

Use an online social network analysis tool such as MentionMapp, Touchgraph, or Klout, or another popular social network mapping software program to monitor and map your own online social network and its influence (you can find a convenient list of these tools by checking this posting: http://www.dreamgrow.com/54-free-social-media-monitoring-tools-update-2012/).

1 Sign in to mentionmapp.com (or another social network mapping online demonstration service) and enter your Twitter or Facebook account name.
2 Explore the resulting maps of your social network and connections. Are you surprised at the results?
3 If you are on Facebook, consider loading your Facebook page. (Read their privacy policy first to make sure you are comfortable with their conditions.)
4 Think about the usefulness of this information for marketers. What sorts of research questions does this data analysis answer? What sort of information and analysis would you like to see? What type of questions is this analysis unable to answer?

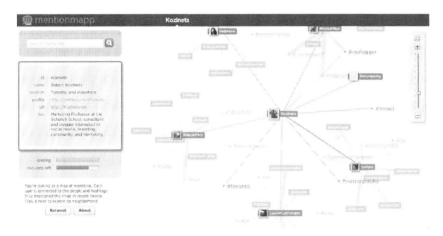

Figure 5.2   A Screenshot of MentionMapp, a Popular Social Network Analysis Online Tool

Introduction to netnography

Both data mining and top-down social network analysis look at the qualitative data on the internet as a type of content that must be decontextualised or processed in different ways in order to reveal more general patterns of common topics, structures, or influence. However, there is another, complementary way to view this qualitative data, called netnography. In netnography, researchers view qualitative online data as indicative of cultures or communities. Using techniques prevalent in anthropology and sociology, marketing and consumer researchers can study social media and online communities as cultural phenomena.

Social media can be defined as media for communication that use accessible and scalable formats and that are generally open to large groups, or even the entire public. If we consider these media to be truly social, then social methods that study the interactions between people as a cultural phenomenon are entirely appropriate, and can reveal important aspects of online behaviour, such as the values, meanings, language, rituals and other symbol systems that consumers create when they share and create culture online.

Researchers have been applying ethnographic methods to online communities and cultures for quite some time now. In 1999, Sterne (1999, p. 269) wrote that 'On-line analyses of Internet culture use a hybrid approach – often combining, in various degrees, ethnography, autobiography, and textual analysis.' Hine (2000, p. 10) defined 'virtual ethnography' as 'an ethnography of, in, and through the Internet [that] can be conceived of as an adaptive and wholeheartedly partial approach which draws on connection rather than location in defining its object.' Without offering particular guidelines, Fernback (1999, p. 216) mentioned that 'ethnographers working in cyberspace must be careful to attempt to a measure of reflexivity, to separate oneself from the subjects being studied; they must develop a sense about the truthfulness and candor of their informants, just as ethnographers of the nonvirtual must; and they must use a theoretically informed framework for their research, just as ethnographers have traditionally done'. For Miller and Slater (2000, p. 21), their ethnography of internet use in Trinidad involved a range of in-person and computer-mediated participant observation and was not limited to a 'purely textual analysis' of 'online "community" and relationships.' Like these past forms and demonstrations of online ethnography, netnography is a form of ethnographic research adapted to the unique contingencies of various types of computer-mediated social interactions. However, using netnography means adhering to a more specific set of guidelines than has been described in these past studies. A netnography is not simply an extension of a 'purely textual analysis', a 'wholeheartedly partial approach', an idiosyncratic 'hybrid', or a loosely specified set of senses and social concepts to which to attend. Instead, netnography offers a common language, a common understanding and a common set of standards for engaging in research practice. This commonality sets the stage for research that is consistent and rigorous.

How can we rigorously employ or adapt the tried-and-true in-person ethnographic techniques discussed in Chapter 4 to the online environment of the internet and social media? To begin, we need some sense about the differences between face-to-face social interactions and online social media interactions. Kozinets (2010a) identifies four critical differences between the two. The first important difference is *alteration*, which simply means that the nature of the interaction is altered – both constrained and liberated – by the specific nature and rules of the technological medium in which it is carried. As an example, consider the learning of additional codes and norms such as 'netiquette'– online and mobile rules of appropriate behaviour, abbreviations such as dot-com and dot-mobi, emoticons, keystroke sets, and other skills and knowledge that are important to transferring and presenting different kinds of social knowledge. There are cultural differences in these conventions as seen, for example, in the different emoticons used in Japan and in North America. For example, most Americans are quite familiar with the simple two-character, 90-degree counterclockwise rotated emoticon for a wink which looks like this ;). However, perhaps because of their complex kanji character set, the Japanese (and Chinese as well) make much more intricate emoticons. An extremely simple wink emoticon for a Japanese person is the following five-character complete facial portait: (^_~). Over time, linguistic and technical conventions such as these become naturalised, as a type of language which in itself expresses a new manifestation of the culture (e.g., Japanese cyberculture versus American cyberculture). Because the technological interface alters the already variegated human interaction experience further, face-to-face ethnographic procedures do not always make sense when applied to understanding online cultural worlds.

The next difference is *anonymity*, which was particularly relevant in the early years of online interaction, but may be less so in a world where Facebook identities are also often public identities. However, the option of anonymity and pseudonymity is still meaningful today and still alters the way that social interactions happen online. As evidence, consider Google +'s recent about face in which they first banned, and then in early 2012 reneged and finally allowed pseudonyms. Anonymity has vexed marketing researchers for years. Many marketers would like to be able to link online consumers with real-world demographics for more precise targeting and understanding. However, anonymity can also be liberating to consumers in a way that is useful and informative. Freed of the inhibitions that accountability creates, they more openly express their opinions, identities, and creativity. This can be valuable not only to participants themselves and their communities, but also to researchers and marketers.

The next difference is the wide *accessibility* of many online forums that are open to participation by anyone or anyone who cares to register using their e-mail address. In general, although there are notable exceptions, online social interactions tend to manifest an ethos of general democracy and inclusiveness. Gaining acceptance and status in social media communities can still be knowledge- and norm-dependent. But social media and the internet, as communications forums, are far more mass and far more global than anything in human history that preceded them. They comprise a hybrid form of public and private communications that is both incredibly broad (e.g., a blog comment) and incredibly narrow (e.g., an e-mail or direct message in Facebook or Twitter). The resulting exhibitionism and voyeurism is something that is unique to the medium, and which requires the adaptation of face-to-face ethnographic techniques.

Finally, there is nothing in the physical world analogous to the automatic *archiving* of conversations and data that we see in the world of social media. Communications take place in a digital format that is instantly stored, and which can be archived indefinitely. Conversation threads can develop asynchronously and last for years. Social interaction automatically becomes an artefact. This is usually done by the applications themselves, but in the case of Twitter, the US Library of Congress has been archiving all Tweets since March 2006. With 250 million Tweets per day, this is obviously a lot of data, even with the application's 140 character limit. For ethnography of content on such media, this means that fieldnotes must take on a different meaning. The way that data are collected, and the amounts of data to collect, radically shift the nature of research. As we consider this alteration in data collection, along with the other three differences, it is useful to turn to a general discussion of the procedures for data collection in netnography, as well as to an overview of general netnographic research techniques themselves.

Data collection in netnography

Netnography is ethnography in the social spaces of online environments. It involves taking an active approach to online research that seeks to maintain and analyse the cultural qualities of online interaction. Netnography is about researcher immersion in the full cultural complexity of online social worlds.

Therefore, data collection in netnography means learning deeply from, and likely communicating meaningfully with, members of an online culture or community manifesting itself through social media. That communication entails an active and relevant involvement, engagement, and connection with a community and its members.

In netnography as in ethnography, data collection happens alongside some basic data analysis. Even if the data is of archival interactions, the netnographer should be noting and interpreting the way that meanings, contexts, and people are influencing one another in a way relevant to the research questions under consideration. Certainly, the act of participating changes the nature of data collection and analysis, and differentiates netnographic techniques from other techniques such as content analysis or social network analysis. Content analysts might move through social media archives (more likely their algorithms would). But they would not be reading them for the kind of meaning-rich information that would help them understand culture membership. And social network analysis might describe patterns of influence between different community members, but it would also fail to build familiarity with the sets of meanings and values of the group being studied.

Netnographic participation drives netnographic data collection. Participation does not necessarily mean reaching out to members with posts which ask them questions, as if the netnographer were conducting an interview with the entire community, or even with certain select other members. Although participation can sometimes be visible to other community members, and preferably it will contribute to their communal interests and well-being, it can also involve other types of actions. The key guideline is that the netnographer should participate in the community at a level that is appropriate for a member. There are many different kinds of members of communities, and for some, it may be appropriate merely to observe the community, to read messages, to follow links and to be engaged in this way on a daily or more frequent basis. For some communities, engagement might require much more commitment in terms of disclosure and content production, for example being on a weight loss community and posting pictures of oneself in a bathing suit, or being a member of a design community and trying one's hand at designing new dresses and posting them for member comments.

Langer and Beckman (2005) have questioned the importance and value of researcher participation in netnography, asserting that 'covert studies' of online communities are sometimes desirable. Often times, researchers have asserted in their methods sections that they are performing 'observational' or 'passive' netnographies (e.g., Beaven and Laws 2007; Brown et al. 2003; Brownlie and Hewer 2007; Füller et al. 2006; Maulana and Eckhardt 2007). When combined with sophisticated qualitative data analysis software approaches, this observational approach to netnography might even come close to content mining and content analysis.

However, the participative role of the cultural researcher is often vital to the experience of learning embedded cultural understandings. As anthropology teaches us, direct experience is the best and perhaps only way to gain the profound understanding of cultural membership. Without it, a netnographer is blind to the cultural meanings of a social media site or community she does not fully understand. Without communal contact, a netnographer has no one to bounce her interpretation off of, and to validate, dispute, or expand upon her many cultural interpretations. The result can often be a retreat into purely descriptive accounts, rather than the profound conceptual understanding for which quality anthropology is renowned (see Boellstorff 2008 for a good anthropological netnography). Like ethnography, netnography is based on the twin and intertwining methodological pillars of participation and observation. Netnography involves coding, but it is not merely coding. Netnography involves data, but at its core it is about weaving strands of data into cultural understanding and deep interpretation. In order to achieve this lofty goal, authentic researcher participation as a culture member is vitally important.

What is netnographic participation?

With so many active social media users online, there has never been a better time to conduct a netnography. The chances are that relevant topics relating to your field of interest are being discussed through social media right now. In fact, your own use of social media can help to make you more aware of social media and how it might be refined and put into use through applying a netnographic approach.

First, write down all of the social media communities you belong to. These might include Facebook, Twitter, YouTube, Foursquare, Flickr, Digg, Reddit, Yelp, Quora, Pinterest and other popular social media sites.

Next, consider which communities you participate in. Write down the names of the communities you participate in.

Please finish this step before you proceed. Do not read ahead.

Now, consider what you just wrote. Did you have any questions about the notion of 'participating' in social media communities? How did you judge 'participation' in those social media communities? Did participation mean only writing and posting? Was it extended to ranking and rating? Or did you consider yourself to be participating in a community even if you merely read the messages?

We adopt the stance that participation in a netnography can take on many forms, as detailed in past work on these methods (Kozinets 2002b, 2006b, 2010). These participative acts can include:

- Reading current messages regularly and in real-time (in netnography this is how it is done for current messages; whereas content miners might download archived messages en masse to be searched and/or automatically coded).
- Reading archives of messages using some sort of temporal or topical pattern.
- Following communally shared links to other pages and communities.
- Following community relevant postings on other sites, such as Twitter, or in Facebook groups.
- Rating and evaluating relevant community-related work.
- Replying to other members via e-mail or other one-on-one communications.
- Offering short comments.
- Offering longer comments.
- Joining in and contributing to the activities of this community, in social media and perhaps outside it in the physical world.
- Becoming an organiser, expert, or recognised voice in the community.

This stance regarding participation may inspire you to recognise that there are many ways to engage with online and social media communities when you conduct your netnographic research. Please keep in mind that participation is about appropriate behaviour in the community, not necessarily extremely active behaviour. When in roaming mode, do as the roamers – or the message posters – do.

Sometimes, introspective self-reflection on cultural matters can be a powerful source of valuable data. For example, consider doing observational work in a new virtual world where a consumer can hear new music and see the pilots for new television shows. Consider the interesting effects of avatar and setting choices on consumer-led brand discussions in online spaces such as virtual worlds. In that case, it might be very useful to understand the new and existing cultures that impact the lived experience of being an avatar in such a marketing-driven virtual event. 'Auto-netnography' is a form of netnography where the data collection is largely autobiographical and consists mainly of personal reflection on social media community membership. This data can be captured in screenshots, recordings, fieldnotes and other subjectively-focused recordings of online experience [for examples of this type of netnography, see Kozinets and Kedzior 2009; Markham 1998; Weinberg 2000; Wood and Solomon 2009).

The useful and prevalent sailing metaphor of 'tacking' to analogise the process of data interpretation applies to online data as well (see Chapters 7 and 8). Netnographers, like ethnographers, constantly tack back and forth between the experience – close, 'emic' 'subjective' involvement with social media community and culture members and the more 'etic' distanced, 'objective', abstract and 'scientific' theory, and research questions/answers. Because of the need to balance cultural experience with abstract insight, netnographic data collection involves the gathering and creation of three different types of data, as outlined below (see also Kozinets 2002, 2006b, 2010a). These three categories correspond approximately to Miles and Huberman's (1994) qualitative research categories of documents, interviews, and observations. They also approximate Wolcott's (1992) categories of watching, asking, and examining.

1 *Archival data*: data that the researcher directly copies from pre-existing files and records or, less often, creates himself or herself. Archival data is purely 'observational' in that it has usually been created and shared by social media community members or by a third party like the Library of Congress. This is data that the researcher has not been directly involved in creating or prompting. There are abundant amounts of data, and the relative effortlessness of its transcription (amounting to downloading) can make acquiring it simple and analysing it daunting. Research filters or sampling can be required to select and manage this storm of data. In particular, this is why

netnographers focus upon particular communities, and then on particular messages or message threads. These close readings can be revelatory of new insights as well as more general insights (see, e.g., Kozinets (2006b) for deep interpretation of a single message posting).

2 *Elicited data*: is data that the researcher co-creates alongside social media community members. This is data produced through social media communications, and thus through relevant personal and communal interaction. Elicited data includes researcher postings and comments. It can also include Twitter feeds, Facebook status updates and messages, Skype conversations, e-mail, chat, or instant messaging interviews. Elicited data is a co-production of the researcher and the community. Because this data has the researcher's influence built into it, it is analysed somewhat differently from data that does not have this stamp of influence, a sorting of data not usually possible in collected ethnographic data. However, this is certainly not 'contaminated' or impure data by any means. Elicited data can be much more focused and much more valuable in the service of answering crucial research questions than other data.

3 *Fieldnote data*: comes from the personal and research-related descriptive and reflexive fieldnotes that the researcher has created. Netnographers, like ethnographers, should be writing their reflections and observations of the fieldsite and culture members throughout their fieldwork (for more on fieldnotes, please see Chapter 4). This inscription process should capture the netnographer's impressions and observations of the social media community itself, its members and memberships, its practices, the members' social interactions and meanings, the researcher's own participation and sense of membership, and much more. During analysis, these observations and impressions can be extremely valuable sources of insight that can help reveal unique and important contexts as well as the cultural processes at work in general and within particular social media communities.

Basic principles of online data capture and collection

Netnographers have a choice between manual data capture and analysis and automated data capture and analysis. Both can be used very effectively. Manual data collection and analysis involve saving computer files on a hard drive and coding either in document programs, such as Word, or in spreadsheets or database programs. These types of capture and analysis make sense when the data is kept to a smaller size, perhaps 500 to 1,000 pages of data. For many projects, and for projects with a tractable focus, manual data coding can be perfectly sufficient.

Automated data collection, which uses qualitative data analysis software programs such as those discussed in Chapter 8 to assist with data coding and organisation, can be used to handle larger and less focused projects with greater amounts of data. When the topic of study is an entire large, active social media community, or when the work seeks to explore a major topic, or is exploratory and insight-driven in nature, this is usually the best technique to use, and the researcher should be prepared and able to handle the large resulting amount of data and the consequent challenges of organising and analysing it.

In terms of actually capturing and storing data, there are two basic ways to capture online data, which we can term saving and capturing. The first is to save the file as a computer-readable file. The second is to capture it as a visual image of the computer screen. Saving is more appropriate for highly textual messages where the researcher considers that other elements of the context, such as page design, visuals, and other elements are unimportant to the analysis and research question(s). Capturing is more appropriate when the reverse is true, i.e., that context, visual elements, and perhaps other elements (e.g., audiovisual links) are important to the research question and eventual analysis. Remember that you will see a lot of data, click through a lot of links, and read a lot of messages in a typical netnographic project. When it comes time to analyse that project, you will not remember every detail. So it is very important during data collection for you to make good judgments about what to save of your netnographic data. It is better to capture information that you later disregard than to speedily move through data collection ignoring details that may later become important but are, by then, excruciatingly absent. In many cases, the captures of online screen grabs can be scanned and the text recognised by OCR programs, and thus capture can be translated back into computer-readable files. Thus, the default decision should probably be, when in doubt about the richness of the data, to capture the image rather than to reduce it by saving the file. It is also noteworthy that content mining and social network analysis deal almost exclusively with textual and relational data. They cannot accommodate the cultural and contextual richness of consumers' sound, image, and audiovisual representations. In this respect as well as others, netnography deals with data that is 'richer' in a linguistic, symbol-driven cultural sense, and holds much greater potential to produce more complex and contextualised understanding of online social worlds.

Getting ready for netnographic data collection

Archiving and accessibility are two of the major differences between online fieldwork and traditional face-to-face ethnography that create a very different research environment when it comes to data collection. These two factors change the way that the researcher locates a relevant site, community, or cultural space. Whereas a traditional ethnographer might travel great distances by air, land, or sea in order to study a culture in a distant land, a netnographer might simply need to sit down at her laptop and open a good search engine. So, for instance, the Google engine can identify many message topic threads across many different media of interest, including blogs and public web-page forums. And twitter.com/search is a search engine that covers posted Twitter feeds. There are also a range of different engines that can search different parts of Facebook and LinkedIn. In addition, many commercial data mining and marketing research services will include access to sophisticated search engines that combine many different types of community information, often allowing the researcher to search within different social media categories (such as blogs, forums, social networking sites, and so on).

One of the main issues surrounding data collection in netnography and, indeed, data collection across the internet in general, concerns where to focus. The enormous opportunity for discovery is why it is crucial for qualitative researchers to begin their work with a general research question and then to adapt and refine that question in response to data collection opportunities and initial analysis results. So, for example, a consumer researcher might be interested in studying the popular consumption of fine art. An appropriate initial research question for such an investigation might be 'What are the main discussions surrounding the popular consumption of fine art? What are the main topics? Who appears to be discussing them? In what context do these discussions occur?' From there, and particularly during data analysis, the research question might develop to focus more specifically on theoretical matters such as European art versus Asian art, the negotiation of aesthetics, and the use of social media to promote consumption-related status distinctions.

Often, marketing and consumer researchers will simply be interested in studying particular online sites. This is similar to an ethnographer who studies in a particular geographical region or a sociologist who is interested in learning about a particular subculture that frequents a certain neighbourhood of a large city. For marketing academics, brand communities pose particularly interesting contexts. So, for example, Muñiz and Schau (2005) were interested in the online communities devoted to the defunct PDA, the Apple Newton. From their study of these communities, they offered a rich theory about the myth-driven and quasi-religious relationship between consumer communities and brands. Brand managers are often interested in understanding the activities and responses of participants in communities and sites that feature or relate to their own brands, consumer lifestyle groupings, or product categories. Netnographic studies of these sites can be useful for benchmarking best practices as well as auditing existing offerings.

After sites have been located, each should be thoroughly investigated. Because netnography is different from data mining, a smaller subset of sites should be considered for deeper, in-person, investigation. The more sites that the researcher searches and investigates and the longer the time she devotes to it, the more likely that a strong cross-section of sites and groups will have been investigated, leading to some interesting and useful findings.

How do you choose specific sites for netnography?

Assume you were about to begin your netnographic project on a given topic. What exactly would you look for in a site to help you choose which place, of all the social spaces online, with which to engage and from which to collect data? This brief exercise will lead you through this crucial stage of the process of performing a netnography.

First, devise a research question for your investigation.

Next, perform a simple Google search using some search terms and keywords related to your topic. Now, use a search on Twitter, such as twitter.com/search. Next, search Facebook for relevant groups.

When the searches return results that seem relevant to your search, click through the first two or three pages of sites or pages. Have a look at from 10 to 20 different sites or locations of social media communities. Try to have at least five from blogs or forums, and at least five from social media such as Twitter and Facebook.

Examine the sites or pages by reading through them in detail. Do not simply scan them, but read each word to try to understand the nuances of what is being said.

Before you read the rest of this box or chapter, answer this question: 'How would you judge which sites, or which parts of these sites to visit?' If you had to choose only one site from the 10 to 20 different sites you have visited, which one would you choose?

Write down what you believe to be the most important criteria you should look for in a site you will investigate.

Did you complete your list? Good! Now, compare it with the list below.

In general, as recommended in Kozinets (2010a, p. 89), the guidelines for deciding to pursue a more detailed and time-consuming investigation of one or more social media sites are that these sites are:

1 *Relevant*, they can inform and clearly link to your stated research focus and question(s).
2 *Active*, possessing both recent and regular communications between members.
3 *Interactive*, manifesting a flow of question–answer or posting–comment responsive communications between participants in the group.
4 *Substantial*, offering a critical mass of communicators and a lively, energised cultural atmosphere.

(Continued)

(Continued)

5 *Heterogeneous*, indicating a good number of different participants; and
6 *Data-rich*, offering data that is significantly detailed or descriptively rich.

How did your list compare with this one? Like social media itself, netnography and all qualitative techniques are constantly changing. Perhaps you came up with some different and more interesting criteria. Keep all of these criteria in mind as you choose a narrower site to engage with and conduct an in-depth netnography.

Do your homework. This means that you should thoroughly read through current messages, archives, community rules and FAQs. This is part of the cultural research process, and you should also be composing detailed fieldnotes about what you are learning as a participant in the process, whether it be your entry into a LinkedIn group, an ongoing Twitter conversation, or a series of related blogs. Good research results from paying careful attention to the characteristics of the online community prior to making first contact.

Notice some important things about your social media site. Cultivating at least a practical working knowledge of the following characteristics, reflected in your observations and your netnographic fieldnotes, will be important as you pursue your netnography and begin to enter the site more frequently.

- What is the software design configuration of the site? How might it influence the social interactions there?
- Who are the site's most active participants?
- What roles do people seem to assume on the site?
- Who are the conversation starters? Who are the 'leaders'? Why do you think of them that way?
- What are some of the most popular topics that are discussed?
- What is the group's history?
- How is this group connected to other groups? Which other groups are the members connected to?
- What can you learn about the demographics, interests, opinions, and values of the people using the site?
- Are there any specialised languages or symbols being use? Acronyms or sayings? What is their meaning and history? What do they indicate about the community?
- Does the community have any common practices, rituals or special activities?

The goal is to be familiar with the social media community's members, topics, language, rituals, norms and processes. If the community seems hostile to researchers and to being researched, it may not be a good candidate for netnography, which includes a participative stance and which demands, because of ethical rules, that the researcher honestly disclose herself and her affiliation where appropriate.

Collecting data and choosing data analysis software

There are no general rules about when to start keeping fieldnotes, but we would recommend getting into a habit of jotting notes about initial sites visited as you begin your investigation. These jottings can be developed into more detailed fieldnotes as your netnography develops. It is useful to begin these practices early, as the insights you will gain as you first enter the social media fieldsite can be enormously valuable when it comes time for data analysis. These initial insights, which occur as you learn about the cultural systems of a new site, are fleeting, and they are crucial to capture immediately.

From the earliest times in your research investigation, you should also be preparing yourself to collect data. Likewise Richards (2005) suggests that researchers should choose a qualitative data analysis package and learn about it even before collecting data. The time to learn about your software package is not when you are awash in your social media site and all of its rich data, but when you can calmly consider how it works and how it can help you. See Chapter 7 for more advice about data capture and analysis software packages that are commercially available.

If you are going to be employing a qualitative data analysis software package, it can be useful to save your initial fieldnotes using the software. You can use these software inputs to keep yourself organised in managing your research design, your readings (many could be stored in the project as pdf files), your field data, your fieldnotes and observations, your initial and more advanced analysis, correspondences, screenshots, downloaded files including video and audio, e-mails, and all of your conclusions and reports. By having all of this information organised and in one place (as well as backed up), you will make your life much easier. For once you begin your formal entrée into the field site, your research work will already be in progress, and places will have already been established for storing that information. Just as is the case with in-person ethnography, it is important to get into the habit of systematically reflecting on your encounters with culture members after these events occur. With a good software package in place, you will already be organising, commenting upon, and perhaps even entering some rudimentary codes in your data.

Online interviews

In ethnography, interviews are frequently involved as a way to deepen the understanding of the lived experience of culture members, to learn about meanings and language, and to build rapport with research participants. Interviews are often described as a special kind of face-to-face oral communication. Online interviews are similar in principle to interviews that are conducted face-to-face, but the reality of their conduct is quite different. In this section we discuss how the principles of interviewing can be adapted and applied to the online context.

We can begin with the realisation that every interview is a structured conversation, a special type of conversation. That is, interviews exist as a set of questions and answers between two or more people who agree that there are generally two roles: that of a questioner and that of an answerer (see Chapter 3). The interview, also sometime called an 'online' or 'cyber-' interview, has been a staple of cultural studies of online worlds from their beginning in the 1990s (see. e.g., Cherny 1999). Although purely observational netnographies can be conducted, interviews are useful when the understanding sought includes consumers' own self-reflections, cultural categories, or expressed narratives.

Although some online researchers report mixed or unsatisfying results from online interviews, and some recommend supplementing online fieldwork with phone interviews (e.g., Bruckman 2006), online interviews still can have a part to play in many online research studies. We do find that synchronous, text-based, chat interviews tend to offer a very thin and often rather rushed and superficial interaction. However, this experience should not preclude the use of other media for interviews, such as e-mail. Indeed, in the age of Skype, a Skype conversation with online audio and visual connections can be quite rich and valuable (see Kivits 2005). Online interviews can also be recorded audio-visually. Is an interview conducted on Skype using Facetime on your iPad an 'online interview'? Technically, it is. So even the meaning of an 'online interview' – e.g., that it is non-visual and does not include body language – is in flux in the age of rapidly increasing technological sophistication.

Traditionally, however, online interviews have been text based, and this has led to some important limitations. In a chat room, who is the actual interview participant (see Turkle 1995)? How can they be understood and socially situated? This lack of individual identifiers has been frustrating to consumer and marketing researchers in the past. In addition, the lack of access to facial expression and body language has hindered the expression of the full cultural and social nature of the interview. It has made that social information more difficult to interpret. This is somewhat less true where both researcher and participants are represented by Avatars, as in Second Life (e.g., Boellstorff 2008) and, as previously mentioned, in iChat, FaceTime, or through an audio-visual link in Skype.

However, as with the notion of adaptation mentioned above, conducting an interview through a computer (or tablet, or mobile device) means that the structure and content of interview communications are going to be modified by the medium used. For some netnographies, in situ conversations or a quick exchange of social information in the form of DM (direct message) or e-mail might suffice to inform your research question. For other purposes, group interviews similar to online focus groups can be employed. For others, depth interviews with single, influential social media participants might be the most useful technique. The type of data that is required should determine the optimal type of interview, and those data needs should in turn be directly informed by the purpose of the research.

In a netnography, we are usually seeking nuanced cultural understandings of the life of a social group and its members. For this purpose, depth interviewing is the best technique we can employ. Depth, or in-depth interviews are intensive interviews with smaller numbers of people that allow a more extensive exploration of their perspective and viewpoints. As noted in Chapter 3, depth interviews are time intensive, labour intensive, and require considerable interviewer skill. They place the most serious demands upon interview participants as well, because they ask for and allow a deeper disclosure of more sensitive, personal matters. As Grant McCracken (1989) usefully describes the grand tour questions in his 'long inter-view' method, the depth interview begins with an understanding of the social situation of the culture member – for example, their age, gender, nationality, family background, schools, ethnic orientation, sexual orientation, and so on – and how it influences their lives. In a netnography, this might be connected to the way that they use social media. For instance, depth interview findings might lead us to theorise that someone who is the eldest sibling, but who was always seen as a creative outsider among their peers and at school, tends to participate more heavily and seek leadership status in social media brand communities such as blogs. Through using depth interviews and the rich personal data they provide, we can understand how brands, communities, and social media intersect with the various contexts and roles that create the human social experience, both in the physical world and online.

Summary

Qualitative data deriving from online and social media interaction are becoming increasingly important to the conduct of consumer and marketing research in the contemporary world. Although the collection and analysis of this data does not necessarily require radical adaptations or departures from extant qualitative research practices, we believe that these existing practices do require careful and systematic adaptation. In providing a broad overview with a number of important details, this chapter has emphasised that taking techniques of content analysis, interviewing, and participant observation into the age of web mining, online interviews, and netnography is a process that is undergoing constant development and rapid evolution. New techniques and tools, and certainly new sites for data collection and research, are available for researchers. It is in this spirit that we can turn towards a deeper examination of some of these tools in our next chapter.

6

Data collection aids

It is often said that the researcher IS the instrument in qualitative research. This is quite true in the sense that the quality and insightfulness of the data obtained depends on the skills of the researcher. It is up to you as the researcher to devise the best and most appropriate data collection techniques for a given situation and to be able to listen and observe attentively, respond appropriately, and guide the interview or other data collection effort with sensitivity, creativity, and in a manner that induces trust and openness. Exactly what this entails will also vary according to the data collection method, with considerable differences between such diverse methods as depth interviews, informal interviews, netnography, archival research, and participant observation. There are no magic gadgets that will compensate or substitute for researcher skills and judgment in such situations. There are however, some aids that can often help a skilled researcher to elicit and capture better data. This chapter will consider the following categories of data collection aids:

1 audio recording;
2 still photography;
3 audio-video recording;
4 participant-produced materials;
5 other high tech and low tech data and devices.

Although such data collection aids need to anticipate analyses intended, data analysis software aids are discussed in Chapter 8 and are largely ignored here. Downloading and screen capture for netnography is discussed in Chapter 5 and amplified in Kozinets (2010), and is not discussed here either. The data collection aids discussed in this chapter will affect the suitability of the material collected for different anticipated means of distributing findings (e.g., print, web-based, audio-visual). But a more thorough treatment of data presentation options can be found in Chapter 9. In other words, everything is connected and this chapter should not be used without considering how the data collection aids discussed fit with the entire research project.

Audio recording

Imagine conducting a depth interview for an hour or longer and then trying to recall the entire conversation verbatim. Even those with the most photographic memories are at best likely to paraphrase most of the interview, recall a few snippets as they were spoken, and forget some material entirely. Yet, this is a situation you may face. Audio recorders may fail, an informant may insist on not being recorded, everything may look fine with the recorder until you play it back and discover that an electrical whine makes it inaudible, or, perhaps worst of all, you accidentally erased or recorded over your prized interview. Such circumstances reinforce the importance of using an audio recorder for a purpose other than recording interviews – you can and should also use an audio recorder for recording rough fieldnotes. Fieldnotes are your subjective notes to yourself about what transpired in the field. In addition to recalling what was said, you should try to capture how it was said, what you saw, what preceded and followed the interview, what the surrounding situation was like (not just visually, but drawing on all the senses), how at ease the informant seemed, how he or she seemed to respond to you, and other informative details, including your initial insights into the meaning of what you are seeing and hearing. This 'dumping' of your recollections and impressions should be done as soon as possible after a significant interview or observation. If you are walking off, duck into a toilet, a quiet grove, or any place you can inconspicuously dictate some impressions. This can even be in the middle of a crowd, as Figure 6.1 shows. If you drive off, pull over to the side of the road as soon as possible and begin dumping fieldnotes. These rough notes may not flow out in sentences, but may be key phrases or events, highlighted by mnemonic references that will help you recall what you have seen, heard, and experienced when you later transcribe these fieldnotes – something that should also be done as soon as possible. So you might spew out phrases and keywords like 'red Porsche', 'salsa dancing', 'boyfriend', 'mother upset', 'throbbing headache'. These may mean little or nothing to someone who was not a part of the interview or observation, but they should be prompts that will allow you to recall the actions and conversation of which they were a part.

Interview transcriptions and even videotapes of interviews and observations cannot capture everything you learn in the field. That is why fieldnotes are so critical. As the key research instrument you know more, including your tacit knowledge of what you are experiencing. Fieldnotes are also the place to make tentative notes to yourself about emerging interpretations while you are in the field. Here is a rough sketch of things to include in your handwritten or dictated fieldnotes; it is not exhaustive and you may well think of others:

1 Where are you? Besides the descriptive name of the town and place, also note the lay-out of the place (a hand-drawn map can be helpful and can later be keyed to photos of the site). What is the weather like? Is there anything like a front stage and back stage at this place?
2 When is this? Date and time may be critical to matching fieldnotes and transcriptions as well as establishing timelines and sequences of events.
3 Who is there? Besides those you interview, what others are present and what are they like (e.g., how might you characterise those in the background of Figure 6.1?). If you have just conducted an interview, how do you think it went? How would you describe the person interviewed? How open or apprehensive was the person interviewed? How honest do you think they were being? If you have a business card from the person, this would be a good place to record that information, just in case it is misplaced or detached from the context of the interview.
4 What is going on? What actions are taking place? What does it sound like? What does it smell like? Who is interacting with whom? What is the mood you sense? Are people happy, excited, bored, tense, eager, relaxed, or in some other state? Are there groups of people (describe them) or do people appear to be by themselves? If this is a retail location, how do service providers act and engage customers? If you have done an interview that was not recorded or had a casual conversation of potential relevance, this is the place to get it down in as much detail as you can. If in doubt, put it down. You never fully know when some incidental observation or comment might become a key piece of information.
5 Why? This involves the category of emerging interpretations, insights, and notes to yourself about things to explore further, follow-up on, and examine more carefully.

These categories should be easy to remember because they involve the basic journalistic questions of who, what, where, why, and when. But you are neither a journalist nor a mechanistic recording device. Rather this is the place to capture details that your recording devices miss and to record your subjective impressions and feelings. Fieldnotes are not only an invaluable addition to interview transcriptions, they are often the only record you have of what you are observing. And even if you are using a camera and camcorder, these devices (see below) cannot capture everything of relevance.

Figure 6.1 Russ Belk and Melanie Wallendorf dictate fieldnotes at a swap meet

━━━━━━━━━━━━━━━━━━━━━━━━ **EXERCISE 6.1** ━━━━━━━━━━━━━━━━━━━━━━━━

Conduct and audio-record a practice interview with someone on a topic of interest to them, but about which you know little. It need not be an hour – 10 or 15 minutes should do. Then without listening to the recording attempt to reconstruct the interview verbatim, including both questions and answers. Now look at your reconstruction while listening to the recording. How accurate are you? A rough guideline is that 70–80 per cent is good, above that is excellent, 60–70 per cent is marginal, and below that means you need to practise more. Also pay attention to what you have missed, anything you have misconstrued, and anything you thought was said that was not. This is an exercise in focused listening as much as it is a test of memory. Try jotting down or recording some keyword fieldnotes as an aid (described above as 'dumping' fieldnotes) before you begin your next reconstruction.

Exercise 6.1 will likely be a good demonstration of the usefulness of audio-recording devices. However, it is also a demonstration of what happens when a recording device fails or cannot be used. Carrying spare batteries and even a spare recorder can help prevent the former situation, but not the latter. To prepare for the inevitable time when someone with something important to say does not want to be recorded, practise, practise, practise. By focusing on what the person being interviewed is saying rather than what you are going to say next, you will be better able to recall what is being said. It will also make you more spontaneous in responding. Active listening also shows you are interested and accepting of what the person has to say.

The other issue that the exercise above brings up is how you transcribe an interview (assuming you are doing transcribing yourself, on which we will say more below). This applies when you are listening to a recording of the conversation as well. Should you try to use some sort of notation system that captures pregnant pauses, emotions, laughter, reticence, and other non-verbal parts of an interview? It depends of the focus of your analysis. If it is important to understand the informant's comfort level, fluency, hesitancy, and emotions, these non-verbals as well as verbal utterances like 'er', 'uh', and 'hum' may be quite important. In other situations they may be less so. If there was an important non-verbal gesture or you have an observation about how something was said, it is a good idea to include this [in brackets like this]. You can hire people to transcribe, but only the interviewer is going to have access to this non-verbal information. Such implicit knowledge on the part of the researcher who was there is also the reason that it is difficult for someone who was not there to fully understand and analyse transcripts. If you do hire someone to transcribe, try to have it done as soon as possible and then go over the transcription not only for accuracy, but also to add [bracketed] comments that only you know because you were there. Fieldnotes help third parties understand more, but they are never able to completely recreate the implicit knowledge of the person who gathered the data.

You also learn a great deal by transcribing and begin to more fully understand your data. But it is highly time consuming (you might figure that it will take four times as long as it took to conduct the interview). So judge accordingly. Translating is another task when dealing with data in a 'foreign' language and requires transcribers who are also skilled (i.e., non-literal) translators. On one occasion while Russ was having a Swedish research agency conduct interviews on consumer ethics, we arranged an audio-video feed to a monitor in another room where a skilled translator did a simultaneous translation into a microphone. This resulted in a video recording in which we had Swedish on one audio track and English on another audio track. This also made it easier to create either an appropriately synced audio translation or to create English subtitles when we later created a video report of the project (Belk et al. 2005). However, we suggest that when possible, you keep the transcript in the original language. If you attempt to use voice recognition software to prepare a transcription, this is even more critical since, at best, it will only capture what was said and not how it was said. Better still, do not transcribe! *Any* transcription is a translation, even when the language remains the same. This is because a transcript cannot capture everything that is on the recording.

So how do you not transcribe and still prepare a data trail and material for analysis? There are computer programs, including the most popular computer programs that facilitate analysis like NVivo and Atlas.ti (see Chapter 8), that allow coding audio and video material directly in their original form. OneNote from Microsoft also allows this. Otherwise we are faced with the problem of pairing analyses of audio and video material (e.g., Rose 2000). Like making marginal notations or codes on text, you can code audio or video material text directly. In this case when you click on codes rather than being taken to the transcript as the context, you are taken to the audio or video material directly. Technology is advancing and this may become the preferred mode of coding data in the future because it omits the transcription step that necessarily loses something as well as takes a large amount of time and effort. But it is still most common to transcribe into written text. Such transcription has the added advantage of allowing you to copy and paste quotes you would like to use in a presentation of your data, assuming that the presentation is to be primarily written rather than audio-visual. Most digital audio recorders today allow transferring data to a computer where you can slow down and pause the playback without affecting the pitch. This allows for easier transcription than attempting the impossible task of transcribing in real time.

We have assumed in discussing transcription that the sound you are recording is the voice of a single person being interviewed. If you are conducting a group interview (see Chapter 3), transcription is trickier because more than one person is responding and they may be talking over one another sometimes. Unless separate microphones and separate audio tracks or separate recorders are used, transcription by the interviewer who was there is even more critical to try to untangle who was saying what. In certain types of research it may not be voices at all that are being recorded, but rather musical instruments, songs, playlists or other types of audio material (e.g., Ayers 2006; Bull 2007). In this case, the advice of coding audio material directly without transcription is even more compelling.

A final note concerns the more mechanical aspects of audio recording. If more than one researcher is present, one person can monitor the sound as it is being recorded. If you are the only researcher present you can do a sound check before you begin to be sure your equipment is set and capturing properly. If possible, lock the file after recording so you cannot record over it. Use separate files for each interview, observation, or set of fieldnotes and label them with names, places, and dates. This filing task is critical if you do not want to search through possibly hundreds of hours of recordings trying to find certain material. Whether you are using a dedicated audio recorder, a smart phone, a portable computer, a tablet computer, or some other device, get the microphone as close to the sound you want to capture as possible. Think about a separate microphone if feasible. A hand-held microphone allows you to direct who speaks by pointing it (see Figure 6.2), while a lapel or boundary area microphone is more readily

Figure 6.2 Melanie Wallendorf using a hand-held microphone to direct the interview

forgotten. If you have a choice, set the microphone pickup pattern to focus narrowly on the participant rather than capture a broader pattern of sound, which will be more likely to pick up background noise. It is more important to get good audio of answers than of your questions. Try to eliminate background noise (radios, televisions, street noise) where possible by moving the interview or turning competing devices down or off. And lastly, get comfortable with your equipment so that it is second nature to watch that the recording light is on, recording levels are adequate, and battery indicators are not indicating imminent death of the recording.

Still photography

The aphorism that a picture is worth a thousand words has a grain of truth to it, but the one that claims that photos cannot lie is itself a lie. More precisely, photos themselves are not the liars, but photographers necessarily 'lie' constantly. They can not only fake a 'candid' photo by staging it, they must also decide what is included and excluded in the photo frame, how the camera focus, aperture, and exposure time are set, what lens and filters to use, and so forth (Goldstein 2007). Photographers can also manipulate the photo after it is taken. Darkroom magic and airbrushing have given way to computer manipulation, making more elaborate deceptions possible with greater ease. In addition when people are the knowing subjects of photographs they can pose and present themselves in ways that are also misleading (Loisos 2000). For example, Indian photo wallahs commonly use backdrops of settings where the photographed subject has never been and pose them with objects like motorcycles that they have never owned, all in an effort to show them as cosmopolitan (Pinney 1997). In photos for Indian matrimonial services, prospective brides sometimes are posed with consumer electronics that are not their own in order to imply higher social status (MacDougall and MacDougall 1996). And wedding photos in much of Asia are elaborately staged in days preceding the wedding, showing the couple in multiple costumes in exotic locations (Adrian 2003). Such practices caution against careless assumptions of veridicality in using photos as secondary data in consumer research (Belk 1998). However, this need not be of quite as much of a concern when photography is being used to gather primary data, because the researcher knows the context and how the photo was taken.

One purpose for using photographs in primary data collection is to record visual details as a part of observation and for triangulation with other data collected. Photos must be logged and catalogued as faithfully as audio recordings and fieldnotes and in a corresponding manner so that they can later be matched to other materials collected. Cameras have become smaller and more flexible and may also be a part of a smartphone, videocamera, tablet computer, laptop computer, or other device. They are likely to be digital and may also provide time, date, exposure, and location information which can make cataloguing easier. The latter details may sound irrelevant when the research interest is on the content of the photos, but (for example) knowing whether a photo was shot with a lens and in a format that is the equivalent of what the eye sees (rather than telephoto or wide angle) can tell something about the degree of intimacy the researcher enjoyed (Heisley et al. 1991).

The photographer may be either the researcher or those being studied. For example, Kelly Tian and Russ (Tian and Belk 2005) studied the meanings of workplace possessions by first sending their informants disposable cameras with which to photograph their favourite possessions in their office or cubicle. Later, at an off-site location, they were asked to discuss the meanings of the objects in their pictures. This subsequent use of the photos is an example of visual elicitation, as discussed in Chapter 3. Just as we said that there is not much purpose in transcribing all of the vocal inflections of recorded interviews unless the purpose is to assess certainty, hesitancy, or similar nuances, there is not much point in photographing those being interviewed unless the purpose is to consider the setting or their non-verbal language. Rather, photographs are better used for capturing 'perspectives in action' rather than 'perspectives of action' (Gould et al. 1974).That is, photos can show behaviour that is only inadequately captured in words or that may be beneath the level of consciousness. For example, Emmison and Smith (2000) show a photo of a professor with a student in his office from which they nicely deduce the following regarding the significance of the use of space and postures:

> Observe how the professor looks relaxed and is adopting an assymetrical posture. By extending his arms and raising one knee he consumes the maximal amount of space. In contrast the student sits bolt upright with her arms by her side. Notice also how the professor's desk furniture creates a barrier which serves to mark out his personal space and thereby dramatise status differences. (p. 221, Figure 6.2)

This was based on a photo that was gathered as a part of primary data collection, but it could just as well have been a part of a secondary data collection. A secondary data use of photographs can be seen in a study by Doan Nguyen and Russ (Nguyen and Belk 2007) who analysed the ways in which American soldiers who had been in what Americans call the Vietnamese war, photographed Vietnamese soldiers and civilians. They found that angles of photography (looking up or looking down) and shot selections tended to heroise the Americans as larger, more powerful, and with more modern weapons and playful attitudes, while locals were portrayed through a figurative lens of Orientalism, making them appear exotic, mysterious, and primitive as well as smaller, weaker, and submissive.

The value of photographic evidence in ethnography is also shown by Arnould and Wallendorf (1994) in analysing their study of American Thanksgiving meals (Wallendorf and Arnould 1991). They found that these observational records often showed discrepancies with what their informants had said about their Thanksgiving. Both overgeneralisations (e.g., 'We always do this') and glosses (e.g., 'homemade' or 'from scratch') were revealed in comparing these accounts to what was actually done (e.g., transferring commercially prepared foods from their original container to family serving dishes might be interpreted as constituting 'homemade'). Such distortions may well be unintentional, but they emphasise the value of observational data and photographic evidence in addition to depth interviews. At the same time, photos and observations by themselves can be very limiting without accounts of what cannot be observed. We need to know about the setting, people, and activities depicted. Otherwise the viewer is reduced to speculation, as would be the case in trying to make sense of an anonymous family photo album acquired at an estate sale.

Bearing in mind that one objective of ethnographic research is to make the strange familiar, an additional research use of photographs anticipating presentation, is simply descriptive. This is especially useful when researching a people, place, or activity that is likely to be unfamiliar to much of the audience. However, for certain sensitive subjects this is sometimes easier said than done. Rana Sobh and Russ (Sobh and Belk 2011a) sought to use photos to reveal the interiors of

Arab Gulf Islamic homes as well as the covering clothing worn by women of the Gulf. They were able to photograph the interiors of the homes of some of the families they interviewed, but few of the women were willing to be photographed in their *abayas* and *shaylas*, even if their faces were completely covered by a *burka* or *niqab*. Most would only allow a photo of the garments by themselves or as modelled by their foreign maids. It should be understood that this is a quite conservative region such that even at all-women wedding receptions, cell phones and cameras must be checked at the door lest anyone photograph another woman and potentially show it to a man outside the subject's immediate family.

This raises more general questions of ethics when using photographs. It is easy enough to supply pseudonyms for people shown or interviewed, but because they can potentially be identified from photos used in presentations or publications, it is not so easy to disguise them without resorting to pixelating or blurring faces as Sandikci and Ger (2010) did in order to show covered women in Turkey. Therefore it is important to not only obtain permissions to interview and quote informants, but also to show their photographs. They should be made aware of just how their photos will potentially be used and who the audience will be. As noted in Chapter 3, we like to have separate informed consent forms for interviews and for uses of materials in presenting and publishing research. In the latter case, informants are given a range of options to check off, ranging from only allowing the researchers to see the photos to allowing public display in journals, books, online, in broadcasts, and in public or professional presentations.

We leave aside the technical questions of how to make good photographs as there are many texts on photography. However, we offer a few hints in the next section on video-recording where many of the same considerations apply. For more theoretical considerations of how to make photographs for qualitative research, some good sources are Pink (2001), Wagner (2007), and Wright (1999). For some more general considerations of how visual images can enhance observational research, good treatments include Abrams (2000), Banks (2001, 2007), and Prosser (1998).

Audio-video recording

What has been said about informed consent for photography of course applies to audio-video recording as well where not only recognition of faces and settings can take place, but voices provide additional means of recognition. Some camcorders are dedicated to audio-video work while others are integrated with cellular phones, tablet computers, laptop computers, and still cameras. Because they have limited capabilities and are difficult to use for steady shots, produce poor sound witout supplemental microphones, and require file conversion prior to editing, cellular phones and point and shoot cameras are not the instruments of choice except in emergencies. There are however supplementary devices to attach to such phones and cameras to stabilise them, allow multiple lenses, and provide off-camera microphones to be attached. Moreover, since they are increasingly our constant companions, smartphone and miniature digital cameras mean that we need never miss a video opportunity, even if totally unplanned. Dedicated camcorders and video-capable DSLR (Digital Single-Lens Reflex) cameras are increasingly able to operate in low light and provide high definition resolution at prices that range from less than US$100 to many thousands of dollars. Higher priced camcorders and DSLRs provide an increasingly sophisticated array of options including interchangeable lenses, solid state recording media, and features such as slow motion, simultaneous multi-media backup, remote operation, and so forth. Still the two most essential things for obtaining high quality recordings are (1) a tripod and (2) an off-camera microphone. A tripod helps to avoid amateurish 'shaky cam' effects while an off-camera microphone, as discussed under audio-recording above, helps get better sound. Generally speaking, good sound is the most important thing separating poor and high quality video. Further guidelines for what makes not only a technically good, but a relevant as well as theoretically and dramatically compelling video can be found in a paper by Rob and Russ (Kozinets and Belk 2006).

That said, for both still and video photography there are visual guidelines that can be mastered with a little practice. These are covered in a variety of manuals and online or DVD videos (e.g., Barbash and Taylor 1997; Heath et al. 2010). Documentaries are an overlapping but different genre than ethnographic video. Documentaries are often intended for a broader audience than ethnographic video and are more apt to be made by journalists and film school graduates than by consumer videographers. But there is much that can be learnt from studying the techniques of documentary filmmaking (e.g., Ellis and McLane 2007; Grant and Sloniowski 1998; Hampe 1997; McCreadie 2008; Nichols 2001; Rabiger 2009; Saunders 2010; Sherman 1998). Documentaries can themselves be used as archival consumer and market research material, see Belk (2011b). So pervasive and significant have videographies become that a *New York Times* article asked 'Is a Cinema Studies Degree the New MBA?' (Van Ness 2005; see also Belk and Kozinets 2005). And the power and prevalence of video as a medium has increased exponentially with online video sites like YouTube and Vimeo (Burgess and Green 2010; Pace 2008; Snickars and Vonderau 2010). A good demonstration of the potential power of YouTube videos is a talk by Michael Wesch (2008) at the US Library of Congress.

Consumer research using video ethnography began in the mid-1980s when a cross-country project called the Consumer Behaviour Odyssey video-recorded a variety of American consumption and produced a video entitled *Deep Meaning in Possessions* (Wallendorf and Belk 1987; see also Belk 2011a). Since 2001, the Association for Consumer Research Conferences have included film festivals (see Belk and Kozinets 2012) and there have been special DVD editions of various marketing and consumer research journals including *Consumption Markets and Culture*, *Qualitative Market Research*, and *International Journal of Culture, Tourism, and Hospitality*, as well as online and DVD videography packages to accompany various consumer behaviour textbooks. Hundreds of consumer behaviour videographies have now been produced covering topics as diverse as Burning Man festivals (Kozinets 1999), modern mountain men (Belk and Costa 2001), Christmas in Japan (Kimura and Belk 2005), and the consumption of souvenirs at Ground Zero in the aftermath of the 9/11 Twin Trade Towers disaster (Marcoux and Legoux 2005). Notably, these are examples of videos involving perspectives in action rather than simply perspectives of action. For example, Alex Thompson (2011) made a compelling video of the difficulties of multiple sclerosis victims in negotiating their everyday environments. Such videos serve not only theoretical interests but can be effective in motivating public policy action as well. They are thus an important tool for transformative consumer research (e.g., Belk 2007). Many of the films that consumer researchers have presented at ACR film festivals or in special issues of journals are available at a video site presently called Films by Consumer Researchers (http://vimeo.com/groups/136972). An examination of some of these videos should provide both ideas and inspiration for the use of video in your research projects. Vimeo also provides a series of online instructional films on making better videos.

EXERCISE 6.2

Take a walk around the block. Have someone silently accompany you with a camcorder set on the widest angle possible and follow your gaze as much as possible, while trying to keep the camcorder steady. The camera person can film from a slow moving car if it is safe. As soon as you complete the walk set down as much detail as possible of all that you can remember in the sequence in which you encountered it. Include sights, sounds, smells, and tactile feelings. When you have finished, compare your recollections to what the camcorder has captured. What did the camcorder capture that you missed or forgot? What did you remember incorrectly? What did you capture that the camcorder did not? The purpose of this exercise is twofold: to show the importance of the camcorder to recording what you would miss, and to show the importance of fieldnotes and the human instrument for capturing what the camcorder misses. It misses some things because they are not audio or visual in nature and other things because they did not enter the frame or

(Continued)

(Continued)

were not captured in sufficient detail. The point is not that one of these instruments, human or technological, is superior, but rather that both have their strengths and weaknesses and they complement each other. It is also a good demonstration of the limitations of even the best observers, mechanical, electronic, or human, to be able to capture everything

---

The use of a separate person to do the camcorder work in the exercise is also good practice for video-recording interviews. Trying to do it all yourself is sure to make the recording, the interview, or both go badly. You can imagine how disappointing it is to conduct a brilliant interview and find that the camcorder has been focused on the person's knees the whole time. Using a separate person to handle the camcorder means that they can monitor both audio (using headphones) and video. If you have the luxury of a three person team, audio and video monitoring can be separated. When a goal is to produce a video as a means of distributing all or a portion of your work, it is also important to gather enough 'B roll' material to be able to show something other than 'talking heads' in your video. This material includes establishing shots of the place where the research takes place, cut-aways to objects mentioned in a video, and shots from different angles to break up the monotony of a long sequence with little movement. B-roll footage can be taken both before and after the primary video. Wherever possible, perspectives in action should also be included. While in some cases arriving with a film crew can seem a bit intimidating, in our experience it makes informants feel even more important. It is still necessary to put people at ease and use good interviewing techniques, but the heightened sense of importance can be an advantage. Often when shooting this way in a public venue like a swap meet or market, people come up and ask if they can be in our movie or on television. Of course, we must disabuse them of these misperceptions of who we are and what we are doing, but it is a good illustration of the power of 'professional' video in a culture where everyone seems to be seeking the 15 minutes of fame that Andy Warhol forecast. And with YouTube, Vimeo, blogs, and social media generally, we are more conscious than ever of this possibility.

Participant produced material

Another data collection aid can be something as simple as a pencil and paper that can be used by participants to draw or map a phenomenon of interest. For example, in studying men's and women's spaces in Qatari homes, Rana and

Russ (Sobh and Belk 2010) had participants draw floor diagrams of their homes. Tellingly, both men and women exaggerated the size of the personal space in the home that was 'theirs', while minimising the size of their partner's spaces. In this way, we also learnt something about what parts of the home were most important to them. For example, the kitchen was marginalised in many drawings and further discussion revealed that it was seen as a place of pollution, bad (food) smells, and maids. Having participants draw a map of a geographic area of interest can also reveal meaningful distortions. We once found that supermarket shoppers in Salt Lake City perceived distances to markets located uphill or downhill as greater than those equidistant on level roads, even though they drove vehicles when they went for groceries. Bridges, railroad tracks, and industrial buildings often form psychological barriers as well.

Participants can also produce rich materials for analysis with cameras or camcorders. Chapter 4 outlines some of the benefits of such a shift in who operates the device. We have also already noted the Tian and Belk (2005) study of personal office possessions involving giving employees cameras to document their favourite workplace objects. More abstract projects might ask research participants to take photographs that express, for example, their world, their identity, or what beauty means to them (Ziller 1990). Various objects might then be the focus of analysis in such photos. For example, Ziller and Lewis (1981) found that students who photographed books as expressing their identity had higher grade-point averages in university than those who did not include books. Ziller (1990) also reports self-photographic studies of shyness, gender concepts, and 'the good life'. He suggests that orientations toward material objects versus people can be detected in the same way and reports differing results across cultures, genders, and age groups. It is easy to envision how such techniques might be used to study participants' perceptions of cool cars, warm homes, healthy food, or friendly stores, for example. And coupled with timing devices or with systematic or randomly timed calls to the participant's mobile phone (which can also double as a camera and a device for e-mailing photos to the researcher instantaneously), it is quite feasible to do time sampling and study a participant's day, evening out, vacation, shopping excursion, or other activities of interest.

Just as participants can be instructed to take photographs, they can be instructed to use small camcorders. Sunderland and Denny (2007) have found this to be highly useful in documenting such topics as how pickup (utility) truck owners use their vehicles, how college students select beers on a group night on the town, and how people clean their houses, use air fresheners, cook dinner, get ready for bed, or purchase consumer electronics. They note that a big part of what makes these projects so successful is the high degree to which participants get involved in actively making the research document rather than more passively responding to questions from observers. To be sure, there can be some less than natural behaviour because of the presence of the camcorder, but this reactivity is lessened by placing the camcorder in the hands of the informant or a known friend or family member rather than an unknown researcher. Sunderland and Denny are two of the principles of Practica, an anthropological marketing research agency, and have good examples of some of their videographies and the autovideographies of participants on their website (http://www.practicagroup. com/pictures_videos.shtml), including an interesting, if disturbing, example of how to eat while driving.

Besides instructing research participants to take photos or videos of themselves engaged in certain types of consumption, it is increasingly possible to examine the photos and videos that people have made accessible on sites like YouTube and Flickr (e.g., Crandall and Snaveley 2011; Nunes et al. 2009; Smith et al. 2012; Van House 2009) or, to the extent it is made publically accessible, on social media sites like Facebook and Google+. There are also better ways of studying social media sites however, as discussed in Chapter 5.

EXERCISE 6.3

Go to YouTube and Flickr and select a dozen sites that come up when you search for 'birthday presents'. It will be useful to do this on both sites (separately) so you can compare the results. Once you have the material, what can you say about what gifts different ages and genders have received (and show)? How do captions, tags, and verbal accounts frame these shows of gifts? What sorts of words do people use in referring to their gifts? What sort of biases do you expect there may be in assuming that these are representative of the sorts of birthday gifts received and how their recipients regard them?

Other low tech and high tech data and data collection aids

If an anthropologist were going to study the textiles of Indonesia, he or she would be very likely to return with some batiks, weavings, and other examples of the artefacts that are the object of study. Depending on the focus of the research, it would also be useful to take photos or video of Indonesians producing, selling, purchasing, wearing, or using these fabrics. There is nothing like having the real thing to be able to examine at leisure and to help capture a multi-sensory impression of the objects of interest. As a consumer or market researcher there may also be consumption or marketing artefacts of interest to try to obtain from your field sites. This is especially likely when the field site is a marketplace site or event. Such a site may provide advertising, menus, business cards, flyers, brochures, packaging, product samples, reviews, newspaper articles, catalogues, or other tangible artefacts. In a study of young Middle Eastern covered women's clothing (the *abayas* and *shaylas* discussed above) by Sobh et al. (2010), informants were asked to wear one of their favourite outfits to the interview. These then became one focus of the interviews. While the clothing could not be retained by the researchers in this instance, the outfits were photographed and the resulting interview conversations were recorded and transcribed. All these objects and images then become a part of the data archive along with audio, video, photographic, and textual material. Such material should all be carefully catalogued with dates, places, and the institutions or people from whom they were obtained. The Nordiska Museet in Stockholm has an archive of photographs, interviews, and artefacts from a program called SAMDOK, intended to document life in Swedish homes, offices, farms, and factories. Because it is a museum-based project, the artefacts gathered can serve in the future not as mute decontextualised objects, but as embedded in the lives and places from which they were obtained (see Belk 1986, 1998). The settings from which they were obtained can also be recreated for display and study in the museum.

Another type of data collection aid, as well as data recording aid, is a tablet or laptop computer, PDA, smartphone, or other device capable of multiple functions often including audio recording, note taking, photography, video recording, internet access, e-mail, texting, instant messaging, and other functions (e.g., Heinet et al. 2011). Such devices can also be very useful for presenting visual and audio stimuli to research participants and recording their responses. In a study of the smile in personal and service contexts across several cultures, Russ and Rosa Llamas used laptop computers to present a series of exercises involving visual elicitation, detecting genuine from staged smiles, and responding to projective stimuli. It is also quite conceivable that such devices could be used for sorting tasks, tracking eye movements in response to an advertisement, package, or other stimulus, capturing drawings, recording demographic characteristics of informants, having informants select alternative virtual merchandise offerings, and allowing informants to construct electronic collages (see Chapter 3). Furthermore, if the informant mentions a website or online store or wants to show something they have put up on a social media site, having such a connected device at hand can make this feasible.

There are other technologies that clever researchers will find ways to fruitfully incorporate into fieldwork, including GPS, geo-location, RFID, and electronic or internet translation. For example, Simone Pettigrew (2011) of the University of Western Australia did research at the Disney World in Orlando, Florida using her own children as informants. She first fitted each of them with heart rate monitors of the sort that runners use. By taking careful notes and photos of where they were as the day progressed, she was later able to compare their heart rates to the attractions they were at in order to see what excited them most. Advances in fMRI and neuro-research may even provide avenues of contact between neuroscience and qualitative consumer research. No doubt there will be additional technological possibilities in the future as well.

Informants may also have their own devices along and be able to display photos and videos stored on the devices or in cloud storage. Rather than try to take a picture of these images, it may be easier to have informants e-mail them to the researcher on the spot. At the very least, obtaining the informant's e-mail address, Skype address, phone number, and other modes of contact makes it possible to easily follow-up after an interview with additional questions as well as provide a thank-you for their participation and eventual distribution of the resulting papers or videos from the project. This also makes it easier to conduct member checks to verify that descriptive information has been recorded accurately. But not everything needs to be high tech. A simple pen and paper can take down informant information, allow the researcher to record detailed technical information (e.g., make, model, and year of automobiles owned) that may not be clear in audio and video recordings, and make his or her own sketches of the research site. After two weeks' fieldwork in an Aboriginal Australian community's women's art collective, Russ transcribed fieldnotes and catalogued photographs on a laptop computer. Then just before leaving for the airport to fly home, the laptop, recorder, and backup materials were stolen from a friend's parked car. In trying to reconstruct as much of the fieldwork as possible, the simple paper and pen proved the only recourse. It was a painful lesson in keeping original and backup materials in separate locations if at all possible. And it was a graphic lesson in the fallibility of high tech and the merit of low tech data collection aids.

EXERCISE 6.4

An ethical issue may exist in the combination of retail surveillance video, consumer relations management (of a particular sort), and facial recognition software. In 2010, the Tate Modern Gallery in London sponsored an exhibition called 'Exposed' about our surveillance society. It is only fitting that this was in London since it was estimated 10 years ago that there were as many as half a million CCTV cameras in the city and at least 4,285,000 in the UK (McCahill and Norris 2002). No doubt there are many more in this post-9/11 era. And this does not include increasingly detailed images from spy planes and satellites. In 1994 a US patent (# 5,331,544) was granted to a scheme for retail stores using in-store surveillance camera data and facial recognition software to identify shoppers in real time and key this information to credit card information, past purchase histories in the store, and other customer information. This information would then be fed to retail sales clerks who could suggest custom-tailored product and service offerings to the consumer. All of this appears to be legal. What benefits might such a system provide to the store and to the consumer? What ethical issues does such a system pose?

Conclusion

At the start of this chapter it was noted that the qualitative researcher is the instrument in ethnographic research. No amount of sophisticated technology can substitute for the astute researcher. Furthermore, such equipment can intimidate informants and create distance between researcher and informant. Just as a tourist can 'hide' behind a camera rather than fully engage with locals, so can a researcher use equipment in a way that becomes a barrier rather than a bridge to understanding. When such equipment is used as a data collection aid, think about whether it is possible to put the equipment and agency in the hands of the informant rather than in the hands of the researcher. Think, too, about truly collaborative possibilities between informants and researcher. At the same time, audio-video equipment and other devices can free the researcher from having to assume that data consists only of written words and numbers.

Visual media help to humanise our informants for the audiences to whom they are presented (Belk 2006). This is also one of the main reasons that corporations respond so favourably to marketing and consumer research produced as videos (Sunderland and Denny 2007; Martin et al. 2006). They help us to capture more detail in more sensory modalities than are otherwise possible. As will be seen in Chapter 9, such media can also help us to disseminate our research far more broadly than traditional market and consumer research journals. And by opening the researcher to additional creative possibilities, visual and other data collection aids can help us to become more creative and insightful researchers.

7

Approaches to data analysis, interpretation and theory building for scholarly research

The real mystique of qualitative inquiry lies in the process of *using* data rather than in the process of *gathering* data. (Wolcott 1994, p. 1)

Most experienced qualitative researchers would agree with the sentiments expressed in this quote from Harry Wolcott. But what is not made clear in the quotation is that the processes of gathering and of using (i.e., analysing, interpreting and building new theory from) qualitative data are deeply intertwined. From the moment you start collecting qualitative data, you can – and you should – begin the process of analysing it. In essence, analysis involves looking for patterns in your data. Some may be patterns you see because of the questions you are trying to answer through collecting the data. Some may be informed by theoretical frameworks you are familiar with. And some may be patterns that are completely unanticipated but that emerge out of the data as you reflect on it.

Looking for patterns within and across individual elements of data *as you collect the data* is vital since it will influence how your research project unfolds. The patterns you see may, for example, suggest new questions to ask of informants, new bodies of literature to read, and new ways of using the data you are collecting. And sometimes, data analysis tells you that the research question you thought you were addressing either is not all that interesting, or cannot be answered using the data you are gathering. It may also suggest another research question that is both interesting (perhaps more so than your original question) and answerable by your data. Thus, analysing data as you collect it is essential for shaping the research project.

Data analysis, moreover, is foundational to your interpretation and theory building. In fact, the lines between data analysis and interpretation/theory building are somewhat arbitrary. The linkage between them is iterative rather than sequential. But if the term 'analysis' is used to refer to finding patterns in the data, then the phrase 'interpretation and theory building' can be used to refer to coming up with an account of what the patterns mean. Compared to description, interpretation and theory building develop a more abstract, more general, or more complete explanation or account of a category of phenomena (the case or context you are studying thus comes to be considered a specific example of that more general category). **When we use the term theory, we follow Bourdieu's (1977) notion and refer to a system of ideas or statements explaining some phenomenon.** We use the phrase 'building new theory' to encompass identifying new concepts or constructs or processes that help us understand something about the phenomenon, identifying new variants in a phenomenon and the factors that help us understand and explain them, identifying exceptions that delineate when an existing theory is relevant, and/or challenging the adequacy of existing theory.

In the remainder of this chapter, we elaborate on techniques for data analysis, and for interpretation and theory building, and provide illustrations. In this chapter we assume that publication of an academic paper is your goal. In the next chapter, we consider analysis with the goal of deriving managerial implications. We also continue below with a series of exercises that are intended to aid in acquiring and practising analytic skills within an academic framework.

Analysing data

Regardless of whether you have started collecting interview data, fieldnotes from participant observation, visual data, or archival data from sources such as blogs, websites, or annual reports, the fundamental step in your data analysis will involve coding. Coding refers to discerning small elements in your data that can retain meaning if lifted out of context (Ely et al. 1997, p. 161). **Codes are concepts and these concepts vary in their concreteness/ abstractness as well as their emic/etic nature. Another way of describing coding is 'reducing data into meaningful segments and assigning names for the segments' (Cresswell 2007, p. 148).** Regardless of whether the data you are coding is textual, visual, aural, or artefactual, the same considerations apply. For ease of discussion and because it is most common, we assume in this chapter that your data are transcribed text transcripts. We will also look at coded elements of interviews taken out of the context of the entire interview as well as out of the entire set of interviews. Nevertheless, it is critical to immerse yourself in the entire dataset so that you are familiar with the context before you start to code. This will help you avoid the problem of coding, interpreting, or quoting people out of context.

For example, the following text is representative of that posted by bloggers who were studied by Eileen and Daiane Scaraboto (Scaraboto and Fischer 2013). In this project, they looked at the online collective of 'plus-sized' consumers who are frustrated with the offerings available from clothing marketers. Bloggers routinely post statements like the following about the difficulties they face in finding suitable fashion options:

> When a favourite dress gets a major stain or tear, I basically feel a sense of panic. Last week, one of my 'go-to' skirts got caught in a car door and developed a tiny hole. My response entailed a surge of pure adrenalin. I rushed to the ladies room, did some elaborate rinsing, then as soon as I left work I went in search for just the right colour of thread at shops all over town. Then I laboured over each stitch required to repair the rip, hoping I could do that invisible stitching thing they taught us a hundred years ago in home economics. Now if I could count on being able to go to a local store and find a new skirt that suits me just as well, I'd have shrugged it off. But NOOOOO. I've learned from bitter experience that it won't work that way. The truth is, if I don't fix it, I'll spend months if not years looking for a replacement. I have no reason to believe I'll ever find one that makes me look good like this one did, and that I am happy to wear again and again.
>
> Those of you who have experienced the pangs of style scarcity will feel my pain. Of course we all know that things could be worse – we could lose our jobs or our homes, or we could lack the basic necessities of life. Fashion famine isn't on the same level. But when our hard-won wardrobes are in any way diminished, we truly do feel a sense of panic rising up. We're not like the women who wear size six or ten or twelve. We can't just stroll into the Banana Republic or Barneys and find some that fits and feels good. No, my friends, fat fashion is in short supply – we are talking resource scarcity here.

In examining a passage such as this one, several codes can be assigned. For example, the sentence 'No, my friends, fat fashion is in short supply – we are talking resource scarcity here' is assigned the code *fashion resource scarcity*. This seems both obvious and important to code as it speaks to the blogger's experience as someone who experiences a shortage of the plus-sized clothing she desperately needs. **It is also worth mentioning that this is an 'emic' code, meaning it draws directly on the language used by the people being studied.** It seems particularly interesting to us, as we rarely think of stylish or fashionable clothing as resource, much less as one that is in scarce supply.

A perhaps less obvious code is associated with the mentions of Banana Republic and Barneys. We code these with the label *mainstream brands*. This is worth noting because it indicates what the writer wants (i.e., to be able to shop at common bricks and mortar retailers), and hints at why she considers herself to be experiencing comparative scarcity (i.e., she lacks the convenient options open to women who can shop at such mainstream stores). **Note that this is an 'etic' code, meaning that we are using language and concepts (e.g., mainstream) that are not necessarily those of the people we study, but that seem appropriate to us within our scholarly field of interest**. A third code is associated with the portion of the passage that self-consciously acknowledges that the style scarcity is a less pressing concern than those facing people who lack a job or a home or basic necessities. We labelled this *legitimacy of desires* as it seems to suggest that the writer fears that her desire for more clothing options is somehow shallow, frivolous, or illegitimate given the scope of other societal issues. This, too, is an etic code.

These codes are not intended to be exhaustive, but rather to illustrate what we mean by identifying meaningful units of data. Codes can be assigned to individual words, to sentences, to paragraphs or to chunks of text of varying lengths. And multiple codes can be applied to the same text.

Keep in mind that coding is iterative. The process typically involves generating an initial set of codes within a dataset (e.g., the transcripts from an initial set of interviews or fieldnotes). As new codes emerge, you have to go back to recode materials that you considered previously. After initial coding, the next step is to examine the set of codes to see which can be collapsed into slightly more abstract categories or expanded into finer codes. This process continues as new data is collected, new codes are identified, and existing codes furthered collapsed and refined into more abstract categories.

To give you a few more ideas about coding, which is so fundamental to the process and so daunting initially, we offer some 'tips' that might help you get started or that might help you find some interesting patterns that you overlooked on first reading.

1   Be alert to metaphors. Coding metaphors can help you figure out how people are making sense of their own reality (cf. Arnould and Wallendorf 1994). In the passage above, likening lack of fashion options to a 'famine' indicates that clothing choices are not experienced as frivolous fancies, but rather as critical necessities.
2   Look for indicators of strong emotion. They provide simple clues as to what is important to those who have produced whatever text you are analysing. In the passage we included above, strong emotions (panic, bitterness, frustration) are attached to the lack of readily accessible fashion options.
3   Listen (watch out) for phrases you have heard in other contexts that seem to be 'imported' into the context you are studying, like the phrase 'scarce resource'. This

may point to context-spanning discourses that structure the ways people think about the particular context you are studying.

4 Identify categories of actors who matter in the context you are studying. In the passage above, mainstream marketers (like Banana Republic, Barneys) are targeted for particular contempt. Thinking about this may lead you to identify other categories of actors, or to code the types of inter-dependencies that may exist or may be perceived as causing conflict between your actors in your context.

5 Notice the kinds of actions that are taken or contemplated. In the passage above, mending clothes is one kind of action that can be juxtaposed with others, in particular shopping. Being alert to actions that are commonly taken or contemplated can also sensitise you to actions that are rare or that are considered illegitimate.

6 Consider motives that lie behind the production of the text you are coding. Alvesson (2003, p. 14) notes that it would be naïve to regard any interviewee or informant in a research project simply as a 'competent and moral truth teller, acting in the service of science and producing the data needed to reveal his or her "interior" (i.e., experiences, feelings, values) ...'. So whether you are coding interview data or some other kind of text, consider what kind of purposes might lie behind the creation of that text. In the passage above, the motives of lobbying for change in the fashion system and against weight-based discrimination in society at large could be considered.

7 Probe for contradictions. Contradictions may be found between seemingly incompatible elements of the text you are coding, or portions of the text may contradict assumptions you had made prior to starting the research. A puzzle related to the passage above concerns the fact that marketers seem to be missing an opportunity to serve a customer need; in 'normal' circumstances marketing theories would predict that some marketer will fill an unmet need so long as they can do so profitably. Coding puzzles like this can help you think out what other data you might need to collect to solve the puzzle, and might open up new research questions for consideration.

▓▓▓▓▓▓▓▓▓▓▓▓▓▓▓▓▓▓ **EXERCISE 7.1** ▓▓▓▓▓▓▓▓▓▓▓▓▓▓▓▓▓▓

1 Examine the passage above and see what other codes you might generate.
2 Get a colleague to engage in the same task, each of you working independently for a few minutes.
3 Compare the codes you have generated. See whether the same chunks of text led to different codes. Discuss between yourselves *why* you thought the code might be significant, and whether you can see why your partner came up with the codes he or she did.
4 See if you can come up with some higher order codes that allow you to collapse or expand the individual ones you have created into slightly more abstract categories.

If there is consensus about the basics of coding, there is less agreement about what can inspire or shape codes. For example, the often-cited (but less often closely read) 'classic' of qualitative research, *The Discovery of Grounded Theory* (Glaser and Strauss 1999), is considered by some to advocate a tabula rasa approach to analysing data; i.e., starting only with the data itself. Many other textbooks on methods seem likewise to suggest that you attempt to come to the data without being 'prejudiced' by outside influences.

While we do not believe you should form strong assumptions or specific ideas about what codes or patterns you will find in your data prior to collecting it, **we do not advocate a tabula rasa approach!** Rather, we believe that your initial and ongoing coding can be influenced both by the data itself and by:

- your initial research purpose or research question;
- prior literature relevant to your research question; and
- the qualitative research tradition in which you are working.

Let us think about how each of these might influence your coding.

Research questions and coding

In Chapter 2, we highlighted the singular importance of research questions in shaping qualitative research projects. Naturally, that means they have some part to play in influencing how you code. Consider a couple of examples related to the project mentioned above, that focuses on the online community of plus-sized fashion consumers. Assume that our research question is concerned with 'coping' – specifically (1) 'How do consumer cope with style scarcity?' and (2) 'What factors influence how consumers cope?' If these were our research questions, we would be looking to code data that identifies coping tactics or strategies, and at individual, group, or cultural level factors that might influence a consumer to use one coping tactic rather than another.

Looked at through the lens of our first research question, we add the code *coping strategies*: the passage above indicates two coping strategies used to deal with style scarcity, one involving mending clothes that cannot be replaced, the other involving venting frustrations, which can be seen to be the purpose, at one level, of the entire passage. Our second research question inspires us to create the code *social comparisons*. We assign this code to the portion of the text in which the writer indicates that she compares herself with 'women who wear size six or ten or twelve', and we flag it since we wonder whether making such comparisons might influence the choice of coping strategies.

Clearly, it is possible that we might have come up with these codes without having formulated research questions related to coping. But had we decided in advance that our research might focus in whole or in part on coping, then we would be sensitised to both different types of, and different influences on, coping. Thus we would deliberately seek out such phenomena in the data transcript. One of the best reasons for letting research questions influence the codes you consider is that it helps you to know if your questions can or cannot be addressed through the data you have collected. If not, it might mean you need other data, or it might mean you need to reframe your research question.

Prior literature and coding

If you have heeded the advice we have offered in previous chapters, you will know we advocate looking at literature that relates to your research question before, during, and after data collection. And if you have done so, then it is both likely and appropriate that there will be concepts that you have identified from your reading that will sensitise you to how you might code portions of your data.

Sticking with the same example, let us assume that our research focus on consumer coping has meant that we have read papers in consumer research and psychology journals on the subject of coping and we are familiar with Goffman's (1963) work on stigma and managing identity. Having done so, we would know that the established literature on coping has created typologies of coping strategies or coping factors, and we might therefore be alerted to code for these. For instance, Duhacek (2005) identified eight coping factors (e.g., action, rational thinking, emotional support seeking, and denial) and we might create sub-codes under the general *coping strategies* code for portions of text that seem to indicate one or more of these coping factors is present in our data. For example, mending clothes as described in the passage above might be coded as a type of *action based coping*.

Looking to the prior literature for codes obviously opens you up to the potential pitfall of 'force-fitting' data. You must avoid assuming that because prior literature has identified (for example) eight types of coping that all or even some of them will be evident in your data. Further, there is the risk that seeing things through the filters of prior research will blind you to original codes and ultimately original insights. **However, the risks associated with not knowing what's in the prior literature far outweigh any benefit you might have from ignoring it**. You risk 'reinventing the wheel' (i.e., discovering what is already established). Further, you risk not seeing how your work can extend or even challenge assumptions that have been made in prior literature. And if you cannot complement or show up the limitations of prior work, you will have a hard time convincing your audience that you are saying and doing something new. So our advice is that you deliberately cultivate a conversation with the prior literature through your coding: see how the insights others have generated might inform your own.

Research traditions and coding

In Chapter 2, we described some of the different types of research traditions. If you have not read that chapter, you might want to scan the pages on research traditions. We bring them up again here because one of the ways in which they shape research projects is in guiding what you pay attention to ... and coding is nothing if not paying close and systematic attention to your data.

Since we have described each research tradition already, here we will just take the opportunity to illustrate how some of them might influence the coding of the data on plus-sized consumers. First, if we were working in the phenomenological tradition, codes related to the nature of plus-sized consumer lived experience would be natural. For example, the code *unreliable marketers* might be generated to reflect the writer's experience of mainstream marketers as unreliable in meeting her perceived needs; the code *enforced self-reliance* might correspond to her experience of wanting to rely on her own skills and initiative in the face of an unreliable market.

If we were working in the hermeneutic tradition, we would be interested in widespread discourses or logics that are shaping the ways that consumers see the marketplace and how they react to it. For example, we might generate the code *consumer sovereignty*. Consumer sovereignty is a term for the culturally pervasive concept that, in a free market, consumers determine the goods that are produced; this makes them 'sovereign' over what is produced in an economy (Henry 2010). We can apply this term to the entire passage, since this implicit cultural discourse appears to be influencing the underlying argument it is making: that consumers of plus-size fashion *lack* sovereignty. Tacitly inspired by the discourse, the writer believes that marketers should be offering them what they want and that fashion should be readily available.

If we were working in a postmodern tradition, we would focus coding on the metanarratives that are taken for granted, and how they might be challenged, inverted, or deconstructed. For example, throughout the post, the writer uses the term 'fat'. Scholars have suggested that there is a dominant narrative regarding fatness, namely that it 'is contextualised as pitiful and/or many of the following: lacking in moral fibre, diseased, potentially diseased, greedy and lazy, not just ugly but disgusting, pathetic, underclass, worthless, a repulsive joke, a problem that needs to be treated and prevented' (Cooper 2008, p. 1). The postmodernist might consider how the passage reflects, reinforces, or challenges the dominant metanarrative associated with fat and fatness.

Turning to a critical tradition, we would want to develop codes that reveal how the focal group (women who wear plus-sized clothes) is marginalised, and which actors or practices in the system contribute to their marginalisation. The passage that refers to the lack of availability of plus-sized clothes at specific retailers that cater to women who wear smaller sizes could be coded *retailer discrimination*. You might also code for the consequences of discrimination. In the passage above, the emotional consequence of the lack of retail selection is described as *panic*, which could be another, more emic, code. In some of the computer software that can be used for data coding (see Chapter 8) we might also have a link to data about the origin of retailers' and bloggers' practices. Later this might help us to compare more easily practices associated with retailers versus bloggers.

A researcher operating within the semiotic tradition might step back from viewing the passage as an indication of the blogger's experiences, and regard the text as a piece of rhetoric crafted with words and phrases that symbolically convey a particular set of meanings, perhaps with persuasive intent. In examining the language of this passage carefully, a semiotician might attach particular codes to the terms with which the writer chooses to describe her fashion choices (Mick and Oswald 2006). She construes fashion as a *resource*; it is contrasted with other vital resources (food and shelter) thus positioning it as a necessity, albeit one that is less critical to survival. A semiotician might further code the rhetorical choice of the term *scarce*. As noted above, it is somewhat unusual to think of fashionable clothing as a scarce resource. In using these terms, and in grouping fashion with (other) necessities like food and shelter, the writer is laying the symbolic groundwork for positioning plus-sized fashion as a political cause, not just a personal frustration.

Finally, someone with a neopositivist approach to qualitative data analysis might look for codes conducive to identifying important constructs in the data, along with the causes and consequences of that construct (Silverman 2011). In the passage above, a focal construct that might be coded is *unmet needs*: the writer seems clearly to be expressing that she, at least, has needs for fashion that are not being met by the marketplace:

> Now if I could count on being able to go to a local store and find a new skirt that suits me just as well, I'd have shrugged it off. But NOOOOO. I've learned from bitter experience that it won't work that way. The truth is, if I don't fix it, I'll spend months if not years looking for a replacement. I have no reason to believe I'll ever find one that makes me look good like this one did, and that I am happy to wear again and again.

In examining the larger database that has been collected concerning plus-sized consumers, a researcher working in the neopositivist tradition could be seeking antecedents and consequences of unmet needs within a segment.

EXERCISE 7.2

1 Drawing on the passage above, identify some codes that would correspond to self-perceptions of *unmet needs.*
2 Compare and contrast your codes with those of a colleague who has undertaken the same exercise.
3 In comparing your codes, consider what theories you have gleaned from other readings that led you to identify additional reasons why needs may be unmet, or that might suggest some individual level or market level outcomes of unmet needs. This might help you to identify other potential codes in the data – which in essence is coding that entails integrating prior literature, as described in the section on prior literature and coding.

Although we have discussed the influences on coding as though they were discrete, in practice they never are. The text itself will always suggest some codes to you, as will your research questions, the prior literature, and the research tradition in which you are working. The trick is not to disentangle these influences, but rather to be open to them all as you generate initial codes, collapse some of those together, and create more abstract codes that integrate a set of lower level codes.

Interpretation and theory building

As we indicated in the introduction to this chapter, data analysis is difficult to distinguish sharply from interpretation and theory building. The process of identifying lower order codes and aggregating them into higher order, more abstract, codes is clearly an interpretive one. However, as you move further along in this process, the emphasis shifts from identifying patterns in the data to attempting to find meaning in the patterns.

In this section we discuss several ways you can develop an interpretation of what the patterns in your data may mean and ultimately build theory. As a reminder, when we use the term theory we mean a system of ideas or statements that help us understand some aspect(s) of the phenomenon in which you are interested. For purposes of publishing in scholarly journals, that is the goal on which you should be focused.

As you are reading what follows, please keep in mind that even though we present analysis, interpretation and theory building as a linear process, in practice you may expand codes, contract them, and revise them as interpretation and theory building progress. You may also tack back and forth between the data, the codes, the literature and your emerging theory. And you may also have *eureka* moments along the way when minor epiphanies send you back to revamp your coding and test an emerging interpretation (Thompson 1990).

Looking for variation

Once you have developed and done some refining of your coding scheme in the analytic stage, you can start to look for variation in your data. When we talk about looking for variation, what we mean is seeking differences between one group and another in terms of the codes you associate with them. For example, when Russ and his colleagues Güliz Ger and Søren Askegaard were analysing data for their study of the phenomenon of consumer desire, they looked for variation in the codes that occurred in the data collected from informants in the three countries they studied: Denmark, Turkey and the USA. They did so in order to assess whether there might be differences in the experiences of desire 'across New World versus Old World, established versus transitional markets, Christians versus Muslims, and social welfare systems versus an individualistic market-based system' (Belk et al. 2003, p. 332). This led them to identify both commonalities and differences in terms of the dimensions of desire that were typical for informants in the distinct cultures.

Where you look for variation depends on your project. If you have collected interview data from a group of individuals, you might think about salient sociological or demographic characteristics that differ between them, such as social class, age, or gender, and see whether the codes that occur in data collected differ between those in one category versus another. If you are studying members of a consumption community, you might study differences between newcomers and those who have long been members. If you are conducting a multi-sited inquiry, you might look at whether the codes you associate with data collected from one locale differ from those you have associated with data collected from another. In general, what makes sense in terms of which groups to compare and contrast will be influenced by the variability in terms of those from whom you have collected data, as well by your research question, the prior literature, and your research tradition.

1   Identify a set of five papers based on qualitative data that have been published within the last five years in either *Journal of Consumer Research* or *Journal of Marketing.*
2   Determine whether the authors' approach to data analysis included looking for variation.
3   If the authors did look for variation, identify the bases on which they looked for variation, and consider the rationale that led them to consider grouping the data as they did.
4   If the authors did not report looking for variation, consider whether there are some bases for variation that they could have considered based on the data set they assembled, their research question, the prior literature they cite, or the research tradition in which they appear to be grounded.

Before we leave the topic of looking for variation, we want to note a suggestion made by our colleagues Eric Arnould and Melanie Wallendorf. In writing about ethnography, they recommend that you look for variation in the codes that you discern in data obtained from interviews versus data from observation or from archival sources (Arnould and Wallendorf 1994). We encourage you to follow their advice in any instance where you have multiple kinds of data. Detecting discrepancies between what people say and what people do, or between what they recall and what the archival record shows, can provide important clues that can contribute to your interpretation and theory building.

Looking for relationships between codes: elements of phenomena, processes, and outcomes

The process of grouping lower order codes into higher order codes entails look-ing for relationships between codes. But you can push further by considering how higher order codes relate to one another in meaningful ways. One very systematic description of how to look for the kinds of relationships between codes has been offered by Strauss and Corbin (1998). They distinguish between open coding (such as that which we have illustrated in Chapter 8) and axial coding. When they use the term axial coding, they mean looking in the data for concepts or constructs that would be related to the central phenomenon or construct under investigation. While some might regard the advice Strauss and Corbin offer as being appropriate only if you are developing grounded theory, our view is that this is useful advice even if you are not 'doing' grounded theory.

We would encourage you to take from their ideas those that are useful to you in interpreting the patterns that exist between elements in your dataset.

(Do note however that if you are going to try to claim to be doing a grounded theory analysis, you should be aware of the disparate ways in which the original proponents of grounded theory, Anselm Strauss and Barney Glaser, independently developed their views on what it actually means to conduct an analysis that leads to grounded theory. As Jones and Noble (2007) note, Glaser is adamant that work that is the product of the grounded theory methodology *must* be created through what he calls 'open', 'selective' and 'theoretical' coding (see e.g., Glaser 2001). Strauss (e.g., Strauss and Corbin 1998) allows that grounded theory may be produced by using some mix of approaches to coding, and recommends not only open and axial coding, but also a 'coding paradigm' that looks for conditions, interactions, strategies, and consequences (Strauss 1987). For an excellent starting point for understanding what it now means to do grounded theory, see Jones and Noble (2007)).

Generally speaking there are three ways that codes you have identified can relate to one another. First, codes can be related to one another because they comprise distinct dimensions of the same construct, or distinct elements of the same phenomenon if you prefer such terminology. Second, they can be related to one another as steps, stages, phases or elements in a process. Third, they can be related to one another in an explanatory fashion: that is, they can be linked based on the premise that some codes can be interpreted as helping to understand why a focal phenomenon exists or has particular characteristics, while others are seen as being explained by, or being a consequence of or response to that focal phenomenon. Interpreting groups of codes as elements of a phenomenon, as processes, or as explanations for/outcomes of a phenomenon can constitute a new theoretical contribution if your insights are novel. To illustrate how this works, we will give examples of studies that built theory in each of these ways.

Elements of phenomena. We can draw once more on Russ, Güliz, and Søren's paper on consumer desire to provide an example of relating codes to one another as elements of a phenomenon. Recall that when they interpreted their data, they identified a set of elements that characterised the experience of desire. (Note that it was on these dimensions that they found that people from different cultures varied.) Specifically, the elements of desire that they found to vary across informants from different cultures were: the extent to which desire was experienced as embodied passion; the extent to which it entailed desire for otherness; the extent to which it entailed desire for sociality; the extent to which is was associated with a sense of danger and immorality; and the extent to which it was associated with distance and inaccessibility. In essence, this identification of the dimensions of the experience of desires constitutes a clarification of the nature of desire as a phenomenon or construct: it helps us understand the complexity of the phenomenon and the variable ways in which it can manifest itself in human experience.

Eileen and her co-author Cele Otnes have referred to this kind of theory building as 'mapping' a construct, and they regard it as a type of theoretical contribution that is particularly valuable when constructs have 'analytical generalisability', in that they account for a large number and range of empirical observations (Fischer and Otnes 2006). Desire is exactly such a phenomenon: it is pervasive across times and cultures. Mapping a construct like desire can help make sense of disparate bodies of research, and it can help structure new research questions on why certain dimensions are more or less prominent in certain contexts.

Processes. One of the most important kinds of contributions that qualitative researchers can make is to develop process theory. Whereas variance theories provide explanations for phenomena in terms of relationships among antecedent and outcomes, process theories provide explanations in terms of the sequence of events leading to an outcome. Temporal ordering is central to process theories, so they require developing an understanding of patterns in events. Anne Langley (1999) describes a number of different strategies for building theory from process data. We would particularly draw your attention to what she defines as a 'temporal bracketing' strategy (pp. 703–704).

This approach to building process theory entails identifying 'phases', not in the sense of a predictable sequential process but as a way of structuring the categorisation of events. Events that cluster within a phase have internal coherence; they are categorically different from events that are grouped together as part of a different phase. Many temporal processes can be analysed in this way, and doing so allows you to compare and contrast conditions that give rise to dynamics in different phases. Langley notes that temporal bracketing strategy is especially useful 'if there is some likelihood that feedback mechanisms, mutual shaping, or multidirectional causality will be incorporated into the theorisation'. And we would argue that in most instances of process theories published in market or consumer research, we would expect to find feedback mechanisms, mutual shaping and/or multi-directional causality.

Again, the paper by Russ and his colleagues Güliz and Søren provides an example of process theorising that features temporal bracketing. In their work, they developed a general account of a process through which desire emerges and evolves. Although they acknowledge that desire is experienced as an emotion, they also posit that there is process during which emotions change, especially when desires are realised. In the 'cycle of desire' (see Belk et al. 2003, p. 344), they argue, based on their data analysis, that the initial stage is an individual self-seductive imagining and an active cultivation of desire. Desire, they conclude, is kept alive until the object is acquired or until it becomes clear that there is no hope that it will ever be acquired. Either the realisation of a desire, or the recognition that desire has been frustrated, can lead back to the beginning of the cycle, i.e., to imaging that which is desired. If you think about the analysis and interpretation that led to this process theory of desire, you can see that Russ et al. found recurring patterns in their data that they ultimately interpreted as being adjacent elements of a process, and as they developed their thinking, a cyclical process theory emerged.

It should be noted that not all data lend themselves to building process theory. Sometimes informants are able to reconstruct a process from memory, particularly if it is one they have gone through recently and or cycled through often (such as the cycle of desire). Ideally, particularly if you are theorising about processes that happen over an extended period of time and that involve a range of actors, it is best to have longitudinal data.

Our colleague Markus Giesler had such longitudinal data acquired through an engagement spanning seven years with music downloaders and music marketers. He conducted his research over the period of time during which downloading exploded in popularity and was ultimately challenged by various marketplace actors. Markus was able to use this data to analyse how markets in the cultural creative sphere evolve through iterative stages of structural instability (Giesler 2008). Markus identified common patterns over time, namely consumers' recurrent attempts to legitimise their preferred music consumption mode which in cyclical fashion provokes corporate reactions that attempt to de-legitimate downloading. Conducting a processual analysis on longitudinal data gave Markus a unique opportunity to develop theories about how markets evolve when consumers' collective actions threaten to destabilise them.

Understanding conditions that give rise to a phenomenon or the consequences precipitated by a phenomenon. Although some regard the notion of conditions that give rise to a phenomenon and consequences precipitated by that phenomenon as relevant only in neopositivist traditions of qualitative work, our observation is that many scholars who are working in other research traditions ultimately develop theories that speak either to conditions (often cultural or social) that give rise to some focal phenomenon of interest, or to outcomes or responses (often the strategies people adopt or reactions that people have) that are precipitated by that phenomenon. We believe that you do not have to eschew the search for conditions and consequences when you are developing theory from the interpretation of qualitative data. Indeed, we think that many of the best theories that have been developed by our peers in the marketing and consumer research communities have explained why things happen the way they do, or why things sometimes turn out one way and sometimes turn out another. These kinds of theories are essentially variance theories, in that they help us understand the conditions under which a phenomenon will/will not occur or the consequences that are likely to come about when a phenomenon occurs versus when it does not.

We will provide an example of a research project that answers a 'why' question through the analysis of qualitative data by describing the study of online word-of-mouth marketing that Rob undertook, together with Kristine De Valck, Andrea Wojnicki and Sarah Wilner. Rob and his colleagues studied the ways that prominent bloggers in online communities communicated about a product when it was 'seeded', that is, given to them by a marketer attempting to generate positive word-of-mouth buzz for the new product (Kozinets et al. 2010). One of the questions that they attempted to answer was *why* bloggers adopt different communication strategies – in other words, they looked for precipitating conditions that would help to explain the variability they observed across bloggers in the communication strategies they adopted. In interpreting the data they collected, Rob and colleagues identified four types of narratives that bloggers create (or more accurately co-create along with members of their community): these were the strategies that they labelled evaluation, explanation, embracing and endorsement. And they found that there were four 'influences' that shaped which type of narrative a particular blogger produced. These included (1) the blogger's own 'character narrative' or enduring personal story; (2) the type of blog forum in which the blogger was embedded (e.g., whether it focused on life crises, relationships, technical issues, or parenting issues); (3) the communication norms within the blogger's forum that govern the expression, transmission, and reception of messages within it and (4) the promotional characteristics of the marketer's campaign, such as the type of product, the product's brand equity, and the campaign's objectives.

It is important to stress that when qualitative researchers develop such explanatory theories by looking at relationships between coded categories of data, they pretty consistently make it clear that they are not suggesting that human behaviour can ever be wholly predicted or fully shaped by a finite set of factors. In the case of Rob and his colleagues, this disavowal was expressed as follows: 'outcomes [forms of blog posts] are complex and underdetermined' (Kozinets et al. 2010, p. 83). Yet, notwithstanding that outcomes are never fully determined by the individual, social, cultural and community factors that are identified through qualitative data analysis, we can, if we choose, distil the relationships we identify into propositional statements. In their article, Rob, Kristine, Andrea, and Sarah included the following proposition:

> A positive communal attitude toward a WOMM [word of mouth marketing] message will be a function of the way that it is (1) consistent with the goals, context, and history of the communicator's character narrative and the communications

forum, or media; (2) acknowledges and successfully discharges commercial-communal tensions or offers a strong reason an individualistic orientation is suitable; and (3) fits with the community's norms and is relevant to its objectives. (Kozinets et al. 2010, p. 86)

It is extremely important to note here that including propositions in research is but one way of expressing its theoretical contribution. Indeed, some eschew this particular way of making a theoretical claim since it can be interpreted as signalling that the knowledge gleaned through qualitative research should be subjected to quantitative testing. Clearly, this is not the case.

In many papers, the expression of theoretical arguments takes the form of a series of sentences that simply lay out the logical connections that have been built through the study. Sometimes figures or diagrams are used as well to convey the logical flow of the theoretical claims being made. We have brought to your attention that fact that you may choose to use propositions, however, since some texts on interpretation and theory building in qualitative research might lead you to conclude this is somehow inappropriate. Our view is that it is neither inappropriate nor obligatory. We have raised it simply because considering logic of the kind expressed in a proposition such as the one Rob and his colleagues articulate may help sharpen your interpretive insight, and increase the theoretical clarity of your thinking. Keep in mind, though, that carelessly worded theoretical claims that make it seem as though you are being overly reductionist in your analysis can cause reviewers to reject your work.

EXERCISE 7.4

1 Go back to that same set of five papers from *Journal of Consumer Research* or *Journal of Marketing* that you used to look for evidence of variation. This time, you will need to look very closely at their findings sections, any figures they have included, and at the discussion section where they summarise and identify implications of their work.
2 Identify the focal constructs or phenomena in their work – that which they seek to understand.
3 Now see whether they have 'mapped' the phenomenon by identifying elements of it, whether they've identified a process through which the phenomenon emerges or changes, and/or whether they have identified some conditions that help to explain the occurrence of the phenomenon, or common consequences of the phenomenon.
4 Try to write a sentence or two that captures the essence of the theory they have developed.

This exercise is intended to help you build up an understanding of how others have developed theory from identifying relationships between coded categories in their data and to give you insight on how you might do so as well. We suspect once you have gone through this exercise, you will find that the next section will help you more fully understand what you observe, since many contemporary scholars are not really just building theory anew from data. They are also using prior theory to modify and build on existing theory, and this requires some explanation.

Drawing on pre-existing theoretical perspectives

Increasingly (though not without exception), qualitative scholars are turning to pre-existing theory to help them develop their own unique conceptual insights into the things they study. We realise this may be a bit confusing, especially since the vast majority of prior texts on qualitative research do not mention using existing theory to build new theory. Indeed, some have asserted that prior theory has little role in qualitative research (e.g., Anfara and Mertz 2006). But a contemporary trend in scholarly research in the fields of marketing and consumer behaviour (and allied fields such as strategy and management) is to embrace some prior theory in order to build new theory. Alvesson and Karreman (2011) are among the most explicit advocates of using pre-existing theory in the theory building process. They argue explicitly for 'theory development through recognising the fusion of theory and empirical material in the research construction process' (p. 3). They challenge the idea that researchers should build theory from data alone and advocate viewing data as a resource for extending and/or challenging existing theories. Given that a growing number of scholars see it is both viable and valuable to use one or more pre-existing theoretical perspectives to develop novel theory, we want to provide some insights into what this means and how it is done.

When we use the term 'pre-existing theoretical perspective' we do not simply mean 'the prior literature' (which may be a rather disjointed set of empirical findings related to your focal phenomenon). Rather, we refer to a set of concepts or a more fully developed theory that has been advanced by earlier scholars to explain a range of phenomena. Often, pre-existing theoretical perspectives can provide a lens through which your focal phenomenon can be viewed, and a set of enabling concepts that may help you answer your research questions. We will illustrate this by talking about just two pre-existing theoretical perspectives that have been used by a range of scholars to address a range of questions.

The first theoretical perspective is the semiotic square. Algirdas Greimas, a structuralist semiotician, introduced the semiotic square as a means of analysing paired concepts in a system of thought or language. In particular, Greimas proposed that concepts might relate to one another not just as binary opposites, but in a range of other ways (for a fuller description of the semiotic square, look at Greimas 1987, pp. xiv, 49). The semiotic square has been used by a number of consumer researchers to help them develop theoretical accounts of relevant phenomena. For example, Rob used a semiotic square to help him address questions about how cultural and social conditions form into ideologies and how these ideologies influence consumers' thoughts, narratives, and actions regarding technology (Kozinets 2008b). He found that using the semiotic square in the context of his study allowed him to see relationships between seemingly disparate ideological elements, and to look at how paradoxical ideological elements interact to inform how consumers think about and use technology.

Others in the field have used the semiotic square for quite different purposes. For example, Paul Henry (2010) adapted the semiotic square to allow him to investigate cultural discourses that encourage or deter consumers from asserting their sovereignty in a market. Doug Holt and Craig Thompson (2004) used a semiotic square to analyse how mythologies of masculinity shape patterns of consumer behaviour and thought among contemporary North American men. And in his study of music downloaders, our colleague Markus Giesler used a semiotic square in order to understand how historical tensions between marketers and consumers arose and were resolved (Giesler 2008). The key point to be stressed here is that the same pre-existing theoretical perspective – the semiotic square – provided a useful means for building theory related to widely varying focal phenomena.

Another pre-existing theoretical perspective that has proven useful for many consumer researchers comes from the work of Pierre Bourdieu. Bourdieu's body of scholarship is vast, and he provided a wide range of 'thinking tools' – that is, conceptual terms which frame his approach to understanding society as a whole, and specific practices and fields of practice within larger societies (for one account of Bourdieu's body of work, see Grenfell 2004). We will focus here on one of his concepts, that of 'habitus', a set of taken-for-granted tastes, skills, styles and habits acquired through early socialisation and subsequent education. The notion of habitus is one of the conceptual tools developed by Bourdieu that has been particularly useful to scholars developing consumption and market related theories.

Douglas Allen (2002) drew on Bourdieu's concept of habitus in developing his theory of how consumers come to make and feel comfortable with major life choices such as selecting a college. His goal was to make sense of choices that cannot well be explained by the rational choice or constructive choice frameworks that are best able to account for decisions made after extensive investment in deliberate and impartial consideration of choice alternatives. Drawing on Bourdieu's notion of habitus, Douglas developed his alternative theory of choice that he labelled the 'Fits-Like-a-Glove' or FLAG framework. It theorises choice as socio-historically shaped practical experience; in other words, as something deeply influenced by the taken-for-granted habitus of the decision-maker. His particular context of investigation was student choice for postsecondary education, but he argues that the FLAG framework is applicable in many contexts.

Others have used Bourdieu's concept of habitus quite differently. One recent paper particularly worthy of note is by Tuba Üstüner and Douglas Holt (2010), who studied how status consumption operates among the middle classes in less industrialised countries. Üstüner and Holt did not simply use the concept of habitus to understand their data, but developed a theoretical contribution by showing that their data enabled them to revise Bourdieu's concept to make it more appropriate for application in a non-Western context. Taken together, these papers show how new theory can be developed either by applying a pre-existing theory and using it to answer a novel research question, or by challenging such theory by applying it in a new and different context.

There are many, many other pre-existing theories that have been used by individual researchers in our field. And often, researchers will use not one but two or more prior theories to inform their analysis and interpretation. For example, Ashlee Humphreys (2010) used concepts from both institutional theory and new social movement theory in order to understand the market creation process that gave rise to the casino gambling industry. The key point we want to make is that you should be aware both of the foundational theories that are used, and of the ways that they help to inform new theory building. To that end, we advise you undertake the final exercise in this chapter.

<hr>

EXERCISE 7.5

1 Review that same set of five papers from *Journal of Consumer Research* or *Journal of Marketing* that you used for the previous two exercises (or pick some new ones).
2 Identify any pre-existing theories that these papers used to develop their novel theoretical contribution.
3 Decide whether they directly applied the pre-existing theory or whether they revised or challenged that theory in examining it through the light of their data. Also consider whether the theories the authors used came from within consumer and market research or from related outside fields.

<hr>

We conclude this chapter on data analysis, interpretation, and theory building by noting something that is often unspoken, but that needs to be acknowledged. What counts as novel theory, and what counts as a valid way of developing a novel theory, is very much socially constructed. We have done our best here to give you some insights into the current state of the art in marketing and consumer research. But if we were writing this paper purely for scholars in, say, operations management, we would be emphasising different things. Approaches to theory building and what counts as an original theoretical contribution are not standard across time or across disciplines. They are very much socially constructed within fields of practice, and they do evolve over time. Call it fashion trends in academic domains if you like. Just as members of different cultures may dress differently, members of academic communities may theorise differently. And just as cultures are continually changing, so are academic disciplines. So if you feel the advice you have been given here is different from what you have read in other domains, there is a reason for that! Our advice here is meant to facilitate the kinds of contributions that will help you publish in consumer or marketing research journals, and will be less relevant if you are targeting journals outside the fields of marketing, consumer research, or management.

8

Analysis, theory, and presentation for managers

Qualitative analysis for managerial decision-making

Qualitative research, in all of its various methodological manifestations, can be useful for developing consumer and marketing insights that managers use to build and strengthen the brand differentiation of a variety of products and services. Current techniques such as focus groups and surveys are still useful, but our world is changing. As technologies such as mobile and social media alter culture and communications, as cultures blend and rapidly transform, and as commercial culture itself intensifies the pace of change across every industry and way of life, we need additional new methods to keep apace of change.

We currently live in a highly competitive global marketplace where even tiny differences in market strategy can be critical to gaining market share. For these reasons, marketing managers have turned increasingly to richer and newer (at least to business) methods such as depth interviews, ethnography, observational methods, videography, and netnography (Sunderland and Denny 2007, p. 25). The ability of managers to follow a marketing orientation of directed consumer desire fulfilment flows from their ability to spot and act in a timely fashion on relevant, evidence-based, and practical consumer insights. This chapter is filled with numerous examples that illustrate how brands and products are developed and repositioned using qualitative marketing and consumer research techniques in order to help companies build sustainable competitive advantage.

Among academic researchers, applied anthropology and other utilitarian inquiry is often cast as problematic. Applied methods are stigmatised as dirty, and often compared by academics to a form of prostitution that 'whores out' pure scientific wisdom to evil corporate purposes. Sunderland and Denny (2007, pp. 31–33) invited advanced anthropology students to assist with an ethnographic study for a fast food company. They later discovered an e-mail trail where the subject heading on their message, as it was passed from one student to another, was 'Selling yourself to the devil for a few days'. On that same project, someone with a master's degree in anthropology refused to work on a task because of the identity of the fast food client, even though the client's stated goal was to help them create healthier options to offer to the public. As Hill and Baba (1997, p. 16) have written about views of business within Western countries, 'practice is viewed as a far removed, downstream and "dirty" activity which may serve utilitarian purposes, but is not relevant or useful to theory-building'. Although we leave the moral choices to the individual researcher and the specific assignment, we certainly disagree that all industry-related work is necessarily irrelevant to theory building.

We can instead think about the 'theory' in management theory in a practical way. For this chapter's guiding framework, we will consider that management and academic theory are both interested in solving so-called 'practical' problems, but that the nature of the exact practice differs. In academic research, as seen in Chapter 7, the 'practical' problems concern the academic practice of theory construction, where theory is a specified relationship between different constructs. As we noted in the previous chapter, compared to description, theory offers a more abstract, more general, or more complete explanation or account of a category of phenomena. It is a system of ideas or statements that help us understand some aspect(s) of the phenomenon in which you are interested. There is, however, a very practical – in the utility sense – side to theory, as the psychological theoretician Kurt Lewin famously stated with his maxim 'there is nothing so practical as a good theory'. By this, he meant that we guide our actions with formal and informal maps of reality that we can loosely call 'theories'. The better those maps of the world are, the better they are able to guide effective and efficient action in the real world. That 'practical' purpose varies. It can certainly include bringing out disempowered voices and guiding public policy. It can also help a multinational corporation to locate healthy menu options that can be sold at a profit.

In the world of managerial practice, the marketing 'theory' we are trying to build should guide marketing action and revolve around an accurate model of some decision-relevant elements of the world of consumers. In much of this book, we have been concerned with contributing to theory, locating and rhetorically exploring gaps in the literature, and specifying the particular relationships that pertain between constructs. For contrast, consider some sample questions that marketers might reasonably ask about consumers.

- Who are these consumers?
- What are their needs or desires?
- How are they different from other consumers?
- How are their behaviours changing?
- How many of them are there?
- How badly do they want this or that thing?
- What matters to them?
- What do they think of my brand?
- What do they think about other brands?
- What desires and wants of theirs are still unfulfilled?
- How do I reach them?
- How do I convince them?
- Where do they congregate?

The answers to these questions reveal different facets of consumer thought, meanings, values, intentions, motivations, or actions. Sometimes, the interests of marketers and academics intersect. Kozinets et al. (2002), for example, sought to understand the factors underlying the appeal of ESP Zone, a themed flagship brandstore. Although theoretical and academic in orientation, that article also sought to build a framework for understanding how the mythological connotations of a complex themed retail space can attract customer loyalty and build brand equity for the long term. As well as informing retail theory about spectacle and mythological themes, it also attempted to provide new ideas to retail managers and marketers.

Sometimes, rather than understanding individual behaviour, qualitative research is designed to detect cultural shifts and meanings. McCracken (2009) gives the negative example of Levi jeans missing the entire hip-hop movement, while Holt (2004) gives the positive example of Mountain Dew successfully shifting from relying on the Redneck myth to utilising the Slacker myth as Generation X consumers adopted new values toward work. Rapaille (2006) and Zaltman and Zaltman (2008) focus on trying to understand differing cultural orientations toward various products and institutions. Using the ZMET technique (see Chapter 3), for example, Zaltman and Zaltman (2008) found that a key meaning of the American hospital involves transformation rather than simply healing an illness. With this perspective in mind the Children's Hospital of Pittsburgh was able to redesign the hospital so that its meanings were much more positive, appropriate, and able to give children and their families optimism and hope.

We must emphasise that the difference between the academic and the managerial approach to qualitative data interpretation and analysis lies in its action and presentation, rather than a publication orientation. Research for this purpose is not intended to pass through double-blind peer review and be published in a scientific journal, book, or chapter. It will not be judged by the criteria of whether it is original and whether it advances a theoretical conversation already in progress in a scholarly community, as academic research must (see Chapters 2 and 7).

Instead, managers rely on this marketing research to make important investment decisions governing the allocation of human, financial, and material resources. The analysis must therefore always be focused on addressing or informing the elements of a relevant marketing decision. For example, in a company that has a number of lines of unprofitable breakfast cereals, marketing research might be used to help inform a decision about which brands of cereal should no longer be produced. In that case, the removal, relaunch or re-branding of one or more cereal brands might be guided by consumer research that assesses whether enough potential exists within an individual brand to revive interest if marketing resources were focused on repositioning the brand.

EXERCISE 8.1

Thinking about managerially-oriented qualitative marketing research

This is a brief exercise intended to get you to think about the type of marketing research that can inform management practice. First, go to your kitchen. Open a cupboard and then pull down a packaged food product. If you were trying to sell more of that product, what questions might you ask? How might you use qualitative consumer and marketing research techniques, such as those described in this book, to answer them? How would the results of your research be applied to management practice? How would you judge whether they were successful or not?

Qualitative consumer and marketing research – particularly ethnographic, netnographic, and other forms of online and offline observational research – have been found to be extremely useful for identifying areas of untapped opportunity for new product development. By 'watching' consumers use, misuse, and even abuse existing products and services (and this 'watching' activity can take place through a variety of methodological techniques, such as the observational methods detailed in Chapter 4), we learn much about the actual behaviours of consumers. For example, when Motorola was developing a voice recognition system for web-connected automobiles, their engineers found that it worked well and was ready for rollout to consumers. However, field tests with consumers in which the device recorded consumers actually trying to use voice commands told a different story. Consumers were continually frustrated and angry when the voice recognition system failed to understand them and they wound up shouting and cursing the device. What the engineers had written off as consumer incompetence was revealed to be a real problem in the natural environment in which it was meant to be used. By observing or questioning consumers during product use we add to this valuable raw material for analysis and product development. Consumer insights can be: (a) translated into new concepts to be tested (this testing now often happens online), (b) built into working prototypes, (c) tested with samples of relevant populations, (d) subject to business model analysis and various types of cost benefit calculations and projections and (e), eventually, for some of these consumer insights, turned into successful new products or services.

Related to specific needs such as new product development, we can think about the creation of different sorts of research analysis outputs that can helpfully be employed to answer a variety of relevant pragmatic marketing questions. We can consider five general categories of results that will drive data analysis and the formation and refinement of 'theories' that can be useful inputs to marketing strategists' decision-making: mapping opportunity space, divining consumption connections, segmenting and sub-segmenting consumer groups, describing target market segments, and decision graphing.

- *Mapping opportunity space.* In this form of analysis, thick description is employed in order to sketch out a detailed portrait of consumption and marketplace experiences. This type of (typically observational) research is often used to identify white space or gaps in the market where new product innovations and extensions can be introduced, and it can reveal consumers' makeshift solutions, product combinations, unarticulated wishes, and other latent practices and desires. Presenting this data can take many forms, including exhibiting photos of consumers' makeshift product, and providing descriptions and vivid accounts of their expressed frustrations or unmet desires.
- *Divining consumption connections.* In this type of research, the analyst is concerned with specifying potential relationships between certain habits, contexts, or behaviours and particular consumption decisions or practices. Understanding how contexts – individual, household, social and environmental – influence and impact consumption can help marketers better understand and respond to the (stated and unstated) expectations of consumers. Here, photos and descriptions of actual lived contexts make powerful rhetorical tools that can tell management the story.
- *Segmenting and sub-segmenting consumer groups.* Demographic, psychographic, and usage-oriented segments can often appear superficially the same to marketing managers. In qualitative data collection and analysis, the subtler differences

between groups such as the brand loyalists and brand switchers can be revealed. By comparing different groups on a range of rich contextual dimensions, qualitative researchers can gain new understandings about which characteristics are and are not relevant to the enterprise of fulfilling particular consumer desires and reaching new customer segments.

- *Describing target market segments.* Qualitative research often intentionally or unintentionally reveals different categories of social, emotional, and action-oriented behaviour. These new qualifications and categorisations can be very helpful in describing, and learning to understand, new and existing groups of consumers and customers. A deeper understanding of the inner lives, everyday habits, and social and cultural worlds of consumers lends valuable insights that can lead to more effective brand management, product development, and advertising and promotion creation decisions. Sometimes a type of personification called a persona will represent segments and targets in managerial presentations. We will discuss this technique in a later section.

- *Decision graphing.* With a naturally-grounded understanding of the way that consumers approach marketplace and consumption decisions, marketing managers can have a much more impactful approach to reaching new and existing customers. For example, driving around in an automobile with consumers can help to reveal how different consumers choose their gasoline providers. Some might always fill up at the same stations, some might be swayed by particular promotions, others might be driven to use stations with car wash facilities, while still others might make their decisions based upon the immediate proximity of the service station as shown on their GPS device. Understanding how these choices are made, by whom, and under which particular conditions can help marketers to better market their products and services. Videos can be especially vivid at portraying shop-alongs such as this one.

Qualitative researchers investigating the worlds, reactions, and interactions of consumers all confront related pragmatic challenges. They enter into a complex cultural and social environment with a toolkit of approaches. Various researchers may specialise in different sorts of techniques. Few can master all of them. So flexibility and a nuanced ability to make adjustments are critical elements to the approach, as is forming alliances with those who have other skill sets that may be useful for a particular project.

Consumption and marketing are extremely dynamic and ever-changing environments; this may require some 'on-the-fly' adaptation on the part of the consumer researcher. In addition, consumers who are relevant to the study may not be so easy to locate. Therefore the procedures that we recommend for analysis and interpretation in the world of management-relevant theory possess considerable generality, flexibility, and an iterative approach that is infinitely adjustable. There is no linear, 'cookie cutter' approach for qualitative consumer and marketing research, in either a managerial or an academic vein. Every single project is different. The skilled input and judgment of the marketing researcher is necessary for reliable and rigorous results. And clients' preferences and budgets will inevitably influence the kinds of research and amount of research that is done.

This book is filled with multiple examples, choices, and exercises regarding the collection of data from consumers in various contexts, ranging from the historical use of artefacts to the technological deployment of various social sites on the internet. What happens to this consumer-generated data once the marketing researcher holds it against the research question? In this chapter, we explore the various options, procedures, and processes that the researcher can use to generate knowledge, understanding and, perhaps most differently from academic and theoretical work, industry decision-making advice, from the qualitative data that has been generated.

Exploring a managerial approach to analysing shopping behaviour

Shopping is one of the most complex and closely considered behaviours in consumer and marketing research because it is one of the most important acts by consumers from the viewpoint of marketers and retailers who desire their business and loyalty. Observation methods are used commercially to help retailers understand the problems and challenges that shoppers face. Such research can reveal opportunities for improving consumers' shopping experiences. In this short section, we introduce a managerial focus by describing a focused approach to solving a managerial problem by collecting, analysing, theorising, and testing using qualitative research to study consumers' shopping behaviours.

Paco Underhill's marketing research agency Envirosell relies almost exclusively on situated qualitative observation methods to generate insights for retail clients including Starbucks, Wal-Mart, Saks Fifth Avenue, and the Gap. Underhill's research consists of careful tracking of what he calls 'the science of shopping' (Underhill 1999). Researchers follow shoppers inconspicuously from their entrance to the store, as they make their way through the store while noting everything they do. These so-called 'trackers' stay with individual shoppers for the duration of their shopping experience in the store (Underhill 1999, p. 13). In addition to various quantitative measures of the shopper's actions, the tracker also records his or her own observations and insights in a set of fieldnotes. These fieldnotes turn out to be especially valuable sources of insight that are used to inform retail management decisions.

'Shop-alongs' are a related and popular consumer and marketing research technique. In the shop-along, or 'accompanied shopping' technique, the researcher will

(Continued)

(Continued)

accompany one or more consumers through a retail setting. Sometimes, the consumer is given a particular shopping goal, and at other times the consumer is left without direction to simply browse and shop as he normally would. The amount of researcher engagement can also vary widely. In some studies, the researcher will attempt to be as invisible as possible, simply observing and noting behaviours and, perhaps, afterwards questioning the consumer about those behaviours in a debriefing interview. In other instances, the researcher can be talking, questioning, discussing and directing through the entire shopping experience, and may even act as a fellow participant in the retail shopping experience.

Let us consider one of the 'scientific' retail consumption principles or practical theories uncovered by Envirosell (Underhill 1999, pp. 17–18). In a study conducted for Bloomingdales in New York City, Envirosell researchers positioned a CCTV camera at one of the main entrances. A nearby sales rack, which happened to be performing far below expectations, was also captured by the camera's angle of view. One of the interesting questions that the researchers were trying to address for Bloomingdales was why that particular clothing rack was performing so far below expectations. What was wrong with it? They needed to develop an interpretation to explain it. As the researchers reviewed the recordings, they noticed that shoppers approached the clothing rack and stopped to look at the clothing that was displayed on it. They seemed interested in the clothing, and would examine it closely. However, because the rack was on an aisle that was near the entrance, people who were moving into or out of the store would bump into these shoppers. After the shoppers were brushed once or twice in this manner, most of them would simply give up and move on. The research analysis suggested an explanation for the problem with the clothing rack's performance. The solution was simply to move the rack to a part of the store where there was less customer traffic.

Then, the research team went further. They coined the term 'the butt-brush effect' to refer to the retail consumption phenomenon wherein shoppers, in general, did not like to be touched, brushed or bumped from behind and would cease their shopping in order to avoid it. They found, on further review, that this effect was especially evident for women, but also held for men. The butt-brush effect was thus a theory about shopper behaviour. Testing this interpretation was the next stage. After Envirosell presented their results to Bloomingdales' management, they began to monitor sales figures. Without changing anything other than the clothing rack's location, sales rose quickly and substantially. Not only were results of this qualitative observation method useful to the management of the store, they also revealed something interesting and potentially generalisable about shopping behaviour as a social activity. In general, the findings emphasise the importance of personal space to Americans and highlight the importance of positioning sales displays (particularly important ones) so that consumers experience less unintentional bodily contact. Finally, we can see from this example that, although Envirosell's results were certainly aimed at increasing sales, the ways that they collected and analysed data, and built as well as tested theory, were no less scientific than any academician's.

Although not all managerial research aims to develop such general theories, managers do frequently seek to understand underlying factors influencing relevant phenomena, just as academicians do. An important difference may be that the type of phenomenon that is considered to be 'relevant' to investigation is directed and constrained by sales and profit making concerns.

Steps in managerially-focused data analysis and interpretation

To perform qualitative consumer and marketing research in a managerially-relevant manner, we can consider a set of general protocols and procedures that might help to guide, but will never completely determine, the approach. We can differentiate qualitative consumer and marketing research analysis and interpretation in regard to a variety of different managerial decision-making purposes, such as the exploration and assessment of consumer insight, consumer reaction, or consumer action. In this section, we briefly discuss how data analysis and interpretation differ when the analysis is intended for managerial purposes.

The first stage of a project will define a particular question that the research is intended to answer. Sometimes, the research might be an exploratory look at a particular topic, such as people's opinions about yogurt. Other times, it may be a deep dive into a particular target segment, such as an attempt to understand the world of mothers who are in their forties who have children under the age of three. And in other situations it might be a profile of a lifestyle such as surfers or Goths. Marketers are also very interested in understanding consumers' opinions of brands. This can require a contextual inquiry into the meanings, values, images, links, and languages surrounding impressions of particular brands.

Understanding management needs

It is very relevant to note that the consumer or marketing researcher must always invest the time up front with the client to fully understand their business and their needs. Meetings are required where the research provider interviews the client as carefully as any research participant would be interviewed.

(Continued)

(Continued)

Questions that can be asked include the following:

- What is the nature of the company, its leadership, its people, its products, and its brands?
- Who does the corporate client believe are their customers?
- What does the company want to achieve in the shorter end of the longer-term?
- What is the company's culture, its vision, and its mission?
- What major challenges and major opportunities does the company currently face?
- What does the company wish to achieve with this research?
- What methods is the company familiar with? What methods is it comfortable with? Not comfortable with?
- What is the budget for the project?

It is only with a sound understanding of the way that the marketing research will fit into the current corporate structure, dynamics, and practices that the marketing researcher can be confident that the research will be understood and successfully deployed to solve real business issues.

It is, as we have noted in a number of places in this book, actually rather difficult to determine when data collection ceases and data analysis and interpretation begin. They are not discrete steps. We would argue that the qualitative analysis and interpretation phase begins long before the first data is collected. In fact, asking questions is a form of analysis. Thus as managers and researchers meet and discuss what constitutes the question to be answered or problem to be solved, this involves a type of analysis, a framing of the problem that will help to determine the methods used and even shape the findings. In this process, the complex world of marketing and business issues must be understood, and a subset of presumably important factors whittled down to just a few areas of investigation. This filtering process places a further limitation upon how the world of consumers will be addressed. Often times, the managerial research focus will be informed by a variety of shared communications, observations, and formal or informal hypotheses and generalisations. Informal data gathering may have begun long before the formal process. The compilation, organisation, and prioritisation of this data have of course been an essential element directing the research endeavour.

During the actual data collection, it is common for researchers to analyse the data in situ. In fact the concept of an inward and outward research design means that ongoing analysis will direct the sampling and data collection process. In observational, ethnographic, and netnographic work, including work that is conducted in teams, it is common for researchers to reflect on their early and ongoing impressions of participants and the field site. In team research, this is called memoing and debriefing. During debriefing meetings, ideas, hunches, organisational categories, ideas for analysis, and tentative conclusions about the implications of particular observations and findings may be discussed, debated, discounted, and delivered. Even side comments and general discussions conducted in the margins of the research can be useful. Treating these ideas as useful tentative conclusions regarding the interpretation and direction of the ongoing research is common. Between debriefing meetings, memos between researchers in the form of e-mails or notes on emerging ideas may be generated and shared. These techniques can also be useful for a researcher who has not been working the field site. Often times, communicating what we think we are seeing to such a third party, as well as among the field team, can be a useful way to see if our hunches and insights are believable, shared, and useful.

Organisational categories will also be used and developed during data collection. Because no research is conducted in a completely tabula rasa form, researchers will come to the field with their own pre-existing categories for analytic interpretation, as noted by anthropologist Grant McCracken (1988). In addition, a hallmark of good research is that it can surprise the researchers by suggesting new insights and novel categorisation schemes. As the research is conducted, researchers will construct categories for interpretation of the data and begin organising it in different ways. Sometimes, in an 'old-school' approach, paper files, perhaps of various colours, perhaps with various coloured and coded tabs, may be used (see Mariampolski 2006, p. 191).

Qualitative data analysis (QDA) software can facilitate and help to organise the often-unwieldy process of handling the output of qualitative consumer and marketing research data collection. As discussed in Chapters 5 and 6, there are many good commercial and even freeware or open source packages available. These packages can be very useful in analysis for locating particular words, images, phrases, video segments, and other specific elements in digital files; as such they can be quite helpful in aiding (but alas, not doing) analysis. Treating the data set as a large digital file enables the researcher to burrow through it using the QDA engine as a search engine. Most commercial packages such as in NVivo and Atlas.ti help the researcher to develop and apply particular coding and categorising templates. They can also do some automated coding, and facilitate trying out different analysis and interpretations. After the data has been searched and categorised, larger order constructs can be discerned from this organised set and conclusions about the meaning and implications of the data can be garnered. From there, various types of representations of the analysis can be generated and original data as well as graphical and infographic diagrams and figures can be easily incorporated into presentations and reports.

QDA software has been found to be extremely useful by some qualitative consumer and marketing researchers. Others shy away from it. There are individual researcher preferences and work styles that may or may not fit with the procedures required for partially automated QDA. Although these programs certainly can reduce and automate repetitive functions for the qualitative researcher, their mechanical operations have also been accused of creating a certain distance between the researcher and his or her data. In qualitative work, insight is key. Thus distance from a particular cultural phenomenon or communal site can be harmful. In addition, QDA software is almost always used to produce a clearly bottom-up analysis resulting from a grounded theory, and a coding-and-categorisation scheme. It can hamper the hermeneutic, creative, and imaginative sorts of interpretive leaps that can lead to deeper understanding. This high level of understanding is a gold standard of quality qualitative research, and when it works it can have major impacts and make important breakthroughs in marketers' understanding of consumers and marketplaces. However, QDA does often produce interesting charts and graphs. These infographics can be extremely valuable in managerial presentations, as clear and usable communication of research results in a corporate context is probably every bit as important as the results themselves.

Twelve focal guidelines for managerially focused marketing analysis

In this section of the chapter, we focus the research analyst's attention on specific elements of qualitative data analysis that can be useful for gleaning rich managerial insights. To be applicable, analysis must be attuned to the various elements of managerial discovery. We can think of managerial intention in the marketing field as directed by various strategic and tactical needs, chief among them the following:

- segmenting a heterogeneous consumer population;
- subsegmenting various consumer populations in meaningful ways;
- understanding the value that consumers place upon various attributes, features, and symbolic characteristics of products and brands;
- understanding consumers' goals and life projects;
- understanding consumers' perceptions of different brands in relationship to one another;

- understanding how consumers respond to various tactical elements such as the product's shape, colour, packaging, size, pricing, placement in a retail setting, discounts, promotions, presence online, and manifestations within the social media sphere;
- other strategic and tactically oriented facets of the purchase and consumption process.

In addition to these elements, a very common objective of research methods such as ethnography and netnography is the uncovering of consumer insights that can help to identify opportunities for new product development (Kozinets 2002, 2010b; Mariampolski 2006; Sunderland and Denny 2007). These opportunities can range from simple product line and brand extensions, such as a new flavour or scent, to the uncovering of insights leading to new platform products and so-called 'radical', 'game-changing', or 'disruptive' innovations.

When we inquire of consumers about their consumption usage or product desires, we often get only a surface-level answer. Consumers are not always aware of their own motivations and are rather poorly equipped to tell managers directly about their consumption or new product wishes. They want lower prices. They want more value. They would like it offered in purple. Unable to articulate their own wants and desires in a way that managers can understand and act upon, consumers are nonetheless the richest and sole source of information about these matters.

Often, but not always, detailed description of a consumer, her behaviours, her language, and her overall experience and world, is inherently valuable information to marketing managers. However, just as theoreticians must sometimes delve beyond the descriptive and the obvious, so must industry-focused marketing researchers. If our research is to help inform urgent managerial needs for strategic and tactical advice, we must sometimes move it to a more profound level of motivational insight. We recommend that the research analyst pay special attention to particular elements of the qualitative consumer and marketing research data. In this spirit, we offer the following 12 guidelines or topics on which to focus data collection and direct qualitative data analysis. The topical guidelines are also applicable to conducting qualitative data collection for work in any managerial vein.

1 *People.* Who consumes the products? What type of person: what age, gender, class, religion, address and location, intelligence, lifestyle, appearance, interest group, or other demographic or psychographic classifiers? Is the product used by a fringe group or by a mainstream one? Do consumers of the product suffer from a consumption stigma? Is the image of the average product user holding back new consumers of the product? Are the consumers a member of a particular community or collective, such as a lifestyle, subculture, brand or consumer tribe? Do they affiliate with one another in person or

through social media? Understanding the various differences among consumers, as well as their differing motivations and uses for products, provides meaningful insights to guide marketing decisions. For example, in a netnographic study of blender discussions, several groups were readily identifiable. There were those who used blenders mainly in the morning for smoothies, those who used them mainly to crush ice to prepare drinks in the evening and to entertain, and 'power user' healthies who put major demands on their blender to make nut butter, soups, and even mill flour. The research revealed these three major segments and suggested marketing strategies resulting in different products, channels, and forms of promotion for each one. The communal affiliations of relevant consumers in social media groups can lead marketers to employ more effective and efficient online promotional and distribution channels. Many such consumer insights are readily available using methods such as interviews and netnography.

2   *Practices.* What are the behaviours that accrete around purchase, consumption, and disposal? Do consumers use products as directed? Do they read instructions? Do they create rituals? Do they progress on experience and learning curves related to the product or service? Do they teach one another? Is there a pre-existing culture or community that helps guide them in their consumption? Understanding what consumers actually do and how they build their physical, emotional, and cognitive routines around their consumption habits can help managers understand where opportunities may lie as well as what problems they need to ameliorate. For example, in-home studies of consumers' use of ketchup revealed that they were often storing bottles upside down in their refrigerators in order to make the ketchup more pourable. This new storage practice became the founding idea behind a packaging innovation in which flat-bottom squeeze bottles were designed to be stored with the spout on the bottom.

3   *Processes.* What are the stages that consumers move through as they progress toward some goal? When and how is the decision to satisfy a desire made? What are the characteristics of the purchase? How does consumption proceed? What happens afterwards? From intention to fulfilment, the entire consumption process is of major interest to marketers. It reveals not only action, but also desire, a rich tapestry of wants, needs, wishes, frustrations, and hopes. As an example, 'a study of laundry practices in Turkey revealed that women, following Islamic custom, separated men's garments from those of women. This observation suggests innovations that could address the needs and expectations of consumers in this market, which are not being met by available brands' (Mariampolski 2006, p. 202).

4   *Parlance.* How do consumers talk about their consumption? What words do they use? Is there a specialised vocabulary? Are acronyms employed? Do they share ideas online and through social media and, if so, what words and language do they use? What phraseology is deployed in their consumption descriptions? During phenomenological interviews, what sorts of tropes and metaphors are used to describe their consumption? By paying close attention to the words and language that consumers use to talk about their consumption, the analyst can decode deeper motivations and meanings that can lead to important consumer insights. For example, a study of a bake-your-own cookie dough product might

reveal that consumers repeatedly use the phrase 'homey smell' when discussing baking cookies. Further analysis of this trope leads to the conclusion that a strong part of the appeal of home-baked cookies lies not in their fresh taste or warmth, but arises from their distinctive and comforting baking aroma. Consumers relate that smell of baking cookies to the meaning of home, family, and mother, and are willing to pay extra not only for the sensation of hot baked cookies, but for that sensuous and evocative smell. Similar types of analysis of consumers' narratives of consumption can reveal strong historical, social, and personal-individual contexts that attach meanings and values to their acts. Understanding the implications of consumers' language leads to important insights about their needs as well as about how to communicate messages to them in ways that will be most meaningful.

5   *Particulars.* Where are particular products stored in the household? Where are particular products used in the household? When are particular consumption tasks performed? What other products or services accompany the use of particular products? Why do people say that they are using particular products at particular times and places? Pantry studies are especially powerful techniques for observing what is actually present in consumers' cupboard and storage spaces. In a pantry study, the researcher has a consumer go to a storage area, for example a bathroom medicine cabinet, and then ask about the different items in that area. Placement is also important in such studies. In the complex consumption environment of the contemporary household, products intended for the garage can end up in consumers' kitchens, while power tools can end up in ensuite bathrooms performing cosmetic tasks. Ethnographers and netnographers should be attuned to shifts of location, changes of timing, and alterations in the role assumed by different household members as indicators of potential insight into new opportunities. Unexpressed meanings and expectations are revealed by these shifts. If a subsegment of macho male consumers is found to be using their electric sanders to rid themselves of corns on their feet, for example, this may be viewed as an opportunity to introduce specially designed machines to more safely and effectively realise the same cosmetic/medical benefit.

6   *Problems.* What sorts of frustrations do consumers have with the products and services that they use? When are consumers not happy with results? Under which circumstances are consumers simply complacent with results? Do consumers 'put up' with unsatisfactory results? Often times, consumers will be unwilling to complain or point fingers about unsatisfactory product performance in any market research setting where they are being compensated for their time. However their dissatisfaction can be disclosed in interviews by the difference between their body language and the words that they utter. As well, ethnographers and observational researchers might see a difference between what people say and what they do. Assume we are drinking beer with twenty-somethings in an (enviable, perhaps) ethnographic research setting. If people are drinking one particular beer, but not seeming to actually enjoy it, this might be indicative of an opportunity to explore their satisfaction or lack thereof. If modern managers aim for delight in consumption experiences, simply settling complacently for a good enough product performance is a clue that the analyst should investigate further.

7   *Plans.* What do consumers wish for? What is their perfect consumption experience? What new objectives would they like their consumption experiences to help them realise? What is the ideal setting for their consumption? What new materials would they like to see incorporated into their products and services? When consumers desire products and services, they build imaginative images of how wonderful the experience of consuming them will be, how it will make them feel, or how it will make them look in the eyes of others. When they use products, they also fantasise about possibilities, identities, and outcomes. Delving into these utopian and idealistic fantasies brings rich insight to the consumer and marketing researcher. For instance, see Dennis Rook's grooming research discussed in Chapter 3. Moving from the mundane and achievable to the imaginative and just-barely-possible is the job of the contemporary marketer. The consumer can be led in her quest by the insightful and thorough consumer researcher. Research for a major musical instrument manufacturer asked guitar players what their perfect guitar would be like. A range of interesting responses, such as ubiquitous guitars, guitars that always stayed in tune or that always played the correct note, or laser sensors that detected finger positions led product engineers and designers to develop innovative new computer chip-equipped guitars to help close the gap between possibility and reality. And the Guitar Hero video games help even the musically inept feel that they are playing classic riffs by talented musicians.

8   *Proxies.* Who performs particular household tasks? Who shops for particular products? Is there a delegation of different consumption and household tasks among different members of a household? Children may be assigned to particular consumption tasks rather than adults, women assigned rather than men, or professionals – such as plumbers or pest control experts – rather than household members. In the case of children, much can be signified by such delegation, such as the desire to educate or inculcate responsibilities, or perhaps even the avoidance of unpleasant chores. Gender distributions can be very revealing as a source of unrealised and untapped potential marketing ideas. For example would a man be more likely to cook meat using an indoor grill built into a high-end stovetop, or would the indoor setting dictate a more feminine touch? Hiring professionals to do household tasks can indicate that consumers are dissatisfied or have low confidence in the ability of existing product offerings to completely reach their expectations. It was this logic that led Procter & Gamble to develop the Dryel product. Dryel promised consumers a dry-cleaning quality level for cleaning delicate clothes in-home. However, some of these proxy-based habits are difficult to change, and product credibility in the face of professional expertise can also be an issue. The failure of the Dryel product by Procter & Gamble exemplifies the challenges of changing some of these consumer impressions.

9   *Prosumption.* How do consumers use existing products to create new products? How do they customise? How do they personalise? How do they add their own touches? Do they invent their own solutions to new problems to address still-unfulfilled desires? Ethnography and netnography have been found to be very useful in revealing a range of consumer-generated creations and playful experiences.

For example, a study of online shoe communities by Munich-based marketing research company Hyve revealed that consumers wanted to customise their shoes with decals and paint. Based on this netnographic study, a shoe manufacturer released a premium-priced limited edition shoe set that came with specially formulated paint and decals so that consumers could customise the shoes. The innovation was profitable, and became one of the company's most successful and high-margin product launches that year.

10 *Pairings.* Do consumers combine different products together? Do they adapt existing off-the-shelf offerings? Do they have their own 'recipes' for particular kinds of consumption? Consumers will often combine products in unique and interesting ways. These combinations are clear indicators that consumption preferences are not being fully met. This information can be very relevant to informing managerial decisions about new or unfilled desires. As an example, early research into shampoos revealed that fashion models [a lead user group for hair care products, according to von Hippel's (1986) useful designations] were cracking an egg and adding it to conventional, detergent-based shampoos before washing their hair. The egg, they believed (correctly, it turns out) added body and shine to their hair. The magical ingredient was, in fact, the protein in the egg. This naturalistic observation led to the development of protein-based shampoos, a highly successful introduction that came to dominate the shampoo category.

11 *Partitions.* Do consumers split larger packages into smaller ones? When, why, how, and where does such unbundling occur? Do consumers develop packaging innovations of their own? Do consumers manipulate the way that the product is delivered to them? Do they adapt existing packaging or change products from one package to another? Are spray bottles and squeeze bottles saved and reused? When and where do such exchanges take place? When consumers were observed feeding particular cereals to their children out of sealed sandwich bags, saving crispy marshmallow rice treats in cellophane wrap, or cutting or repacking snack foods so they were in smaller-calorie bundles, marketers got the idea to offer alternative packages for these products. From such alterations and customisations emerge ideas about consumer needs and new opportunities.

12 *Pleasures.* Where was the positive energy in the consumers' experience? Where and among whom did it flow? How did consumers anticipate their purchase and consumption experiences? How did consumers enjoy the consumption experience? What different emotions surround the specific form and elements of the consumption experience? How do consumers act playfully with products? Because consumers' experiences of product benefits are influenced by such a variety of personal and social factors, qualitative researchers are challenged to explore all the facets of consumers' subjective experiences with product and service usage. Consumers using social media often reveal and show off their new product innovations and their playful use of existing products. Netnographic research on the benefits of the mouthwash brand Listerine revealed not only that consumers enjoyed its harsh, almost toxic germ-killing abilities, but also gathered nostalgic benefits from its history and inspiration from its many unexpected 'home remedy' type uses (Kozinets 2010b). In a conceptually

related study, marketing researchers working for a major food company undertook a qualitative study to examine unexpected uses of food. They were surprised to find that families with young children – perhaps in reaction to their own parents' restrictive injunctions against doing so – often encouraged the children to have fun and play with their food. As a result of the study, the manufacturer developed and tested different coloured forms of ketchup (including bright green and purple) in a specially designed squeeze bottle that fitted into children's hands and could be used by them to paint with the ketchup.

These 12 guidelines can help the analyst to focus on areas of high potential. Like any qualitative research endeavour, data collection will exhibit many emergent characteristics such that adjustments are made during the rich and contextually driven research encounters. Staying in close contact with the client, and checking and vetting the insights gained from the research on a regular basis, is a key to a successful project (see the box 'Understanding management needs', above). Just as with qualitative data analysis for theoretical purposes, great insights may come from the discovery of a single 'black swan' (confirming that not all swans are white; see also Chapter 4). If the analyst finds a single instance of inspiring consumer creativity, or finds during in-home study a particularly rich 'revelatory incident' that gets to the heart of consumers' relationship with a product or brand, these single instances can lead to extremely impactful contributions to marketing management. Generalising is generally not the goal with such findings. It is sometimes completely sufficient to find a single managerial idea worth exploring further.

Judging the quality of managerially-relevant analysis

How can we judge the quality of managerially oriented qualitative research? Sometimes, unlike the position taken in Chapter 7, a detailed and descriptive study can have high value in a managerial context. Sometimes managers just want to understand and recognise the consumers that are using their products or services. Sometimes, the simple recognition of the mindset or behavioural set of an otherwise unfamiliar consumer can be an extremely useful source of insight.

Another type of qualitative research analysis can offer creative, integrative, and insight-inspiring leaps of recognition, transforming the mundane into the unexpected. Although the precise and cogent incorporation of the relevant forms and movements of the context are often a valuable part of the insights derived from qualitative consumer research, it is the blending of penetrating analysis and organisation with management needs that, in the final analysis, defines the successful managerially-oriented qualitative research project.

In terms of judging the output of a piece of managerially-oriented qualitative consumer marketing research, Sanjek (1990) suggests that there are three basic criteria we can use to assess ethnographic quality. These are theoretical honesty, transparent representation of the way the ethnographer moved through data collection, and accounting for the relationship between fieldnotes and ethnographic interpretation (p. 485). For managerial presentation, we can develop these ideas a bit further. There are three generally useful categories constituting clarity in the output of a managerially focused qualitative consumer or marketing research project.

First, the outcome should have a clear answer focus that addresses the question drawing from management's need for specific decision-making input. Second, the outcome should clearly link the methods used in the study or studies with the question that the research is intended to answer. Finally, the outcome must lucidly link the data collected and represented, the findings as analysed, and the relevant, focused advice provided in order to guide management action. Analysis should focus on the management decisions it is required to inform. There is no other purpose for managerially oriented qualitative consumer and marketing research.

Sometimes our research may not answer the exact question that we originally set out to investigate. Considerable value can sometimes be gained from the fact that qualitative research often reveals unexpected insights. This is one of qualitative research's great advantages: because it is conducted in a naturalistic setting and examines the dynamic realities of a complex and changing cultural and communal environment, it can be completely up-to-date and can inform our understanding of issues that we may previously have never even suspected. However, such off-the-beaten-path analyses should always be taken with full management buy-in. Managing the political process of providing marketing research data is ever-important, although suffice it to say that the subtle details of this process are beyond the scope of this chapter.

Good analysts often begin their work with some sense of what they may be looking for and how they might locate it. If they have already been involved with data collection and organisation, the findings will not be entirely new to them. In addition to attending to the 12 focus guidelines offered in the section above, the following are some general suggestions we find helpful for creating high-quality managerially oriented interpretations and presentations.

1 *Contextualise the data.* Consumer behaviours take place in context. When observations are placed in their context, new insights can be generated from the juxtaposition and interrelation of often-unexpected constructs. For example, taking care of one's pet

might involve a range of hired services, pet store products, different types of hoses and water treatment, medicines, table food, special cuts of meat, and toys. Attempting to link up these different types of products into the consumption of pet care can reveal novel behavioural constellations and patterns of consumer action that structure consumer decisions and thoughts. Another example comes from Barbara Olsen's (1995) study of childhood memories of brands. A 22-year-old man in her study recalled:

> My parents were always loyal to Colgate, Listerine, and Ivory products. I find myself automatically picking these items when I am at the supermarket; it makes me feel sort of at home in my own bathroom in sunny California. I remember my mom bathing my sister and me and we always used to play with the bubbles of the Johnson & Johnson baby shampoo; well I still use the same product. When I feel down with a cold and alone in my apartment with no mother to care for me, a whiff of Vicks VapoRub always reminds me of my grandmother by my side and my mom's never-ending pampering.

Based on such associations, a 1988 printed advertisement by Richardson-Vicks for VapoRub featured the familiar blue jar as 'hero' of the ad and stated, 'Recent clinical studies prove your grandmother was right'. It continued, 'Today it's a known fact that Vicks VapoRub not only relieves congestion like a pill, it also relieves coughs like a cough syrup. And nothing can match that warm, soothing VapoRub feeling. All of which goes to show that your grandmother did know what was best for you'. Nostalgia and intergenerational brand loyalty were thus fused in this campaign thanks to insights based on recollections of brands from childhood.

2 *Analyse figures of speech, such as tropes and metaphors.* Arnould and Wallendorf (1994, p. 498) discuss and illustrate the importance of noticing and analysing meaningful symbolic links between various behaviours and their verbal expression in consumers' use of language. These relationships can include paradigmatic, syntagmatic, metaphoric, and metonymic relations. The example that they use in their study is the use of the term 'homemade' to refer to different kinds of celebratory meal elements prepared and served to family and guests on Thanksgiving Day in America. When the analyst explores the importance of words such as 'homemade', and the exact meaning and consumer-generated definition of the term ('So what *exactly* do you mean when you say something is "*homemade*"?'), new insights about the values of particular kinds of consumption are revealed. Insightful analysis and perspicacious managerial application can lead to a variety of practical implications for such cultural understandings. In this case, homemade was found to apply to simply removing a product from its commercial packaging and placing it on the family's own dinnerware. Similarly, 'made from scratch' could mean using a mix and adding water and an egg. As noted earlier, metaphoric analyses are the specialty of Zaltman and Zaltman's (2008) ZMET technique.

3 *Attend to contradictions in the data.* Often times qualitative researchers will find that their data can support multiple and even contradictory points of view. This is

interesting and useful because it draws from the fact that cultures, meanings, and values are not single-sided phenomena, but complex and multifaceted ones. By paying attention to the conjunctures and divergences in the data (or, as Arnould and Wallendorf (1994) term them, 'convergences and disjunctures') and by contextualising these and watching for their patterns (as in the first suggestion, above), a qualitative research analyst can sometimes locate unexpected new insights. Such attention can also help to identify different segments of consumers who behave quite differently with regard to the focal product or service.

4 *Reveal moments of revelation.* Culture members often will reveal some of the deepest secrets of their existence in *eureka*-like moments that anthropologist James Fernandez (2000) has termed and developed as 'revelatory incidents'. Mariampolski (2006) describes an ethnographic study of paper towel users. During the study, the researchers observed paper towels being used in situations that would usually require paper napkins. When the ethnographer probed this behaviour, research participants revealed that it was driven by dissatisfaction with the results from using paper napkins when eating different categories of 'finger foods' that were becoming increasingly popular in America, such as burritos. Those findings led to the identification of a number of opportunities for new products that were developed in reports to the clients. The ideas came from one set of revelatory incidents occurring at the dinner table.

5 *Explore discontinuities between talk and action.* As mentioned in Chapter 4, observant observational researchers may find that consumers say one thing but do another. Consumers may make unrealistic claims, or make statements about product use for which there is little or even contradictory evidence. For example, a research participant might claim to 'eat healthy, most of the time' but be found to have a kitchen cupboard fully stocked with multiple brands of potato chips, cookies, candies, and chocolates. When asked, the consumer might embarrassedly explain that those snacks are 'for guests', 'for the kids', or 'only for when we watch movies together'. Exploring these sorts of discontinuities between what people say and what they do can help clarify the categories that they use to think about and describe their consumption. Those categories can have profound implications for a marketer's understanding of consumer thought and action.

6 *Maintain some productive contact with academic theory.* Finally, although it can certainly be overdone, there is still much to be gained by interfacing with academic work that relates to a project's theoretical and substantive domain. For example, in a study of ethnic fast food, anthropological studies of a particular ethnic food culture, as well as sociological studies of contemporary fast food culture might usefully inform and illuminate various aspects of the project. In particular, the theoretical domain can be valuable when consulted at an early stage of the project. At that time, it can familiarise the researcher with a broad range of thinking about the given topic. Although managerial clients tend to be more focused on concise and action-oriented conclusions, an academic grounding can add legitimacy and also contribute to a higher level of thinking that can result in imaginative breakthroughs. As with all

such hybridisations, however, a 'Goldilocks principle' of theory-practice combination should pertain, where the researcher brings in not too much abstract theory, nor too little, but just the right amount.

Presenting qualitative consumer and marketing research to managers

Qualitative researchers working for managers have a responsibility to make the results of their investigations useful and accessible. Many, perhaps most, managers are not conversant with research methods or theoretical language and they tend not to have the interest or time to spend on learning about method or theory. To be blunt, they are paying for results. The key to a successful management presentation then, is to present usable and relevant conclusions in a succinct, relevant, and easily distributed format. There will be some specific hints provided in a later section of this chapter to help guide you in constructing and delivering your research results.

Staying in close contact with the client will help the researcher to prepare a report and presentation that meets the needs of the clients and also facilitates the use of the research results. If a written report is required, the results in it should always be succinctly summarised. In a written report, the key element is a tightly written, concise, and actionable executive summary or highlights. They should be provided to managers in an easy-to-read, easy-to-understand, and easy-to-use form: because managers are always under extreme time pressure, the key word is easy. Avoid methodological or theoretical descriptions and move straight to the findings and their implications. Methodological detail can be placed in an appendix, if need be. If the report is to be distributed, a draft report should be submitted prior to distribution and discussed with the client for its applicability.

The standards for contemporary marketing research are currently quite high. Corporate clients are accustomed to a high level of client service and a keen level of analytic insight. They seek originality, imagination, creativity, and invention that move well beyond conventional, familiar, and overused ideas and formats (an example of a banal and overused analysis might deploy Maslow's hierarchy of needs to explain data). Clients want to use research to develop new visions of consumers' collective reality, their driving forces and social behaviours. Bringing this to light and to life is your task. Fortunately, the rise of methods like videography and netnography means that you have many more options to present your data in visually and audio-visually compelling ways.

Marketing research clients expect attractive and informative presentations of the data. Often times, the PowerPoint slideshow or video that the client commissions will become the key deliverable shared and used in the corporate setting. It is therefore no surprise that marketing researchers, especially those who come from a more patient and less time pressured academic environs, are pressured by clients to decrease the jargon, minimise the methodological babble, simplify every aspect of their presentation, and deliver it in an engaging manner.

Aspiring marketing researchers are advised to pay close attention to the quality of their slides or video and every other aspect of their presentation (for excellent advice, see Duarte 2008). This often means offering a cutting edge PowerPoint presentation. So, if you are still writing on overhead transparencies with the same non-permanent marker you used in 1989, it might be time to spruce things up a little. The following are eight important tips for presenting qualitative consumer and marketing research to managers.

1 Tell a story. Think about the narrative you want to convey before you begin. Craft a powerful story that gets across your central point. If you are not a confident presenter, then read some books on the topic and perhaps take a course. The standards of management presentation are high.
2 Be useful. Always focus in on management's questions and your findings. Link up their need for action with the information you have found that can direct that action.
3 Keep it tight. Aim for fewer, stronger slides. Do not overload your audience.
4 Make it visual. There is nothing worse than sitting through a two-hour presentation filled with PowerPoint slides crammed with black words on a white background. Much more powerful is the visual image.
5 Insert life. Nothing adds energy to a qualitative presentation as much as good quality video in the right places. Do not overuse it, but use it if you can.
6 Use infographics. Representations of your data can be powerful. Think about using maps of online social relationships and networks such as Mention Mapp and others to represent social structure in netnographic data and findings.
7 Devise personas. Where it is possible, create a persona image of your typical target consumer. Tell her story, her hopes, her dreams, her fantasies, as well as her frustration and her fears. Stir the imagination. And then tell the relevant facts about her actual behaviours.
8 Make it easy to share. Provide elements of the presentation that are easily communicated. Can you make it into a two-minute video? Can you summarise it in a powerful diagram? The more you can do to create a 'research meme' the better chance your presentation has of being utilised.

Remember that a high quality analysis and plenty of time for presentation preparation are key elements to achieving such impact. Heaps of detail, quantities of under analysed research participant contributions, and albums of observational photography are not welcome if they substitute quantity of detail and overwhelming description for impactful single insights. Instead, keen and clear minded focus will help the researcher focus on a small set of meaningful and well-integrated insights that can deliver major benefits to clients. By following the advice and guidelines in this chapter, consumer and marketing researchers can help to apply these powerful methods to help managers improve their businesses and serve consumers better by more deeply understanding the worlds of consumers.

9

Presenting, disseminating, and sharing

Presentation and dissemination of qualitative research findings commonly entails presentations at conferences, film festivals, and to other face-to-face audiences, publication in books, journals, working papers, and proceedings, broadcast on television, radio, or other broadcast media, creation of videos or photo essays on DVDs or other distribution media, or posting in online journals, websites, research archives, or other internet sites. Each of these means of presentation and dissemination can be regarded as sharing findings with potentially interested others. So, too, can e-mailing papers, photos, slide presentations, and videos to interested colleagues. Findings can also be shared with a corporate group, class, seminar, or colloquium, or workshop. Besides these more conventional forms of expression there are also alternative forms of prose, poetry, and novels, as well as participation in online forums, creating online expressive photo albums, composing and performing music, and engaging other media often regarded as 'artistic'. Still less common, but also feasible is disseminating and sharing something closer to raw data rather than polished findings. In this chapter we will consider both older and newer means of presenting, disseminating, and sharing qualitative research outcomes. We will also consider alternative outlets for your work and the process of getting successfully published in more traditional media as well as the process of getting credit for dissemination in less traditional media.

Goals

One goal: moving people emotionally

In general, the goal of qualitative consumer and market research is to enhance, deepen, broaden, or otherwise advance our understanding of a particular phenomenon, process, group, or institution of interest to marketers, consumers, scholars, public policy makers or other stakeholders in market-related phenomena. But qualitative research can also be intended to critically problematise an area of interest, to prompt action, or to move an audience emotionally. This is something more than the illustrative role that Basil (2011) sees for 'photoessays'. For example, writers, researchers, photographers, and filmmakers like Jacob Riis (1971), Lewis Hine (Freedman and Hine 1994), Upton Sinclair (2003), and Frederick Wiseman (Grant 2003) all used their work to advocate for change in areas such as slum housing, child labour, unsafe working conditions, and poor mental health-care facilities.

In photography, for example, Hine showed children as young as nine running power knitting looms expressly made short so that they were able to be operated by the very young (Feenberg 2010). James Agee and Walker Evans (1941) combined photographs and prose in a moving portrait of poor and predominantly white Americans in the South during the 1930s. The Farm Security Administration photographs of this era provide a portrait of American life during the Depression (e.g., Hagen 1985; Lang 1981). Maharidge and Williamson (1989) provide a portrait of the cycle of poverty in a follow-up to Agee and Evans's work 40 years later focusing on the next generation in the same area, again combining photography and prose. In a compelling series of photos Jim Goldberg (1985) shows the equally forlorn lives of the rich and their servants and the poor and their children. After photographing them he returned with copies of the photographs and asked those portrayed to write something as if that and the photo was all people had to remember them by. It is difficult to find a more convincing portrayal of the emptiness of materialism. Another quite different track was taken by Daniela Rossell (2002) who succeeded in portraying the excesses and decadence in the lifestyles of Mexican nouveau riche women.

In filmmaking, Wiseman's 1967 film *Titicut Follies* is an observational documentary about the patients/inmates of the Bridgewater State Hospital for the criminally insane in Bridgewater, Massachusetts. The depiction of poor patient care was so upsetting to the state that the film was ordered to be destroyed by a Massachusetts Superior Court judge in 1968. It was only in 1991 that the decision was overturned and the film was allowed to be shown and distributed (Grant 2003). Although not quite so controversial, a number of recent documentaries have focused a similarly critical spotlight on General Motors (Moore 1989), the American health-care system (Moore 2007), gun ownership (Moore 2002),

McDonald's food (Spurlock 2004), Enron (Ellwood 2005), the personality of the corporation (Achbar and Abbott 2005), global warming (Gugenheim 2006), natural gas extraction by 'fragging' (Fox 2010), and various Wal-Mart business practices (Greenwald 2005; Hawes-Davis 2002; Kirby 2006; Young 2004). One award-winning film from the Association for Consumer Research Film Festival, *A Right to Life: Reducing Maternal Death and Morbidity in Pakistan* by Marylouise Caldwell, Paul Henry, and Stephen Watson (2008) was so emotionally moving that some members of the audience actually fainted when it was shown. And Al Gore's *An Inconvenient Truth* (Gugenheim 2006), is widely acknowledged to have aroused a disbelieving public from complacency regarding global warming.

Ethnographic writing also has action potential when it is emotionally arousing. Upton Sinclair's (2003) treatment of the Chicago meat-packing industry, written in 1906, led to several Federal laws in the USA to improve public health, even though Sinclair's intent was more on improving the working conditions of the labourers in the stockyards. However, exposés and critical ethnographies are not the only way to precipitate emotion and prompt action. It is also possible to humanise 'the other' and create a more empathetic portrait of other people and other cultures. Ron Hill's ethnographies of homeless and incarcerated consumers are good examples (Hill 1991; Hill and Stamey 1990; Szykman and Hill 1993). Such portraits stand in contrast to popular culture depictions of the Other that have often relied on colonialist, racist, and sexist depictions that valorise 'us' at the expense of 'them' (e.g., Goffman 1988; Lutz and Collins 1993; McClintock 1995; O'Barr 1994; Sivulka 1998).

Another goal: creating understanding

Although not mutually exclusive of precipitating audience emotion, the more commonly acknowledged goal of qualitative research is to create understanding. This goal stands in contradistinction to the more positivist goal of explaining behaviour in terms of cause and effect relationships. In interpretive research it is normally assumed that behaviour is shaped by multiple causes, is dependent on the context, and is influenced by the researcher's presence. Thus, it is not thought to be possible to explain behaviour in terms of the reductionist causal linkages usually specified by hypotheses, tested in simple experimental designs, and diagrammed with conceptual and behavioural boxes linked by causal arrows. Instead, the understanding that is generally sought by qualitative research is of one of two sorts. At a more descriptive level the effort is to create what anthropologist Clifford Geertz (1973) called thick description. Gertz also reminds us that it is 'not necessary to know everything in order to understand something' (1973, p. 20). Thick description in Geertz's presentation of the concept has three characteristics: it is complex, specific, and circumstantial (1973, p. 23). That is, at the descriptive level, we are seeking a narrative that is appropriately detailed, that names people, places, and brands (although they may well be pseudonyms in order to provide informants with anonymity), and that also creates a picture of the surrounding context.

If successful, a thick description helps the reader or viewer come to feel that they know the people, places, and phenomena of interest. They not only understand in terms of facts such as 'she is a 30-year-old school teacher in a small New England village', but also in terms of feelings such as 'she is already becoming bored and frustrated with her life and with the prospects of finding a mate in this small town; she dreams of moving to the big city where she imagines that life is a constant whirlwind of parties, clubs, and new people'. Langer (1963) called this type of knowledge, 'knowledge of' rather than 'knowledge about'. Denzin (1989) called it 'emotional understanding' versus 'cognitive understanding'. And Russ (Belk 1989) refers to it as 'experiential knowledge' as opposed to 'propositional knowledge'. Thick description thus calls on the researcher/writer to create a rich, interiorised, and intimate story; ideally one that is engaging enough that the reader or viewer can suspend disbelief and imagine themselves in the narrative (Davies and Harré 1990). This is the objective that Martin et al. (2006) use in helping managers to get a concrete image of their target consumers. Management-oriented qualitative research very often must paint a compelling portrait of a consumer or target consumer in order for managers to better understand their behaviours, their needs, and their social world. A persona is an often used technique for conveying this understanding (see Chapter 8).

The second type of understanding that good qualitative research seeks to provide is interpretation. Although description stays pretty close to the data – the *who*, *what*, *when*, and *where* of the phenomenon – interpretation goes beyond the facts of what was observed and said in order to provide a more abstract, conceptual, and theoretical understanding of *how* or *why* something has occurred in a particular way (Wolcott 1994). The interpretive researcher has certain advantages relative to those studied. He or she usually has a broader vantage point based on observing and talking to different people on different occasions and perhaps in different places in the case of multi-sited ethnography (e.g., Ekström 2006; Kjeldgaard et al. 2006). The interpretive researcher has taken a careful and systematic approach to gathering data, often using multiple methods and sometimes with multiple researchers, thus allowing two different sorts of triangulation. The researcher has read related literature and knows the accounts and theories that others have provided to interpret similar phenomena. And the researcher has knowledge of and experience with making sense of qualitative data (see Chapters 7 and 8). Thus, the researcher is hopefully in a privileged interpretive position relative to that of those studied.

We interpret all the time in everyday behaviour. If someone says to us 'I love you', we try to interpret what they mean. Context and knowledge of the speaker help. Is this a casual friend, someone we are dating, a parent, a child, or a long-time partner? Is this spoken at a public gathering or when we are alone? At what time of day and with what tone of voice? Are they smiling or laughing as they say this? How unusual is this statement given the person's prior conversations with us and with others? What ulterior motives might the person have for saying this? What might we have done to prompt this confession? How does it seem that the person expects us to respond? In order to interpret such a statement we might further interrogate the person, ask them to clarify, or perhaps ask directly how they mean that. We might triangulate with other behaviours. And we might try out alternative interpretations: romantic love, brotherly love, sexual love, or casual love (in the sense of appreciate, like, or enjoy).

In the film, *To Sir with Love* the teacher, Sidney Poitier, receives a love note from an infatuated female student. Rather than react to the note on a personal level he maintains his role as teacher and corrects the message for grammar before returning it to the now heart-broken student. It is not that he misses the intent of the situation, but rather that he chooses to redefine it as a classroom exercise and keep within a professional teacher–student relationship. As this example suggests, when communication takes place, we also need to ascertain the degree of co-orientation of the source and the target of the message. This includes communications between researchers and informants. People do not always say what they mean. They may be giving us socially desirable answers that flatter one or both of us. Behaviours can also be less than natural when people know they are being observed. Probing, projective questions, prolonged engagement, trust building, triangulation, and other techniques of good fieldwork are designed to minimise or discover such distortions, but interpretation still needs to be judicious in evaluating the available evidence. This includes researcher reflexivity in which the authority of the author to speak for informants is questioned with one outcome being a critical pluralism in which there is an attempt to present multiple and sometimes conflicting points of view (Joy et al. 2006). Spiggle (1998) refers to this approach as creating multivocal framing. This does not fully solve the problem of representation because the other voices introduced may well have their own biases. But it does call attention to the multiplicity of possible alternative perspectives on the phenomenon – male/female, young/old, rich/poor, core/periphery, and so forth.

Wolcott (1994) makes the distinction that whereas analysis transforms data, interpretation transcends data. That is, interpretation is more data-distant, abstract, and only partially derives from the data. The remainder of the interpretation comes from the researcher and is shaped by training, experience, reading, and – for better or for worse – biases. Biases are inevitable and it is no sin to put your personal stamp on what you are writing. There must be some warrant in the data or in prior research for the interpretation you are arguing, but some speculation and idiosyncrasy is inevitable and should not be ignored with a veneer of 'scientific objectivity'. For example, metaphor and analogy are commonly employed in creating and communicating an interpretation. For the critical audience, the proof of the pudding is in the tasting and it matters not only what you say, but how well you argue for your interpretation by presenting evidence, argument, citations, and plausible and convincing logic linking the data and your interpretation. You are asking the audience to make a leap of faith with you, to buy into a metaphor or analogy, and to suspend their disbelief long enough to hear you out. It helps that in qualitative research the interpretation is contextualised and is not offered as a universal pronouncement about human nature. But still, we hope that our interpretation is not restricted to the context studied and will have some usefulness in understanding other people, other places, and related phenomena. Stated differently, while good thick description gives your research legs to stand on, good interpretation gives it wings to soar.

Creating something to share

The roles of prior literature and theory

As noted in Chapter 7, while some advocates of truly discovery-oriented research grounded in data suggest that you stay away from literature that may shape your viewpoints prior to entering the field, we beg to differ. As we suggested in Chapter 3, an open mind need not mean an empty head. By all means read or view everything you can on the phenomenon of interest and potentially related theoretical perspectives. This should take place before, during, and after fieldwork as your ideas develop and as you tack back and forth between literature and data, like a sailing ship heading into the wind (we, too, use metaphors in an attempt to communicate more effectively). Creative ideas come from drawing on eclectic sources, not least of all your own introspection to see whether a theory, observation, or insight resonates with your own sense of the world. The best ideas are simple without being obvious.

A literature review of prior related work is common and expected in academic marketing and consumer research journals, chapters, and books. It is uncommon to find such a review in a video. This is both because videos may be more descriptive and because the medium does not lend itself to citations. However if video outputs are to be regarded as research products rather than pedagogical vehicles, theory is expected in this medium as well, even though it will likely use references more subtly and adroitly (Kozinets and Belk 2006). In written formats, it is customary for the literature review to precede methods and findings sections. Unfortunately this makes the theoretical perspective adopted seem more a priori and disguises the tacking between data, literature, and theory that has almost certainly taken place in the planning, data collection, and analysis. It remains for an innovative project to better represent the actual process employed in your discovery-oriented qualitative research.

The general purpose of a literature review is to situate the present study within the streams of related research and theory that have gone before. In so doing the contribution of the present research should be identified and foreshadowed. The literature review should be a critical synthesis of relevant work and not a mere listing of 'A said X', 'B found Y', and 'C said Z'. By critiquing as well as identifying gaps that your research fills, you provide a synthesis rather than a mere summary. But filling gaps or doing something that has not been done before is not a good enough reason to publish your research. It merely indicates that there is something new here. More important is to identify what your research contributes to our understanding; what new insights it derives, and how this should help to change the course of future research.

If the contribution of your research is to develop a completely new theory of how and why something important happens, great! But this is extremely rare in consumer and market research. Chances are far better that you will extend someone else's theory, show an exception to what someone else has found, or apply an existing theory in a new and interesting way.

On being interesting

Murray Davis (1971) suggests that the greatness of great theories lies not in their profundity, meaningfulness, or truthfulness, but rather in their interestingness. Being interesting, he maintains, is a matter of denying rather than affirming the assumptions of the audience. Zaltman et al. (1982) give numerous examples of how to do this. One of their many examples is Caplovitz's (1963) *The Poor Pay More*. Common sense would have it that because of lower incomes, the poor should pay less than the rich for the goods and services they buy, because they can ill afford superfluities and luxury versions of products. But because of their lower geographic mobility and lack of access to the lower cost goods in the megastores of the affluent suburbs, the poor actually wind up paying more for equivalent merchandise compared to the rich. That is interesting! (And, for those of a critical bent, it is a stimulus for seeking ways to ameliorate the price inequities facing poor consumers.)

This insight is another argument for interpretation as a leap of faith beyond a literal interpretation of the data. But making research interesting can also occur by bringing to bear disparate literature and insights that are not a part of the common knowledge of the audience, saying or showing things in new and interesting ways, and crafting an account in a compelling fashion. The latter point is driven home by marketing's writer extraordinaire, Stephen Brown (1998), in commenting on Arnould and Price's (1993) paper 'River Magic'. After noting that the paper is much celebrated and 'ranks among *the very best* of its type' Brown (1998) continues:

> Nevertheless, the question still has to be asked: does 'River Magic' capture the magic of the river magic experience? And the answer, regrettably, is no. The 'River Magic' paper *tells* us about river magic, certainly, it simply doesn't *show* us any … Sadly, there is nothing magical, supernatural or even mildly thaumaturgic about Arnould and Price's ponderous piece. Although, to repeat, the paper ranks amongst the *very best* of the genre, it unfailingly reminds me of the rhetorical question posed about ethnography by literary critic Mary Louise Pratt (1986: 33), 'why do such interesting people, doing such interesting things, in such an interesting domain, produce such dull books and articles?' (pp. 374–375)

Notably, Brown himself has at least temporarily set aside ethnographic journal and book writing in order to complete a trilogy of novels about marketing and consumption (Brown 2006b, 2008, 2009). Others like Rob (Kozinets 2008a), Schouten (1991a, 1991b, 1993), Sherry (1991b, 1998, 2008), Stern (1998), Wijland et al. (2010), and Zinkhan (1998) have embraced poetry as a writing genre for conveying their insights into consumption and marketing. Several of Rob's poems, like the one cited above, are performed to music – either pre-recorded or with a live DJ. As these examples begin to suggest presenting research – any research – is a form of storytelling (Elliott 2005). And the most interesting presentations are interesting in both form and content. Van Maanen (1988) discusses the different types of stories we typically tell as ethnographers: realist tales (narrated in a dispassionate third person voice), confessional tales (highly personalised and self-absorbed including the melodrama of fieldwork hardships), and impressionist tales (dramatic, reflective, and meditative accounts privileging fieldwork). Each of these has obvious problems and Van Maanen (1988) also considers correctives he terms literary tales, jointly told tales, focused formal tales, and critical tales. Which literary style will work best for your storytelling is something you will have to work out, but we encourage both experimentation and serious attention to the craft of writing (or video editing) well. Write, write, and rewrite! Try to develop a voice of your own rather than attempting a formulaic approach.

When creating a video there are additional considerations that are absent in most writing. These include decisions about whether to include music, and if so what music at what points in the video, whether to include titles, inter-titles, or subtitles, how to do transitions, how to pace the video, what sort of tone the film should have, whether to include a voice-over and if so what to say, how much theory to bring in, how to acknowledge relevant prior work, and how to put the video together. The tendency with the ease of non-linear editing programs is to get too elaborate. It is better to keep it simple, with lots of straight cuts and as little narration and use of titles as possible. There are books and classes on video editing that can help and some of the former have been cited in Chapter 6. But another trick is to watch how others have done it in documentaries, films, YouTube, and television. Selectively imitating the techniques you see and like is one good way to start. You will probably do this subconsciously anyway, but by studying others' work you will become better faster as well as a better critic of what you see in various media.

When Russ and Rob co-chaired the Association for Consumer Research Film Festivals during its first ten years, they developed guidelines used in jurying the films shown in these festivals (Kozinets and Belk 2006). The Consumer Culture Theory conference features both film and poetry and the now defunct Heretical Consumer Research conferences also featured interpretive plays conveying research and theory in yet another way. Another part of the rationale for presentations using such expressive media is that such forms can help us to 'say' things that would be difficult or impossible to say in another manner. When asked what her dance meant, the famous interpretive dancer of the early twentieth century, Isadora Duncan, reportedly replied 'If I could say it, I wouldn't have to dance it!'

EXERCISE 9.1

Find a journal article or chapter by someone whom you feel writes with flair and who has developed a distinctive voice – perhaps someone like Stephen Brown or Morris Holbrook or John Sherry. Carefully study the paper and analyse what writing conventions the author employs in order to write with such flair. When you think you have him or her down pretty well, take another paper from the same volume or issue and try to rewrite a few paragraphs in the style of the author you have chosen to imitate. This will likely come out as a somewhat stereotyped piece of writing, but that is fine. Now turn to a colleague who is familiar with the author you have chosen. Give them your writing example and see whether they can discern who you are emulating. Ask for their constructive feedback in terms of how to make it more like the writer who inspired it. This exercise is meant both to free yourself from convention and to begin to develop an appreciation of what it might mean to cultivate a distinctive voice. See Brown's (2005) analysis of marketing writer styles for inspiration and ideas.

What should a presentation of qualitative research include?

Exactly what you include in presenting your qualitative research and findings depends on the audience and the presentation medium. Clearly an academic presentation based on analyses like those discussed in Chapter 7 will include different material from a managerial presentation based on analyses like those that are the focus of Chapter 8. Generally you will include decreasing amounts of detail in moving from audiences consisting of dissertation committees, academic audiences, and corporate audiences, to general public audiences. This decrease in specificity will likely include decreasing the extent of literature review, methods description, quotations from research participants, theoretical discussion, general discussion, and references. And the findings that remain may be presented in an increasingly simple vocabulary as the audiences become more general. However, you should always write-up qualitative (as well as quantitative) research in a straightforward, simple, and direct manner. Use short sentences, short paragraphs, an active first person voice (e.g., 'I found that', not 'It was found' or 'It was revealed that'). Avoid jargon and big words unless they are absolutely needed to convey your findings. Wolcott (2001) gives some good advice on what to include, what to cut, how to write, and even how to choose titles.

In terms of media, generally you will include declining amounts of detail in moving from books to journal articles, to book chapters, to conference papers, to PowerPoint presentations, to videos, to web presentations, to blogs. All of these media allow the inclusion of visual material and the latter media also allow the use of audio. We suggest gearing the message to the medium and taking advantage of multi-media capabilities whenever possible. This is not to say that you need to include video in each of your PowerPoint presentations (or that you always need to use PowerPoint in making presentations), but if you have compelling audio-visual material, why not show it rather than describe it?

Whenever possible it is also a good idea to make your presentation interactive, especially when you have an audience that is likely to be involved in the topic and a medium that facilitates interactivity. For example, in an online or DVD presentation, rather than turn a non-linear medium into a linear presentation, why not allow the audience to skip to the portions they want to see, hear, or read in the sequence that they prefer? This takes a bit more work on your part, but it potentially allows the audience the opportunity to go into methods, themes, informants, settings, references, photos, and so forth in as much or as little detail as they wish. One example is Peter Menzel's (1994b) interactive CD-ROM version of his (1994a) book, *Material World*. Both report the findings of a 30-country photographic, videographic, and ethnographic study of families and their possessions. Although the book has an index, it is organised by country and presents photos, narratives, and brief descriptions of each country and each family, including photos and descriptions of their possessions. There are also photo depictions of televisions, meals, and toilets of the world comparing most of the countries studied. There are photographers' notes, statistical comparisons of the countries, and an introduction and afterword. The CD-ROM has this information as well as video clips and additional photos showing family members' daily activities, schools, musical instruments, and comparisons of kitchens, transportation, and leisure activities. Moreover, the CD-ROM allows users to access information more or less as they wish. If you want to follow one family member or compare music of the world, or see an inventory of each possession keyed to its meaning to different family members, each of these are possible by clicking the right buttons. Not much use has been made of interactive CD-ROMs (but see Keshenboom 1995) and newer technologies like DVDs and the internet have largely superseded the CD-ROM, but the same potential remains in each new medium. As Farnell and Huntley (1995) observe:

> If the results of scholarly production can be almost as multi-media as cultural events themselves, then conducting fieldwork with a CD-ROM in mind means collecting data in as many forms as possible – video, sound tape, photographs, pictures, maps, drawings, songs, interviews – and imaging creative ways to re-present them, bearing in mind that the ethnography so produced will be structured somewhat differently each time, depending upon the inquisitive choice of the user. I find that exciting! (p. 10)

Belk (1998) further discusses these possibilities.

In the user-directed possibilities of interactive presentations of qualitative research findings we begin to see a decline in the dictatorial control of the researcher to impose a certain interpretation on the audience. It also makes more of the raw data available to the interested viewer. A still more radical shift in the balance of power between the researcher and others is to share raw data itself (e.g., Sieber 1991). Given the enormous investment of time and talent in gathering qualitative data and the likelihood that different people will find different aspects of the data theoretically or pragmatically interesting, it makes a great deal of sense that we should share data, especially after we have done all we intend to do with it ourselves. Yet this very rarely happens. There are several reasons for this – some weak, some strong. The weaker arguments are based on proprietary attitudes that the data are ours. We may fear that someone else is potentially getting an easy publication without putting in all the work that we have. Or we may fear that someone will challenge our interpretations using our own data. But there are stronger reasons for objecting. For ethical reasons, there is likely to be a greater chance that informant confidentiality will be compromised if raw data are shared. While there may be safeguards to avoid this, we cannot be sure. More compelling is the argument raised in Chapter 6 that the researcher who has conducted the fieldwork always has tacit knowledge that third parties will not have. Yet sometimes data *are* shared – if less often openly and publicly then more often with invited colleagues who potentially bring something to the interpretation (e.g., theoretical expertise, experience, writing skills, video editing skills) that we lack. Sharing of this sort is more common and may lead to a win-win situation of collaboration and joint authorship. And our collaborators can also be the research participants themselves, solving or at least ameliorating issues of representation that were such a concern in anthropology in the 1980s (Clifford and Marcus 1986; Clifford 1988).

████████████████████████ **EXERCISE 9.2** ████████████████████████

Good research begins with a strong opening that cues audience expectations, gets their attention, and makes them want to learn what you have to say and show. Your title and abstract are the critical decision points that help readers determine whether to engage or ignore your work. You have 150 words, exclusive of title, to convince us that the research you are currently pursuing is worth our attention. Go!

Publishing

Choosing an outlet and preparing your contribution

Although good ethnographies require book length monographs to fully do them justice, the norm in marketing academia is to write journal articles. If you decide to follow this tradition, it means that you will have a relatively small number of pages (generally no more than 50 or 60 double spaced pages in the most liberal of journals) to present your research. Business journals increasingly demand theory, to the extent that the context is now secondary. Thus you need to focus from the outset on the theoretical advance that your paper makes. Conference papers and videos may allow you to concentrate more fully on your descriptive findings, but these outlets are even more restricted in terms of how much you will be able to present. Although videos may go an hour or longer, 20 minutes is more common, and those online are often a fraction of this. An hour may sound long, but unless you load the video with your words (boring!) you will probably be able to say less than you can in a 40-page paper. On the other hand, you will be able to privilege the voice of the consumer (or marketers, if they are they focus) to a greater degree than in print media. Juried consumer research film festivals too are looking for theory as well as context.

Another consideration in selecting video is how you will distribute the product of your video editing work. Marketing and consumer research film festivals and special online or DVD issues of journals have the advantage of jurying, which may be more convincing evidence of quality and competitive peer review for promotion and tenure committees at universities. Still, such presentations are somewhat ephemeral. It may be best to not only think of submission to film festivals and special issues of journals, but also posting your video online (e.g., YouTube, Vimeo) in order to assure wider access. As noted in Chapter 6, the Vimeo site presently called Films by Consumer Researchers (http://vimeo.com/groups/136972), provides a lasting outlet for films that have been accepted into refereed journals or juried flm festivals. You can always send out DVD copies, but that involves more effort, greater cost, and narrower distribution. Inclusion of your video in a consumer behaviour or marketing text media package may gain a larger audience, but may also stigmatise the video as being pedagogical in nature rather than a research document. On the other hand, there are generally awards given for best video in film festivals and this too can provide evidence of the quality of your work.

For journal submissions in marketing and consumer behaviour, the first two of our three major journals (*Journal of Consumer Research*, *Journal of Marketing*, and *Journal of Marketing Research*) are receptive to qualitative research. There are also a number of other good journals that are receptive to qualitative work, both in the USA and Europe and both in English and French. There may be more strict page limits in some of these journals however. Although some of these journals are more specialised (e.g., tourism, ethnography, marketing theory, consumer culture), they provide good distribution choices if the research is not likely to make it into the top three journals.

If you are seeking to publish from your dissertation, our colleague Markus Giesler gives some good advice: throw away your dissertation! While this may sound extreme, it means that you should start over writing something for a journal and not assume that it can merely be extracted from your thesis. This advice may pertain a bit less in a multiple essay dissertation where the intent is to be able to calve-off pieces in their entirety, but it is still important to recognise that journal conventions and writing styles are likely not the same as dissertation conventions and styles. Be certain to cite relevant papers that have appeared in the journal and make your paper conform to the journal's style sheet. Look at other interpretive articles in the journal and the relative amount of space they devote to literature, methods, and findings. What level of theory familiarity do they expect from readers? If in doubt, keep it simple. Referencing significant sources you cannot take the space to review will show your familiarity with things that reviewers might otherwise criticise a paper for missing. And most importantly learn to write well! If you are seeking to publish in English and

English is not your first language, you might do well to seek a copy editor whose mother tongue is English to go over your manuscript before submission.

Be sure to distinguish what you intend to be descriptive from that which you intend to be interpretive. Thick description will need to be illustrative without attempting to include too much interesting but inessential detail. Interpretation can take greater liberties in omitting interview and observational detail, but needs to provide some plausible basis for the interpretations offered, including referring back to the descriptive data presented earlier in the paper. Your literature review should not be conducted in your presentation of findings and interpretations. You can cite a few papers in these portions of the paper, but it should primarily be based on your own work. You can do more citation in the discussion section to bolster your arguments and draw links to related work that supports your conclusions or potentially expands their applicability to other contexts.

In the case of books, potential publishers usually require a prospectus and sample chapter or two along with an assessment of the audience and market for such a book. Some publishers are more receptive to qualitative marketing and consumer research, and an examination of existing titles will be a good clue. Besides books, conference papers, journal articles, and videos, book chapters are other potential outlets. If you do not know who may be contemplating editing a relevant volume, presenting your work at conferences is a good way to meet like-minded others. You can also join listservs, websites, and discussion forums in relevant areas and seek others to form a session or book proposal. The latter case envisions editing such a volume yourself, alone or with co-editors. In that case, the prospectus you write should either enumerate authors or give sample authors who have already agreed to participate by contributing chapters.

If you are maintaining a blog or website or if you are self-publishing on YouTube, Vimeo, or other social media sites, you do not have to meet the additional concerns of the review process considered in the next section. This is all the more reason to be critical of your own work. On one hand maintaining such a self-publication effort is a great way to reach a broader audience with your work. Especially if the site allows viewer comments, you may 'meet' a variety of interesting people you would not otherwise encounter. But keep in mind that the academic and corporate audience will likely be judging your work as well. Grant McCracken's CultureBy blog (http://www.cultureby.com/) and Rob's Brandthroposophy blog (http://kozinets.net/) are some good examples to emulate or inspire you.

Responding to reviewers and editors

When you have finished writing, writing, and rewriting your paper, book proposal, or video and sent it off for review, you can finally breathe a sigh of relief – but only for an anxiety-filled few weeks until the reviews come back. Nothing ever gets accepted in the first round of reviews and some papers get 'desk-rejected' without ever making it to the first round of reviews. A revision opportunity, or even a 'reject and resubmit something substantially different', is a very good thing and brings you much closer to acceptance. If you do have a chance to revise, you should generally respond to the editor and/or associate editor rather than the individual reviewers. These intermediaries between you and the reviewers should have prioritised the reviewers' comments and told you what is really important for a successful revision. Take this advice seriously, but feel free to disagree with some of it. The least likely tactic for success is to try to please all of the reviewers on all of the points they raise. They may often have different visions of what your paper should be and this is a good reason for having the intervention of an editor and/or associate editor. If you disagree with certain points, make the reasons for your disagreement clear. For example, you cannot do everything in the space available; they have misunderstood your intent or the evidence; you can see what they would like you to do but cannot accommodate it without completely redoing your study, and so forth. If you have conducted your fieldwork in another country or location, it may not be feasible for you to go back and collect more data. If this is a deal breaker, so be it. You can only do so much.

Perhaps the most important trait when it comes to getting published is persistence. This does not mean contacting the editor and begging for understanding, although if you feel there has been a communication problem or you are confused by the review, by all means try to clarify. But it does mean pursuing any hope that is left open. Too many would-be authors give up at the first sign of negative feedback. This is your baby. Be realistic, but be tenacious. Do not be afraid to completely change your ideas. The review process is a collaborative effort and the reviewers and editors will try to help you with alternative theories, alternative explanations for your observations, and recommendations of alternative literatures. Be selective in accepting such advice, but fully explore it before you reject anything and be prepared to justify your choices. Just as the interpretive process does not stop with manuscript submission, neither does the literature review or theorising. Be open minded and thankful for good advice, no matter how painful it may sometimes seem. Each of the present authors has served as an editor or associate editor and we agree that by far the most common reason for rejecting qualitative research papers is the lack of sufficient depth and originality in the paper's theoretical contribution. Do not be afraid to be bold in your interpretations. This is seldom something that emerges fully born from the data. Rather it is apt to be something that occurs to you at times when you have left the data and may be thinking about something different. It may even occur in your sleep, so keep a pencil and paper or recorder handy by your bedside just in case. Otherwise the idea will almost certainly be gone in the morning.

Journal pages in the 'best' journals are precious and it is very likely that the editor and perhaps the reviewers will call for reducing the number of pages by 10–20 per cent or even more. When forced to cut you will need to decide how to say things more succinctly and what is really important. If you are giving references of the (e.g., A, B, C, and D) sort, do not list more than two or three – these are meant as examples, not an exhaustive list. Here, too, is where you will learn the virtue of short simple sentences. You can also cut down on the number of quotations from participants you are using and do more paraphrasing or summarising. Remember to draw on the observational part of an ethnography as well as the interviews.

EXERCISE 9.3

Suppose you get the review below on a paper you submitted to a leading consumer research journal. Further suppose that you agree with about half the points raised in the review (you can choose which ones) and believe that the other comments are misdirected, either because they have misunderstood what you are trying to do, they would compromise what you see as the integrity of your research, or because they would unnecessarily add to the length of the already too long manuscript and are peripheral to what you are trying to do in the paper. Prepare a set of constructive responses to the review. You can assume that you have already made the changes called for in the subset of comments that you accept.

The Review: Thank you for sending your work to *XYZ*. It has been read by three knowledgeable reviewers. I summarise their comments in what follows, privileging those that I feel are most important. All three reviewers agree that how people bathe is an important and neglected topic in consumer research. At the same time, each of the reviewers raises serious concerns about how the research was carried out, theorised, and presented. The major concerns, in my view, are these:

1 The manuscript is too long, especially your literature review and findings sections. Do we really need to know the history of bathing and hygiene to appreciate your study? After you have presented results from two men and two women, do we really need to learn about the slight variations in additional informants? And it does not seem necessary to include both showering and tub bathing. Can you concentrate on one or the other? See Reviewers A and C on these points.
2 The reviewers and I acknowledge that this is a sensitive topic and that it may well have been necessary to pay professional models to bathe before you and allow you to take photographs and videos of them doing so. But this raises two issues: (1) Would it not have sufficed to have clothed informants take a mock bath or shower (without water) in order to demonstrate their bathing and drying procedures? (2) Is there a need to show these photos or is this just gratuitous nudity? What do you hope to accomplish with these photos that words cannot

handle? Reviewer B raises a moral concern in this regard and I expect that some readers of the Journal will share this perspective.

3   More basically, was it necessary to conduct observations at all? Could this study not have been conducted by having people describe their showering and bathing experiences rather than also enact them? None of the reviewers explicitly raises this point, but it seems to underlie their critical treatment of your methods.

4   The bulk of your current theoretical contribution in the paper lies in pointing out the various ways in which Mary Douglas's (1966) concepts of pollution and taboo affect the bodily cleaning rituals of contemporary North Americans. Yet the bulk of her work was based on Biblical proscriptions and the lives of 'primitive' people. How do you justify using these concepts? If you cannot do so, as Reviewers A and B suggest, an alternative perspective is needed. In this regard, Reviewer B suggests Elizabeth Shove's (2003) work on the commodification of cleanliness. In any case, something is needed to advance your contribution beyond that of Douglas, which is well known and brings nothing new to the table.

5   There is one additional issue that Reviewer C brings up that I also think is important. You (or perhaps your informants) tend to take a moralistic tone toward cleanliness and order, valorising these as unassailably good things. Yet, as this reviewer notes, excessive cleaning practices are also associated with OCD (obsessive-compulsive disorder). As Abrahamson and Freedman (2006) have argued, disorder, clutter, and dirt may provide benefits in our lives and too much order and cleaning can shut us off to creativity and change. I think you need to take a hard and critical look at your data with this alternative moral perspective in mind. At the very least, you need to counter-argue the points raised by Abrahamson and Freedman and by Reviewer C.

I won't reiterate the other points raised by the reviewers, but I believe these are the more significant ones. In light of the points above, I must reject the paper in its current form, but we would be receptive to a substantially different paper. If you decide to revise, please prepare a brief response summarising the changes you have made from the current paper and specifically responding to the points made above. Thank you for sending us your work and best wishes.

Yours sincerely,
The Editor

Conclusion

One thing we have sought to do in this chapter is to expand the ways you think about outlets for your work and genres in which you might communicate. Although we would like to see a broader set of ways of communicating, we also realise that realistically publishing in top journals will remain first priority for many qualitative researchers in academic positions. If your institution only counts 'top tier' journals, this may well restrict your scope for a few years until you obtain the promotion you are seeking. But it is all too easy to put off doing the things that you really want to do and that might fulfil your life as well as enrich the lives of readers, students, and viewers. We are reminded of the following story attributed to George Bernard Shaw. On meeting a London socialite at a party he reputedly asked her, 'would you sleep with me for ... for a million pounds?' 'Well', she said, 'maybe for a million I would, yes'. 'Would you do it for ten shillings?' said Bernard Shaw. 'Certainly not!' said the woman 'What do you take me for? A prostitute?' 'We've established that already', said Shaw. 'We're just trying to fix your price now!' The point is that if you start compromising your ideals you have already given up on the self you would like to create. And the longer you do this, the harder it will be to take the creative chances your imagination aspires to.

So we encourage you not to foreclose your options in presenting your qualitative work. Find a way to do what you must as well as what you want to do. Think broadly, 'publish' widely, and seek to communicate with diverse audiences. If instead your work becomes narrower and narrower and your audiences become more and more concentrated, you may be speaking to a very focused enclave of compatriots, but missing the opportunity to make a more profound impact that will really affect lives.

10

Final thoughts

This is the final chapter, but hardly the final word on qualitative research. Given the dynamic state of qualitative research and consumption, this book offers an extension more than an ending in the evolution of consumer and market research. With this book, we have had a rare opportunity to examine a burgeoning, but still in many ways nascent, field of research, and to do it at a particular period in time. As researchers with different genders, different perspectives, and coming from different generations, we have struggled to represent these differing points of view in a somewhat consistent manner within the pages of a single book. We have also attempted to write a book that will be relevant to different audiences, including seasoned academic researchers as well as newcomers, managerial marketing researchers and consumer insights personnel, as well as teachers in academic classrooms. In this final chapter, we would like to offer some 'sage' words of advice that both summarise and extend the lessons, debates, and considerations we have tried to offer in this volume. These insights, which we share as injunctions and challenges offered to fellow researchers, cover the following areas: investigating new communications technologies, developing an expanded methodological toolkit, the time-consuming nature of qualitative research, the value of hands-on experience, the usefulness of teamwork, the need for duplicate equipment, the emotionally involving nature of qualitative research, and the nature of scientific research as a language.

The practice of qualitative consumer and market research, whether in academia or industry, involves practices initiated in Herodotus' ancient Greek ethnographies as well as those that have only recently emerged to study social media and online interactions. It is thus with one foot firmly planted in the well-established ethnographic practices of the past and the other in the rapidly advancing data mining and netnographic practices of the present and future, that we would like to offer a few thoughts in the form of admonitions, encouragements, and brief insights that did not find their way into the preceding chapters or that deserve re-emphasis.

Although it is undeniable that the digital revolution that has been underway for the past decades has had a tremendous impact on our lives, our consumption, and the ways in which we are able to conduct qualitative and other research, we should not get too carried away with the impression that our lives are transforming as never before. Similar waves of technophilia (and technophobia) have greeted many past technologies including the telegraph, telephone, radio, television, the automobile, and many others (e.g., Gietlman 2008; Marvin 1988; Nye 1994; Standage 1998). Each of these technologies *did* have a profound effect on our lives, but they were not as totally disruptive as their early enthusiasts forecast. For instance, consider the breathless enthusiasm of the following forecast of the effects of cable television:

> Cable TV … had the potential to connect people like no other technology. It would bring about ubiquitous two-way communication, and it would likely usher in a Wired Society governed by Electronic Democracy. The multichannel universe would revitalise communities, enrich schools, end poverty, eliminate the need for everything from banks to shopping malls, and reduce dependence on the automobile … In short, cable TV would transform the world (Mosco 2004, p. 1).

If this forecast sounds familiar, it is because we have heard something very similar about the internet. And although we may have passed through the dot com bubble at the end of the millennium, some people contend that in 2012 with the ascendance of Apple to the world's most valuable company, we are in the midst of bubble 2.0. So our first admonition is: **Do not get too carried away with the great potential to do qualitative research using new technologies and investigating new media.**

By all means *do* consider that many consumption phenomena these days have some internet presence whether in the form of online word of mouth, online rating services, online purchase or access, or other online manifestations. In fact, a number of researchers have noted that it is increasingly impossible to fully study particular cultural and social groups and phenomena without moving to an examination, connection, and analysis of their online communications and social behaviours (e.g., Garcia et al. 2009). But we should not make the mistake of looking only at these manifestations when there is still a real world manifestation of these phenomena. For example, some department and clothing stores are installing computer and camera devices in their dressing rooms or displays that facilitate photographing oneself in new outfits and posting the pictures to

Facebook so that friends can instantly give their feedback. This is a potentially interesting phenomenon to study in that it seems to involve the co-construction of self. But it would be a mistake to overlook other aspects of clothing and other relevant social fields in which to investigate fashion. To do so would be to ignore the importance of context, anticipated audiences, and other day-to-day influences on the clothing we buy and wear. Observational studies of fashion choices in situ, wardrobe studies in which we go through items worn and not worn with informants, studies of second-hand clothing stores, examinations of atmospherics in retail clothing spaces, clothes diaries, projectives, and other qualitative research possibilities all offer different sorts of behaviours and insights than those available online.

This also leads to a second recommendation: **Develop a big methodological toolkit and select the appropriate tools for the problem or research question at hand.** The old saying that when the only tool in your toolkit is a hammer, all you can do is pound away, regardless of the problem, certainly applies here. By a full toolkit, we mean not only all or at least a substantial number of the qualitative methods described here – observation, depth interviews, projectives, ethnography, videography, netnography, content analysis, data mining, etc. – but also quantitative tools. In this book we have briefly illustrated some methods that have quantitative components, and a potential to combine qualitative and quantitative approaches, such as data mining and content analysis. Computerised data 'analysis' packages can also facilitate a quantitative approach to previously qualitative data. Even though the enthusiasm of some qualitative consumer and market researchers may sometimes make it seem like a religion, complete with sacred rituals, deities, and devils (in the quantitative camp), to curse quantitative methods as somehow wrong, inherently manipulative, or 'evil' is as much of a mistake as when quantitative researchers disparage qualitative methods as shallow, journalistic, or incomplete. Both antagonisms are unproductive in many ways, and stand against the interdisciplinary and unbounded spirit of scientific inquiry.

So, given the undeniable fact that there are inevitable constraints on aptitude and reputation, we would advise you to approach research by first identifying an interesting context, theory, or concept and then to pick appropriate tools to match it. Otherwise you are pursuing a method in search of a problem. This is not the best approach. It restricts the problems you can address, leads to mismatches of tools and problems (the law of the hammer), and very likely leads to less passionate research than is the case when you get excited by a context or theoretical perspective. This recommendation also means that you are never finished learning or inventing new research approaches. Both ingenuity and changing technologies mean that there will continue to be changing opportunities to employ methods that do not currently exist and that therefore have not been discussed here. We find that you will be much more likely to be able to create a new approach within qualitative research than is the case with quantitative research. We also find that the Consumer Culture Theory community is quite open to new methods of collecting data, analysing it, and presenting your research conclusions. In fact, as Arnould and Thompson (2005, p. 870) note 'Consumer culture theory researchers embrace methodological pluralism whenever quantitative measures and analytic techniques can advance the operative theoretical agenda (e.g., Arnould and Price 1993; Coulter et al. 2003; Grayson and Martinec 2004; Grayson and Shulman 2000; McQuarrie and Mick 1992; Moore and Lutz 2000; Sirsi et al.1996). Why not enjoy this relative methodological freedom? Be ecumenical in choosing the methods you employ and be inventive in developing a fruitful approach to a research problem at hand.

A third caution applies to those who may be new to qualitative methods, and especially those who have only done quantitative research previously. It is that: **Qualitative methods are more time-consuming, require more active participation, and are quite likely more challenging and difficult to master than quantitative methods**. We are by no means saying 'don't try this at home kids; leave it to the pros'. We fully encourage you to do qualitative research and that is why we have written this book. But anyone who expects qualitative methods to be easier than quantitative methods or who turns to them because they have trouble with quantitative skills is in for a rude awakening. Qualitative research can sometimes be quickly and superficially applied by, for example, doing a couple of focus groups. But such an approach is also certain to lead to superficial understandings of the phenomenon being considered.

Conducting a high-quality depth interview or a quality observational session with detailed fieldnotes is a skill that does not come automatically from being able to talk, listen, see, and write. In fact, we would estimate that learning strong interview techniques probably requires that the researcher have at least 50 long interviews under his or her belt. Ethnographic skills transcend things that you can learn in a book and include subtle social and political skills, and the ability to remember and resonantly record what happens in the field. Acquiring these skills is something that requires significant practice. Whether face-to-face or online, qualitative research requires active engagement and generally cannot be delegated to the qualitative equivalent of a lab assistant who can 'run subjects' through a study. We also do not mean to belittle experimental and survey researchers as they, too, require skills, knowledge, and interpretative ability. However, in qualitative research, the apprenticeship and data collection period are longer. Moreover, the data produced cannot be input into a statistical program that will spit out results that seem definitive and concrete. Therefore, aspiring researchers should be prepared to invest more time in any given study – longer than with most quantitative methods and longer than you may initially anticipate. This relative time frame also holds in applied market research, even though it will most likely take place under greater time pressure than most academic studies.

A fourth recommendation also flows from, and even contradicts some of, the preceding points. In the words of an old Nike slogan: **'Just do it!'** That is, while we can offer hints, tips, methods, and suggestions, the only real way to learn qualitative methods is to use them. Having mentioned an apprenticeship in the prior paragraph we also recommend that accompanying an experienced qualitative researcher can be a great learning experience. But until you face the challenges of building trust and rapport in a depth interview, choosing what to observe amidst what may initially appear to be a bewildering chaos of action and talk, and trying to make sense of the limitless text and images of the internet in order to study a particular topic, you have not fully experienced the reality of 'doing research'. It is for this reason that we have tried to provide a bank of hands-on exercises in each of the preceding chapters. These exercises constitute a key part of the potential learning you can accomplish with this book. We are planning to extend these exercises with a social media component that will allow you to share your exercise findings with others online in a communal format. Regardless of how you approach it, knowledge and skill in becoming a better qualitative researcher cannot be taught as much as co-created by teachers and learners, to the extent that the distinction melts.

Learning by doing is the primary way of learning to do qualitative research, and probably any other form of, research. Until the last decade or two, anthropology students were essentially exiled to the field with little or nothing in terms of ethnographic training and few if any means of contacting their supervisors at their universities. They may have learnt the language fairly well and read prior ethnographies of a place before stepping into another culture, but, after that, the rest was making it up as they went along. That is, having only read a number of prior ethnographies, they were forced to use their imaginations in order to head toward such an end result themselves. In both anthropology and consumer research today, students are unlikely to be thrown to the wolves quite so harshly, and contact with the 'outside world' is far easier and instantaneous. When Gülnur Tumbat was a doctoral student being supervised by Russ she was isolated for months doing her research in the remote location of Mount Everest base camp. But still she was able to occasionally have e-mail contact with him and even, on one occasion, a telephone conversation via a satellite phone. Even so, it is fair to say that she had to use considerable ingenuity and fortitude in order to have a fieldwork experience that eventually led to an award-winning *Journal of Consumer Research* article and other publications from the dissertation-based study.

Something that has been alluded to in earlier chapters but that bears repeating is: **It is often easier to work as part of a research team than to go entirely solo.** No doubt Gülnur would have found it easier both emotionally and logistically if a research partner or team had been able to accompany her to Everest. But because it was a dissertation, because getting to base camp is quite expensive, and because this was hardly a location where researchers could pop in for a few hours and then go home to write-up fieldnotes, this was simply impossible. Even with a support team of fellow researchers, Russ reported that in his initial fieldwork experience on the Consumer Behavior Odyssey pretest:

> I had conducted focus groups before and had just completed a video class, but doing depth interviews in the field was *terra incognita*. I was simultaneously excited and frightened. We ate, slept, and breathed the swap meet and each successive interview became a little less terrifying as I learned that people are basically friendly, helpful, and rewarded by someone who takes a sincere interest in what they have to say. (Belk 1991b, p. 7)

The fact that Melanie Wallendorf and John Sherry were a part of the research team made this a far easier and more instructive initiation than it would otherwise have been. Furthermore, having a team of at least two to do video interviews with one person operating the large three-quarter-inch tape camcorder and one conducting the interviews made it far more feasible than attempting it alone. In addition, and as discussed in Chapter 7, having a research team allows memoing, debriefing, and otherwise comparing notes – a collaborative process that can be highly productive of new ideas as well as supportive of the team members.

Another recommendation that came from the Consumer Behavior Odyssey (Belk 1991a) was to: **Bring two or more of each essential piece of equipment**. As we have noted in Chapters 3 and 6, equipment like recorders, camcorders, smartphones, tablet PCs, and laptops can all fail or run out of batteries at the most inopportune times. Even pens can run out of ink and pencil leads break. For cameras and digital storage media camcorders, extra memory cards are another supply to always keep in reserve. Even with modern communication equipment available at Mount Everest base camp, Gülnur Tumbat was unlikely to find back-up equipment if she did not bring it along. This advice also applies to the researcher being prepared to retrieve entire interviews and more from memory when equipment is lost or stolen, as recounted in Chapter 6. Because the researcher is the instrument in qualitative research and because we too are fragile vessels, it is good to have backup people (the research team mentioned above) in case of sickness or other emergencies. On the Consumer Behavior Odyssey, Hal Kassarjian's wife's medical emergency kept him from the pretest, and Tom O'Guinn's injury en route on the main Odyssey took the chief camera operator out of action. Once again, a cross-trained research team saved the day.

On a more human level: **Be prepared to become emotionally involved with informants.** Unlike the hands-off approach of experiments, surveys, and analysis of secondary data, in dealing with human informants, using participant observation, prolonged engagement, depth interviews, and rapport building, we develop human relationships with our informants. This sometimes involves two-way exchanges of information and help. For example, when Russ and colleagues were doing research with gay consumers in a heavily HIV-infected region in Thailand and many revealed no knowledge of what were and were not safe sex practices, they felt it incumbent to share this information with them before leaving (Belk et al. 1998). Thus qualitative research can shade almost effortlessly into what has been called 'action' or 'participatory action' research that seeks social change (see Ozanne and Saatcioglu 2008). On other occasions, we find ourselves continuing to exchange e-mails with informants who have become friends. We have had informants invite us for meals in their homes, stay at our homes, and continue to send us material after we leave the field. We have sent or given them promised papers and videos. Rob has built an entire social network, including affiliations with a number of interesting scholars across multiple disciplinary fields, through his fieldwork at Burning Man, which required him to live and camp with groups of fellow event attendees. These sorts of socialising stories are not always the case, but researchers should be aware of the level of social engagement, particularly from ethnographic research. Although it would be surprising if any such close contact resulted from experimental or survey work, it is not all that unusual in qualitative research.

Another important injunction that you will hear repeated explicitly and implicitly through the pages of this book is: **Keep it real and stay close to your data**. You will learn many lessons and techniques as you practise qualitative research data collection and analysis methods. You will also develop your own unique style of conducting and representing your research. In fact, much like an artist, the more unique your research style, the greater is your opportunity to develop your own voice and your academic career. The University of Ulster's Stephen Brown, for example, has not only developed his own unique writing and presentation style, he has also analysed and written about the unique styles of other scholars in the marketing field (e.g., Brown 2005).

In terms of pursuing your own muse, for example, some scholars in this area of qualitative consumer and marketing research will prefer to conduct their analysis using computer programs like NVivo and Atlas.ti, while others will eschew them. We have all used these methods and all prefer to work without them using simpler data search and coding programs. Our biggest concern is that the more sophisticated programs can get between you and the data and lead to a fully grounded approach that we try to avoid. They make it difficult to transcend the data as is needed for richer etic interpretation. But do try these programs and see what they can do for you. The more powerful programs do not need to be used in their full complexity and portions of them can be used without trying all the bells and whistles. Find what works best for you and do not just rely on our advice. We suspect that in the future the tedious task of transcribing will be rendered old-fashioned due to better voice recognition software as well as the ability to code sound and video directly without the need to transcribe. With most smartphones capable of still photography, high definition video, and sound recording, there is no excuse to be unprepared for an opportunistic interview. And for the alert qualitative consumer or market researcher, you are never 'off'. There is always a chance, and often a very good chance, that you will happen upon an interesting consumption phenomenon, a great potential informant, an interesting and inspiring piece of research that you want to make note of, an interesting photo opportunity involving something unexpected, or other serendipitous research opportunities. Even (perhaps especially) if you are a doctoral student, pursue multiple research projects, be ever alert for new phenomena of interest, and be prepared to do fieldwork unexpectedly 24/7 and wherever you may happen to be.

Finally, we offer a piece of advice that we have also reinforced in various ways through the pages of this book, and that is: **Remember that research itself is a language**. We follow Wittgenstein's philosophy to its logical conclusion and see the universe of research in general, and the world of qualitative consumer and marketing research in particular, as a field of culturally-constituted meanings and dynamic social conventions. What is in style in one year, in one decade, within the pages of one journal, in one corporate environment, under one consumer insight manager, under one editorial regime, may change with the next. Thus it is extremely important that you as a researcher learn the languages, norms, and customs of this perhaps strange group of persons you call, or will call, your peers, and others who will both evaluate your work and be evaluated by you. Although we have gone to sometimes painstaking lengths to assert what quality work is in this area of investigation, and how to represent and judge it, these standards are in constant flux. Your only sustainable strategy is to learn the relevant language of research and then to keep up with the current conversations.

The way to do this in an academic context is to continue to read top research journals, to review for them, and to attend and participate in at least some top conferences. If you are primarily an academic researcher, plan to attend the annual *Association of Consumer Research* and *Consumer Culture Theory* conferences. If you are working with industry and doing applied qualitative research, *EPIC* (the annual Ethnographic Praxis in Industry Conference – http://epiconference.com/) should be on your agenda: it is where applied qualitative researchers come together to discuss how best to integrate qualitative methods in business practices and to develop a mutual understanding of the evolution of 'best' practices.

Understanding the current language and form of consumer and marketing research will also keep you from thinking that one form or another research technique or method provides an inside pathway to a truth, even though it can never be 'the Truth'. Science involves a grammar, an accent, a mastery of inflection. Like language itself, acceptable views of ostensibly 'objective', but always consensual, 'reality', are constantly changing, diverse, and multifaceted. Yet they intelligibly underpin all our research.

Qualitative research can be a process of self-discovery. We mean this both in the sense of discovering new qualitative techniques for yourself and in the sense of discovering yourself via qualitative research. Because we are most often prone to study things that pique our curiosity, that we become aware of and find interesting, or that we have been involved in but have not had the chance to study and reflect upon, you may have many opportunities to explore yourself in the course of conducting qualitative research. And because we define ourselves in contrast to others, by learning about others who are similar to and different from us, we also learn about ourselves. Often times we learn more about a consumption phenomenon by beginning at extremes. For example, if you were interested how people relate to money, it would be useful to begin with one or several self-labelled misers and one or more self-labelled spendthrifts. You can later study people in the middle, but going to extremes helps patterns to emerge sooner and more clearly. The same goes for interpretation. Unlike quantitative research where extreme cases are regarded as 'outliers' and omitted from analysis, in qualitative research they are often the most interesting and informative cases as we seek to understand why people engage in extreme consumer behaviours.

We could go on, but we do not want to spoil the fun of your own voyage of discovery using qualitative research methods. We hope that this book has broadened your horizons about what constitutes contemporary qualitative consumer and market research. We hope that it has provided enough examples and exercises to inspire your confidence and either get you started or advance your skills in qualitative research. And we hope that we have opened you to the different types of qualitative research, the different audiences (e.g., academic and corporate, differing research traditions and journal expectations), and different possibilities for presenting qualitative research. We know that if you embrace qualitative methods as we have that you will find a community of kindred spirits in colleagues who have also embraced such methods. They may not be in your company or university, and in that case it is all the more necessary to reach out and find them. We three have been extremely fortunate to have wound up on the same faculty and to also share our predilections for qualitative methods with insightful and similarly disposed colleagues like Sammy Bonsu, Markus Giesler, Detlev Zwick, various visiting faculty and doctoral students, and a revolving set of Schulich doctoral students, the majority of whom pursue qualitative dissertations. But we realise that we are the exception more than the rule. Chances are that you will find your enthusiasm for qualitative methods something you need to explain to your department or company. We hope that we have given you some useful material for doing so.

References

Abrahamson, Eric and David H. Freedman (2006) *A Perfect Mess: The Hidden Benefits of Disorder*, New York: Little, Brown and Company.

Abrams, Bill (2000) *The Observational Research Handbook: Understanding How Consumers Live With Your Product*, Lincolnwood, IL: NTC.

Achbar, Mark and Jennifer Abbott (2005) 'The Corporation', 145:00 minutes, Zeitgeist Films.

Adrian, Bonnie (2003) *Framing the Bride: Globalizing Beauty and Romance in Taiwan's Bridal Industry*, Berkeley, CA: University of California Press.

Agee, James and Walker Evans (1941) *Let Us Now Praise Famous Men*, Cambridge, MA: Riverside Press.

Allen, Douglas (2002) 'Toward a Theory of Consumer Choice as Sociohistorically Shaped Practical Experience: The Fits-Like-A-Glove (FLAG) Framework', *Journal of Consumer Research*, 28 (March), 515–532.

Alvesson, Mats (2003 'Beyond Neo Positivists, Romantics and Localists: A Reflexive Approach to Interviews in Organizational Research', *Academy of Management Review*, 28 (1), 13–33.

Alvesson, Mats and Dan Kärremann (2011) *Qualitative Research and Theory Development: Mystery as Method*. Thousand Oaks, CA: Sage.

Anderson, Paul (1983) 'Marketing, Scientific Progress and Scientific Methods', *Journal of Marketing*, 47 (Fall), 18–31.

Anfara, Vincent and Norma Mertz (2006) *Theoretical Frameworks in Qualitative Research*, Thousand Oaks, CA: Sage.

Angrosino, M. (2007) *Doing Ethnographic and Observational Research*, London: Sage.

Arbitron (no date) 'The Bedroom Study'. Available online at http://www.thebedroomstudy.com/.

Arnold, Stephen and Eileen Fischer (1994) 'Hermeneutics and Consumer Research', *Journal of Consumer Research*, 21 (1), 55–70.

Arnould, Eric J. (1989) 'Toward a Broadened Theory of Preference Formation and the Diffusion of Innovations: Cases from Zinder Province, Niger Republic', *Journal of Consumer Research*, 16 (September), 239–67.

Arnould, Eric J. and Craig J. Thompson (2005) 'Consumer. Culture Theory (CCT): Twenty Years of Research', *Journal of Consumer Research*, 31 (March), 868–882.

―――― and ―――― (2007) Consumer Culture Theory (And We Really Mean Theoretics) in Russell W. Belk and John F. Sherry (eds) *Consumer Culture Theory* (Research in Consumer Behavior, Volume 11), Emerald Group Publishing Limited, pp. 3–22.

Arnould, Eric J. and Linda L. Price (1993) 'River Magic: Hedonic Consumption and the Extended Service Encounter', *Journal of Consumer Research*, 20 (June), 24–45.

Arnould, Eric and Melanie Wallendorf (1994) 'Market Oriented Ethnography: Interpretation Building and Marketing Strategy Formulation', *Journal of Marketing Research*, 31 (November), 484–504.

Arsel, Zeynep and Craig Thompson (2011) 'Demythologizing Consumption Practices: How Consumers Protect Their Field-Dependent Identity Investments from Devaluing Marketplace Myths', *Journal of Consumer Research*, 37 (February), 791–806.

Ayers, Michael P. (ed.) (2006) *Cybersounds: Essays on Virtual Music Culture*, New York: Peter Lang.

Baker, Stephen (2009) 'Netflix Isn't Done Mining Consumer Data, Company's Goal is to "Predict People Earlier" – When they First get to Site', *Business Week*, 22 September, accessed online at http://www.msnbc.msn.com/id/32969539/ns/business-us_business/t/netflix-isnt-done-mining-consumer-data/#.T0pybUret1A.

Banks, Marcus (2001) *Visual Methods in Social Research*, London: Sage.

Banks, Marcus (2007) *Using Visual Data in Qualitative Research*, Los Angeles, CA: Sage.

Barbash, Ilisa and Lucien Taylor (1997) *Cross-Cultural Filmmaking: A Handbook for Making Documentary and Ethnogaphic Films and Videos*, Berkeley, CA: University of California Press.

Barbour, Rosaline (2008) *Doing Focus Groups*, London: Sage.

Basil, Michael (2011) 'Use of Photography and Video in Observational Research', *Qualitative Market Research*, 14 (3), 246–257.

Baym, Nancy (2010) *Personal Connections in the Digital Age*, Cambridge: Polity.

Beaven, Zuleika and Chantal Laws (2007) '"Never Let Me Down Again": Loyal Customer Attitudes Towards Ticket Distribution Channels for Live Music Events: A Netnographic Exploration of the US Leg of the Depeche Mode 2005–2006 World Tour', *Managing Leisure*, 12 (April), 120–142.

Belk, Russell (1978) 'Assessing the Effects of Visible Consumption on Impression Formation', in H. Keith Hunt (ed.), *Advances in Consumer Research*, 5, pp. 39–47.

—— (1985) 'Materialism: Trait Aspects of Living in the Material World', *Journal of Consumer Research*, 12 (December), 265–280.

—— (1986) 'Art Versus Science as Ways of Generating Knowledge About Materialism', in David Brinberg and Richard J. Lutz (eds), *Perspectives on Methodology in Consumer Research*, New York: Springer-Verlag, pp. 3–36.

—— (1989) 'Visual Images of Consumption: What you See and What you Get', in Terrence Childers and Richard Bagozzi (eds), *1989 AMA Winter Educators' Conference: Marketing Theory and Practice*, Chicago: American Marketing Association, 122.

—— (1991a) 'Epilogue: Lessons Learned', in Russell Belk (ed.), *Highways and Buyways: Naturalistic Research from the Consumer Behavior Odyssey*, Provo, UT: Association for Consumer Research, pp. 234–238.

—— (1991b) 'The History and Development of the Consumer Behavior Odyssey', in Russell W. Belk (ed.), *Highways and Buyways: Naturalistic Research from the Consumer Behavior Odyssey*, Provo: Association for Consumer Research, pp. 1–12.

—— (1992) 'Moving Possessions: An Analysis Based on Personal Documents from the 1847–1869 Mormon Migration', *Journal of Consumer Research*, 19 (December), 339–361.

—— (1994) 'Battling Worldliness in the New Zion: Mercantilism Versus Homespun in 19th Century Utah', *Journal of Macromarketing*, 14 (Spring), 9–22.

—— (1998) 'Multimedia Approaches to Qualitative Data and Representations', in Barbara B. Stern (ed.), *Representing Consumers: Voices, Views and Visions*, London: Routledge, pp. 308–338.

—— (2006) 'You Ought to be in Pictures: Envisioning Marketing Research', in Naresh Malholtra (ed.), *Review of Marketing Research*, 3, Armonk, NY: M.E. Sharpe, pp. 193–205.

—— (2007) 'I See What You Mean: The Role of Video in Transformative Consumer Research', 30:00 minutes, Toronto: Odyssey Films.

—— (2011a) 'Consumer Behavior Odyssey Redux', 20:10 minutes, Toronto: Odyssey Films, (for Marketing Science Institute).

—— (2011b) 'Examining Markets, Marketing, Consumers, and Society through Documentary Films', *Journal of Macromarketing*, 31 (December), 403–409.

Belk, Russell, Kenneth Bahn, and Robert Mayer (1982) 'Developmental Recognition of Consumption Symbolism', *Journal of Consumer Research*, 9 (June), 4–17.

Belk, Russell and Janeen Arnold Costa (1998) 'The Mountain Man Myth: A Contemporary Consuming Fantasy', *Journal of Consumer Research*, 25 (December), 218–240.

Belk, Russell and Janeen A. Costa (2001) 'The Rendezvous as Bounded Utopia', 22:00 minutes, Salt Lake City, UT: Odyssey Films.

Belk, Russell, Timothy Devinney, and Giana Eckhardt (2005) 'Consumer Ethics Across Cultures', *Consumption, Markets and Culture*, with Timothy Devinney and Giana Eckhardt, 8 (September), 275–290, with accompanying 26:00 minute video; also in working paper form. Available online at http://repositories.cdlib.org/crb/wps/23, http://www.inpsicon.com/elconsumidor/archivos/consumer_ethics_eng.pdf (English), and http://www.inpsicon.com/elconsumidor/archivos/consumer_ethics.pdf (Spanish).

Belk, Russell W. and Güliz Ger (1995) 'Art and Development: Socio-Economic, Cultural, and Historical Perspectives', (abstract), in Annamma Joy, Kunal Basu, and Zheng Hangsheng (eds), *Marketing and Development*, Beijing: International Society for Marketing and Development, pp. 447–450.

—— and —— (2005) 'Emergence of Consumer Cultures: A Cross-Cultural and (Art) Historical Comparison' (abstract), *The Future of Marketing's Past: Proceedings of the Twelfth Conference on Historical Analysis and Research in Marketing* (CHARM), 337.

Belk, Russell, Güliz Ger, and Søren Askegaard (2003) 'The Fire of Desire: A Multisited Inquiry into Consumer Passion', *Journal of Consumer Research*, 30 (3), 326–351.

Belk, Russell W. and Robert V. Kozinets, (2005) 'Videography in marketing and consumer research', *Qualitative Marketing Research*, 8 (2), 128–141.

—— and —— (2012) 'The Last Picture Show', Advances in Consumer Research.

Belk, Russell W., Per Østergaard, and Ronald Groves (1998) 'Sexual Consumption in the Time of AIDS: A Study of Prostitute Patronage in Thailand', *Journal of Public Policy and Marketing*, 17 (4), 197–214.

Belk, Russell W., Joon Yong Seo and Eric Li (2007) 'Dirty Little Secret: Home Chaos and Professional Organizers', *Consumption, Markets and Culture*, 10 (2), 133–140.

Belk, Russell, John Sherry and Melanie Wallendorf (1988) 'A Naturalistic Inquiry into Buyer and Seller Behavior at a Swap Meet', *Journal of Consumer Research*, 14 (4), 449–470.

Belk, Russell and Gülnur Tumbat (2005) 'The Cult of Macintosh', *Consumption, Markets and Culture*, 8 (September), 205–218.

Belk, Russell, Melanie Wallendorf and John Sherry (1989) 'The Sacred and the Profane in Consumer Behavior: Theodicy on the Odyssey', *Journal of Consumer Research*, 16 (1) 1–38.

Belk, Russell W. and Joyce Yeh (2011) 'Tourist Photography: Signs of Self', *International Journal of Culture, Tourism, and Hospitality*, 5 (1), 345–353.

Berger, Peter and Thomas Luckmann (1966) *The Social Construction of Reality: A Treatise in the Sociology of Knowledge*, Garden City, NY: Anchor Books.

Berkowitz, S.D. (1982) *An Introduction to Structural Analysis: The Network Approach to Social Research*, Toronto, ON: Butterworth.

Boellstorff, Tom (2008) *Coming of Age in Second Life: An Anthropologist Explores the Virtually Human*, Princeton, NJ: Princeton University Press.

Bonoma, Thomas (1985) 'Case Research in Marketing: Opportunities, Problems and a Process', *Journal of Marketing Research*, 22 (May) 199–208.

Bourdieu, Pierre (1977) *Outline of a Theory of Practice*, Cambridge: Cambridge University Press.

Bradshaw, Alan and Stephen Brown (2008) 'Scholars Who Stare at Goats: The Collaborative Circle Cycle in Creative Consumer Research', *European Marketing Journal*, 42 (11/12), 1396–1414.

Brown, Jane D., Carol Reese Dykers, Jeanne Rogge Steele, and Anner Barton White (1994) 'Teenage Room Culture: Where Media and Identities Intersect', *Communication Research*, 31 (6), 813–827.

Brown, Stephen (1998) 'Unlucky for Some: Slacker Scholarship and the Well-Wrought Turn', in Barbara B. Stern (ed.), *Representing Consumers: Voices, Views, and Visions*, London: Routledge, pp. 365–383.

—— (2005) *Writing Marketing: Literary Lessons from Academic Authorities*, London: Sage.

———— (2006a) 'Autobiography', in Russell Belk (ed.), *Handbook of Qualitative Research Methods in Marketing*, Cheltenham, UK: Edward Elgar, pp. 440–452.

———— (2006b) *The Marketing Code*, London: Cyan.

———— (2008) *Agents and Dealers*, Singapore: Marshall Cavendish.

———— (2009) *The Lost Logo*, Singapore: Marshall Cavendish. Available online at http://www.sfxbrown.com/books_list.php?category_name=All.

Brown, Stephen, Robert V. Kozinets, and John F. Sherry, Jr. (2003) 'Teaching Old Brands New Tricks: Retro Branding and the Revival of Brand Meaning', *Journal of Marketing*, 67 (July) 19–33.

Brownlie, Douglas and Paul Hewer (2007) 'Culture of Consumption of Car Aficionados: Aesthetics and Consumption Communities', *International Journal of Sociology and Social Policy*, 27 (January), 106–119.

Bruckman, Amy (2006) 'Teaching Students to Study Online Communities Ethically', *Journal of Information Ethics*, Fall, 82–98.

Bull, Michael (2007) *Sound Moves: iPod Culture and the Urban Experience*, London: Routledge.

Burgess, Jean and Joshua Green (2010) *YouTube*, London: Polity.

Burrell, Gibson and Gareth Morgan (1979) *Sociological Paradigms and Organizational Analysis: Element of the Sociology of Organizational Life*, London: Heinemann.

Calder, Bobby and Alice Tybout (1987) 'What Consumer Research Is …', *Journal of Consumer Research*, 14 (1), 136–140.

Caldwell, Mary Louise, Paul Henry, and Stephen Watson (2008) 'A Right to Life: Reducing Maternal Death and Morbidity in Pakistan', 58:48 minutes, University of Sydney Film Unit.

Caplovitz, David (1963) *The Poor Pay More*, New York: Free Press.

Catterall, Miriam (1998) 'Academics, Practitioners and Qualitative Market Research', *Qualitative Market Research*, 1 (2), 69–76.

Catterall, Miriam and Pauline Maclaren (2006) 'Focus Groups in Marketing Research', in Russell Belk (ed.), *Handbook of Qualitative Research Methods in Marketing*, Cheltenham, UK: Edward Elgar, pp. 255–267.

Chalfen, Richard (1987) *Snapshot Visions of Life*, Bowling Green, OH: Bowling Green State University Popular Press.

Chan, Kara (2006) 'Exploring Children's Perceptions of Material Possessions: A Drawing Study', *Qualitative Market Research*, 9 (4), 352–366.

Cherny, Lynn (1999) *Conversation and Community: Chat in a Virtual World*, Stanford: Center for the Study of Language and Information.

Cios, Krzysztof J., Witold Pedrycz, Roman W. Swiniarski (2007) *Data Mining: A Knowledge Discovery Approach*, New York: Springer.

Clark, Cindy Dell (1995) *Flights of Fancy, Leaps of Faith: Children's Myths in Contemporary America*, Chicago: University of Chicago Press.

Clifford, James (1988) *The Predicament of Culture: Twentieth-Century Ethnography, Literature, and Art*, Cambridge, MA: Harvard University Press.

Clifford, James and George Marcus (eds) (1986) *Writing Culture: the Poetics and Politics of Ethnography*, Berkeley, CA: University of California Press.

Collett, Peter (1984) 'History and the Study of Expressive Action', in Kenneth Gergen and N.M. Gergen (eds), *Historical Social Psychology*, Hillsdale, NJ: Lawrence Erlbaum, pp. 371–396.

Cooper, Charlotte (2008) 'What's Fat Activism?' Working Paper, University of Limerick, Department of Sociology Working Paper Series. Available online http://www.ul.ie/sociology/docstore/workingpapers/wp2008-02.pdf (last accessed 05/11/2011).

Cote, Joseph A., James McCullough, and Michael Reilly (1985) 'Effects of Unexpected Situations on Behavior-Intention Differences: A Garbology Analysis', *Journal of Consumer Research*, 12 (September), 188–194.

Coulter, Robin (2006) 'Consumption Experiences as Escape: An Application of the Zaltman Metaphor Elicitation Technique', in Russell Belk (ed.), *Handbook of Qualitative Research Methods in Marketing*, Cheltenham, UK: Edward Elgar, pp. 400–418.

Coulter, Robin, Linda Price, and Lawrence Feick (2003) 'Rethinking the Origins of Involvement and Brand Commitment: Insights from Postsocialist Central Europe', *Journal of Consumer Research*, 30 (September), 151–169.

Coupland, Jennifer Chang (2005) 'Invisible Brands: An Ethnography of Households and Their Brands in their Kitchen Pantries', *Journal of Consumer Research*, 32 (June), 106–118.

Crandall, David and Noah Snaveley (2011) 'Networks of Photos, Landmarks, and People', *Leonardo*, 44 (June), online journal.

Cresswell, John (2007) *Qualitative Inquiry and Research Design: Choosing Among Give Approaches*, 2nd edn, Thousand Oaks, CA: Sage.

Danes, Jeffrey E., Jeffrey S. Hess, John W. Story, and Jonathan L. York (2010) 'Brand Image Associations for Large Virtual Groups', *Qualitative Market Research*, 13 (3), 309–323.

Davies, Bronwyn and Rom Harré (1990) 'Positioning: The Discursive Production of Selves', *Journal for the Theory of Social Behaviour*, 20 (1), 44–63.

Davis, Murray S. (1971) 'That's Interesting! Towards a Phenomenology of Sociology and a Sociology of Phenomenology', *Philosophy of the Social Sciences*, 1 (2), 309–344.

Denzin, Norman K. (1989) *Interpretive Interactionism*, Newbury Park, CA: Sage.

Dichter, Ernest (1947) 'Psychology in Marketing Research', *Harvard Business Review*, 25 (4), 432–443.

Douglas, Jack (1986) *Creative Interviewing*, Beverly Hills, CA: Sage.

Douglas, Jack, Paul Rasmussen, and Carol Ann Flanagan (1977) *The Nude Beach*, Beverly Hills, CA: Sage.

Douglas, Mary (1966) *Purity and Danger: An Analysis of the Concepts of Pollution and Taboo*, London: Routledge and Kegan Paul.

Duarte, Nancy (2008) *Slide:ology: The Art and Science of Creating Great Presentations*, Sebastopol, CA: O'Reilly.

Duhachek, Adam (2005) 'Coping: A Multidimensional, Hierarchical Framework of Responses to Stressful Consumption Episodes', *Journal of Consumer Research*, 32 (June), 41–53.

Durgee, Jeffrey F. (1991) 'Interpreting Dichter's Interpretations: An Analysis of Consumption Symbolism in *The Handbook of Consumer Motivations*' in Claus Alsted, David Mick and Hanne Larsen (eds), *Marketing and Semiotics: The Copenhagen Symposium*, Copenhagen: Handelshojskolens Forlag, pp. 52–69.

Durgee, Jeffrey and Manli Chen (2006) 'Metaphors, Needs and New Product Ideation', in Russell Belk (ed.), *Handbook of Qualitative Research Methods in Marketing*, Cheltenham, UK: Edward Elgar, pp. 291–302.

Eckhardt, Giana M. and Anders Bengtsson (2010) 'A Brief History of Branding in China', *Journal of Macromarketing*, 30 (September), 210–222.

Ekström, Karin (2006) 'The Emergence of Multi-Sited Ethnography in Anthropology and Marketing', in Russell Belk (ed.), *Handbook of Qualitative Research Methods in Marketing*, Cheltenham, UK: Edward Elgar, pp. 497–508.

Eisenhardt, Kathleen (1989) 'Building Theories from Case Study Research', *Academy of Management Review*, 14 (4), 532–550.

Ellen, R.F., ed. (1984), *Ethnographic Research: A Guide To General Conduct*, London: Academic Press.

Elliott, Jane (2005) *Using Narrative in Social Research: Qualitative and Quantitative Approaches*, Thousand Oaks, CA: Sage.

Elliott, Richard and Andrea Davies (2006) 'Using Oral History Methods in Consumer Research', in Russell Belk (ed.), *Handbook of Qualitative Research Methods in Marketing*, Cheltenham, UK: Edward Elgar, pp. 255–267.

Ellis, Carolyn (2004) *The Ethnographic I: A Methodological Novel about Autoethnography*, Walnut Creek, CA: AltaMira Press.

Ellis, Jack C. and Betsy A. McLane (2007) *A New History of Documentary Film*, New York: Continuum, pp. 61–81.

Ellwood, Alison (2005) 'Enron: The Smartest Guys in the Room', 110:00 minutes, Los Angeles, CA: Magnolia Pictures.

Ely, Margot, Ruth Vinz, Maryann Dowling, and Margaret Anzu (1997) *On Writing Qualitative Research*, London: Falmer Press.

Emerson, Robert M., Rachel I. Fretz and Linda L Shaw (1995), *Writing Ethnographic Fieldnotes*, Chicago and London: University of Chicago Press.

Emmison, Michael and Philip Smith (2000) *Researching the Visual*, London: Sage.

Epp, Amber M. and Linda L. Price (2010), 'The Storied Life of Singularized Objects: Forces of Agency and Network Transformation,' *Journal of Consumer Research*, 36 (February), 820–837.

Farnell, Brenda and Joan Huntley (1995) 'Ethnogaphy Goes Interactive', *Anthropology Today*, 11 (October), 7–14.

Feenberg, Andrew (2010) *Between Reason and Experience: Essays in Technology and Modernity*, Cambridge, MA: MIT Press.

Fernandez, James (2000) 'The Wild Man and the Elephant: A Revelatory Incident', *Anthropology and Humanism*, 25 (2), 189–194.

Fernback, Jan (1999) 'There is a There There: Notes Toward a Definition of Cybercomunity', in Steve Jones, (ed.), *Doing Internet Research: Critical Issues and Methods for Examining the Net*, pp. 203–220.

Fetterman, David M. (2010) *Ethnography: Step by Step*, 3rd edn, Thousand Oaks, CA: Sage.

Firat, A. Fuat and Alladi Venkatesh (1995) 'Liberatory Postmodernism and the Reenchantment of Consumption', *Journal of Consumer Research*, 22 (December), 239–267.

Fischer, Eileen and Stephen Arnold (1990) 'More Than a Labor of Love: Gender Roles and Christmas Gift Shopping', *Journal of Consumer Research*, 17 (December), 333–345.

Fischer, Eileen and Cele Otnes (2006) 'Breaking New Ground: Developing Grounded Theories in Marketing and Consumer Behavior', in Russell Belk (ed.), *Handbook of Qualitative Research Methods in Marketing*, Cheltenham, UK: Edward Elgar.

Fischer, Eileen, Cele Otnes, and Linda Tuncay (2007) 'Pursuing Parenthood: Integrating Cultural and Cognitive Perspectives on Persistent Goal Striving', *Journal of Consumer Research*, 34 (3), 425–440.

Flick, Uwe (2007) *Using Visual Data in Qualitative Research*, London: Sage.

Fournier, Susan (1998) 'Consumers and their Brands: Developing Relationship Theory in Consumer Research', *Journal of Consumer Research*, 24 (March), 343–373.

Fox, Fiona E., Marianne Morris, and Nichola Rumsey (2007) 'Doing Synchronous Online Focus Groups with Young People: Methodological Reflections', *Qualitative Health Research*, 17 (April), 539–547.

Fox, Josh (2010) 'Gasland', 107:00 minutes, HBO Documentary Films.

Freedman, Russell and Lewis Hine (1994) *Kids at Work: Lewis Hine and the Crusade Against Child Labor*, New York: Clarion Books.

Fullerton, R.A. (1990) 'The Art of Marketing Research: Selection from Paul F. Lazarsfeld's "Shoe buying in Zurich"', *Journal of the Academy of Marketing Science*, 18 (4), 319–327.

Füller, Johann, Gregor Jawecki, and Hans Mühlbacher (2006) 'Innovation Creation by Online Basketball Communities', *Journal of Business Research*, 60 (1), 60–71.

Garcia, Angela Cora, Alecea I. Standless, Jennifer Bechkoff, and Yan Cui (2009) 'Ethnographic Approaches to the Internet and Computer-Mediated Communication', *Journal of Contemporary Ethnography*, 38 (1), February, 52–84.

Garfinkel, Harold (1967) *Studies in Ethnomethodology*, Englewood Cliffs, NJ: Prentice Hall.

Gaskell, George (2000) 'Individual and Group Interviewing', in Martin Bauer and George Gaskell (eds), *Qualitative Research with Text, Image and Sound: A Practical Handbook for Social Research*, London: Sage, pp. 38–56.

Geertz, Clifford (1973) *The Interpretation of Cultures*, New York: Basic Books.

Giesler, Markus (2008) 'Conflict and Compromise: Drama in Marketplace Evolution', *Journal of Consumer Research*, 34 (April), 739–753.

Gietlman, Lisa (2008) *Always Already New: Media, History and the Data of Culture*, Cambridge, MA: MIT Press.

Giorgi, Amedeo (1985) 'Phenomenological Psychology of Learning and the Verbal Tradition', in Amedeo Giorgi (ed.), *Phenomenology and Psychological Research*, Pittsburgh, PA: Duquesne University Press, pp. 23–85.

Glaser, Barney. (2001) *The Grounded Theory Perspective: Conceptualization Contrasted with Description*, Mill Valley, CA: Sociology Press.

Glaser, Barney and Anselm Strauss (1967) *The Discovery of Grounded Theory*, Chicago: Aldine.

Goffman, Erving (1963) *Stigma: Notes on the Management of Spoiled Identity*, Englewood Cliffs, NJ: Prentice-Hall.

—— (1988) *Gender Advertisements*, New York: Harper Collins.

—— (1989) 'On Fieldwork', *Journal of Contemporary Ethnography*, 18, 123–132.

Goldberg, Jim (1985) Rich and Poor, New York: Random House.

Goldstein, Barry M. (2007) 'All Photos Lie: Images as Data', in Gregory C. Stanczak (ed.), *Visual Research Methods: Image, Society, and Representation*, Thousand Oaks, CA: Sage, pp. 61–81.

Goodenough, Florence (1926) *Measurement of Intelligence by Drawings*, New York: Harcourt, Brace and World.

Gordon, Wendy and Roy Langmaid (1988) *Qualitative Market Research: A Practitioner's and Buyer's Guide*, Aldershot, UK: Gower.

Gosling, Sam (2008) *Snoop: What Your Stuff Says About You*, New York: Basic Books.

Gould, Leroy C., Andrew L. Walker, Lansing E. Crane, and Charles W. Lidz (1974) *Connections: Notes from the Heroin World*, New Haven, CT: Yale University Press.

Gould, Stephen Jay (1991), 'The Self-Manipulation of My Pervasive, Vital Energy through Product Use: An Introspective-Praxis Approach,' *Journal of Consumer Research*, 18 (September), 194–207.

—— (1995) 'Researcher Introspection as a Method in Consumer Research: Applications, Issues, and Implications', *Journal of Consumer Research*, 21 (March), 719–722.

—— (2006) 'Unpacking the Many Faces of Interpretive Research', in Russell Belk (ed.), *Handbook of Qualitative Research Methods in Marketing*, Cheltenham, UK: Edward Elgar, pp. 186–197.

Goulding, Christina, Avi Shankar, Richard Elliott, and Robin Canniford (2009) 'The Marketplace Management of Illicit Pleasure', *Journal of Consumer Research*, 35 (5), 759–771.

Grant, Barry K. (2003) *Five Films by Frederick Wiseman*, Berkeley, CA: University of California Press.

Grant, Barry K. and Jeannette Sloniowski (ed.) (1998) *Documenting the Documentary: Closed Readings of Documentary Film and Video*, Detroit, MI: Wayne State University Press.

Grayson, Kent and David Shulman (2000), 'Indexicality and the Verification Function of Irreplaceable Possessions: A Semiotic Analysis', *Journal of Consumer Research*, 27 (June), 17–30.

Grayson, Kent and Radan Martinec (2004) 'Consumer Perceptions of Iconicity and Indexicality and Their Influence on Assessments of Authentic Market Offerings', *Journal of Consumer Research*, 31, (2) (September), 296–312.

Greenwald, Robert (2005) 'Wal-Mart: The High Cost of Low Price', 97:00 minutes, Retail Project LLC.

Gregson, Nicky (2007) *Living with Things: Ridding, Accommodation, Dwelling*, Wantage, UK: Sean Kingston.

Greimas, Algirdas (1987) *On Meaning: Selected Writings in Semiotic Theory*, trans. Paul J. Perron and Frank H. Collins, London: Frances Pinter.

Grenful, Michael (2004) *Pierre Bourdieu Agent Provocateur*, London, England: Continuum.

Gugenheim, Davis (2006) 'An Inconvenient Truth', 100:00 minutes, Lawrence Bender Productions.

Hagen, Charles (1985) *American Photographers of the Depression*, New York: Pantheon.

Haire, Mason (1950) 'Projective Techniques in Marketing Research', *Journal of Marketing*, 14 (April) 649–656.

Hamilton, Gary G. and Chi-kong Lai (1989) 'Consumerism without Capitalism: Consumption and Brand Names in Late Imperial China', in Henry J. Rutz and Benjamin S. Orlove (eds), *The Social Economy of Consumption*, Lanham, MD: University Press, pp. 253–279.

Hampe, Barry (2007) *Making Documentary Films and Reality Videos: A Practical Guide to Planning, Filming, and Editing Documentaries of Real Events*, New York: Holt.

Han, Jiawei, Micheline Kamber, and Jian Pei (2012) *Data Mining: Concepts and Techniques*, Waltham, MA: Elsevier.

Havlena, William J. and Susan L. Holak (1996) 'Exploring Nostalgia Imagery Through the Use of Consumer Collages', *Advances in Consumer Research*, 23, 35–42.

Haythornthwaite, Caroline (2005) 'Social Networks and Internet Connectivity Effects', *Information, Communication and Society*, 8 (June), 125–147.

Hawes-Davis, Doug (2002) 'This is Nowhere', 67:00 minutes, Missoula, MT: High Plains Films.

Heath, Christian, Jon Hindmarsh, and Paul Luff (2010) *Video in Qualitative Research: Analysing Social Interaction in Everyday Life*, Los Angeles, CA: Sage.

Heisley, Deborah and Sidney Levy (1991) 'Autodriving: A Photoelicitation Technique', *Journal of Consumer Research*, 18 (December), 257–272.

Heisley, Deborah D., Mary Ann McGrath, and John F. Sherry, Jr. (1991) '"To Everything There Is a Season:" A Photoessay of a Farmer's Market', in Russell W. Belk (ed.), *Highways and Buyways: Naturalistic Research from the Consumer Behaviour Odyssey*, Provo, UT: Association for Consumer Research, pp. 141–166.

Hen, Wendy and Stephanie O'Donohoe (2011) 'Mobile Phones as an Extension of the Participant Observer's Self: Reflections on the Emergent Role of an Emergent Technology', *Qualitative Market Research: An International Journal*, 14 (3), 2011, 258–273.

Henry, Paul (2010) 'How Mainstream Consumers think about Consumers' Rights and Responsibilities', *Journal of Consumer Research*, 37 (December), 670–687.

Hill, Carole and Marietta Baba (1997) 'The International Practice of Anthropology: A Critical Overview', in M. Baba and C. Hill (eds), *The Global Practice of Anthropology*, Williamsburg, VA: Dept of Anthropology College of William and Mary, pp. 1–24.

Hill, Ronald Paul (1991), 'Homeless Women, Special Possessions, and the Meaning of "Home": An Ethnographic Case Study', *Journal of Consumer Research*, 18 (December), 298–310.

Hill, Ronald Paul and Mark Stamey (1990), 'The Homeless in America: An Examination of Possession and Consumption Behaviors,' *Journal of Consumer Research*, 17 (December), 303–321.

Hirschman, Elizabeth (1986) 'Humanistic Inquiry in Market Research: Philosophy, Method and Criteria', *Journal of Marketing Research*, 23 (August), 237–249.

——— (1988) 'The Ideology of Consumption: A Structural-Syntactic Analysis of Dallas and Dynasty', *Journal of Consumer Research*, 15 (December), 344–359.

——— (ed.) (1989) *Interpretive Consumer Research*, Provo, UT: Association for Consumer Research.

Hobbs, Dick (2006) 'Ethnography', in Victor Jupp (ed.) *Sage Dictionary of Social Research Methods*, Thousand Oaks, CA and London: Sage.

Holbrook, Morris B. (1988) 'An Interpretation: Gremlins as Metaphors for Materialism', *Journal of Macromarketing*, 8 (Spring), 54–59.

——— (1998) 'Journey to Kroywen: An Ethnoscopic Auto-Auto-Auto-Driven Stereographic Photo Essay', in Barbara B. Stern (ed.), *Representing Consumers: Voices, Views and Visions*, London: Routledge, pp. 231–263.

——— (2005) 'Customer Value and Autoethnography: Subjective Personal Introspection and the Meanings of a Photograph Collection', *Journal of Business Research*, 58 (1), 45–61.

Holbrook, Morris and Mark Grayson (1986) 'The Semiology of Cinematic Consumption: Symbolic Consumer Behavior in Out of Africa', *Journal of Consumer Research*, 13 (3), 374–381.

Holbrook, Morris B. and Elizabeth C. Hirschman (1993) *The Semiotics of Consumption: Interpreting Symbolic Consumer Behavior in Popular Culture and Works of Art*, New York: Mouton De Gruyter.

Holstein, James A. and Jaber F. Gubrium (1994), 'Phenomenology, Ethnomethodology, and Interpretive Practice,' in *Handbook of Qualitative Research*, eds Norman K. Denzin and Yvonna S. Lincoln, Thousand Oaks, CA: Sage, 262–272.

Holt, Douglas B. (1995), 'How Consumers Consume: A Typology of Consumption Practices,' *Journal of Consumer Research*, 22 (June), 1–16.

——— (2002) 'Why Do Brands Cause Trouble? A Dialectical Theory of Consumer Culture and Branding', *Journal of Consumer Research*, 29 (June), 70–90.

——— (2004) *How Brands Become Icons: The Principles of Cultural Branding*, Cambridge, MA: Harvard Business School.

Holt, Douglas B. and Craig J. Thompson (2004) 'Man-of-Action Heroes: The Pursuit of Heroic Masculinity in Everyday Consumption', *Journal of Consumer Research*, 31 (September), 425–440.

Hopkinson, Gillian C. and Margaret K. Hogg (2006) 'Stories: How they are Used and Produced in Market(ing) Research', in Russell Belk (ed.), *Handbook of Qualitative Research Methods in Marketing*, Cheltenham, UK: Edward Elgar, pp. 156–174.

Hudson, Laurel Anderson and Julie L. Ozanne (1988) 'Alternative Ways of Seeking Knowledge in Consumer Research', *Journal of Consumer Research*, 14 (March), 508–521.

Humphreys, Ashlee (2006) 'The Consumer as Foucauldian "Object of Knowledge"', *Social Science Computer Review*, 24 (3), 296–309.

Humphreys, Ashlee (2010) 'Megamarketing: The Creation of Markets as a Social Process', *Journal of Marketing*, 74 (2), 19.

Hunt, Shelby (1990) 'Truth in Marketing Theory and Research', *Journal of Marketing*, 54 (July), 1–15.

Iacobucci, Dawn (ed.) (1996) *Networks in Marketing*, Thousand Oaks, CA: Sage.

Jackson, Bruce (1987), *Fieldwork*, Chicago: University of Illinois Press.

Jayanthi, Rama K. and Jagdip Singh (2010) 'Pragmatic Learning Theory: An Inquiry-Action Framework for Distributed Consumer Learning in Online Communities', *Journal of Consumer Research*, 36 (April), 1058–1081.

Jayasinghe, Laknath and Mark Ritson (forthcoming) 'Everyday Advertising Context: An Ethnography of Advertising Audiences in the Family Living Room', *Journal of Consumer Research*.

Jones, Robert and Graham Noble (2007) 'Grounded Theory and Management Research: a Lack of Integrity?', *Qualitative Research in Organizations and Management*, 2 (2) 84–103.

Joy, Annamma, John F. Sherry, Gabriele Triolo, and Jonathan Deschenes (2006) 'Writing it Up, Writing it Down: Being Reflexive in Accounts of Consumer Behavior', in Russell Belk (ed.), *Handbook of Qualitative Research Methods in Marketing*, Cheltenham, UK: Edward Elgar, pp. 345–360.

Karababa, Eminegul and Güliz Ger (2011) 'Early Modern Ottoman Coffeehouse Culture and the Formation of the New Consumer Subject', *Journal of Consumer Research*, 37 (February), 737–762.file://localhost/notes/::pan:852571BC005137D6:8C0869D12E8BE6F085257058 00561F2D:79627B87C351C9086EDA2D234F0D2DAB

Kassarjian, Harold H. (1977) 'Content Analysis in Consumer Research', *Journal of Consumer Research*, 4 (June), 8–18.

—— (1994) 'Some Recollections from a Quarter Century Ago', in Frank R. Kardes and Mita Sujan (eds), *Advances in Consumer Research*, 22, pp. 550–552.

Kershenboom, Saskia (1995) *Word, Sound, Image: The Life of the Tamil Text*, Oxford: Berg.

Kimura, Junko and Russell W. Belk (2005) 'Christmas in Japan: Globalization versus Localization', 14:00 minutes, in special 2-DVD issue of *Consumption Markets and Culture*, 8 (3).

Kirby, Sergeo (2006) 'Wal-Town: The Film', 67:00 minutes, Ottawa, ON: National Film Board of Canada.

Kivits, Joëlle (2005) 'Online Interviewing and the Research Relationship', in Christine Hine (ed.), *Virtual Methods; Issues in Social Research on the Internet*, Oxford: Berg, pp. 35–50.

Kjeldgaard, Dannie, Fabien Csaba, and Güliz Ger (2006) 'Grasping the Global: Multi-Sited Ethnographic Market Studies', in Russell Belk (ed.), *Handbook of Qualitative Research Methods in Marketing*, Cheltenham, UK: Edward Elgar, pp. 521–533.

Kozinets, Robert (1999) 'Desert Pilgrim', presented at Heretical Consumer Research Conference, Columbus, OH, 20:00 minutes.

—— (2001) 'Utopian Enterprise: Articulating The Meanings Of Star Trek's Culture Of Consumption', *Journal of Consumer Research*, 28 (1), 67–88.

—— (2002a) 'Can Consumers Escape the Market? Emancipatory Illuminations from Burning Man', *Journal of Consumer Research*, 29 (June), 20–38.

—— (2002b) 'The Field Behind the Screen: Using Netnography for Marketing Research in Online Communities', *Journal of Marketing Research*, 39 (February), 61–72.

—— (2006a) 'Netnography 2.0', in Russell W. Belk (ed.), *Handbook of Qualitative Research Methods in Marketing*, Cheltenham, UK and Northampton, MA: Edward Elgar Publishing, pp. 129–142.

—— (2006b) 'Click to Connect: Netnography and Tribal Advertising', *Journal of Advertising Research*, 46 (September), 279–288.

——— (2007) 'Inno-tribes: Star Trek As Wikimedia', in Bernard Cova, Robert

——— (2008a) 'Stigmatic Enterprise-Spoken Word, Theorizing with Poetry: An Exercise in Transmutability'. Available at http://kozinets.net/archives/204/stigmatic-enterprise-spoken-word/.

——— (2008b) 'Technology/Ideology: How Ideological Fields Influence Consumers' Technology Narratives', *Journal of Consumer Research*, 34 (April), 864–881.

——— (2010a) *Netnography: Doing Ethnographic Research Online*, London: Sage.

——— (2010b) Netnography: The Marketer's Secret Weapon, White Paper. Available online at http://info.netbase.com/wp-netnography.html.

——— (2012), 'Me/my research/avatar,' *Journal of Business Research*, 65 (April), 478–482.

Kozinets, Robert V. and Belk, Russell W. (2006) 'Camcorder Society: Quality Videography in Consumer Research', in Russell W. Belk (ed), *Handbook of Qualitative Research Methods in Marketing*, Northampton, MA: Edward Elgar Publishing, pp. 335–344.

Kozinets, Robert, Kristine De Valck, Andrea Wojnicki, and Sarah Wilner (2010) 'Networked Narratives: Understanding Word-of-Mouth Marketing in Online Communities', *Journal of Marketing*, 71 (March), 71–89.

Kozinets, Robert V. and Richard Kedzior (2009) 'I, Avatar: Auto-netnographic Research in Virtual Worlds', in Michael Solomon and Natalie Wood (eds), *Virtual Social Identity and Consumer Behavior*, Armonk, NY: M.E. Sharpe, pp. 3–19.

Kozinets, Robert V. and Avi Shankar (eds) (2007) *Consumer Tribes*, London: Butterworth-Heinemann, pp. 194–211.

Kozinets, Robert V., Sherry, John F., Jr., Diana Storm, Adam Duhachek, Krittinee Nuttavuthisit and Benét DeBerry-Spence (2002) 'Themed Flagship Brand Stores in the New Millennium: Theory, Practice, Prospects', *Journal of Retailing*, 78 (Spring), 17–29.

Lang, Dorothea (1981) *Dorothea Lang*, New York: Aperture Foundation.

Langer, Roy and Suzanne C. Beckman (2005) 'Sensitive Research Topics: Netnography Revisited', *Qualitative Market Research: An International Journal*, 8 (2), 189–203.

Langer, Suzanne K. (1963) *Philosophy in a New Key: A Study of the Symbolism of Reason, Rite, and Art*, 3rd edn, Cambridge, MA: Harvard University Press.

Langley, Ann (1999) 'Strategies for Theorizing from Process Data', *Academy of Management Review*, 24 (4), 691–710.

Latour, Bruno (2005) *Reassembling the Social: An Introduction to Actor-Network Theory*, Oxford, UK: Oxford University Press.

Laudan, Larry (1984) *Science and Values*, Berkeley, CA: University of California Press.

Lazarsfeld, Paul F. (1934) 'The Psychological Aspect of Marketing Research', *Harvard Business Review*, 13 (1), 54–71.

Lee, R.M. (2000) *Unobtrusive Methods in Social Research*, Buckingham: Open University Press.

Leonard, Hillary (2005) 'Imaginative Consumption: The Construction, Meaning and Experience of Consumer Fantasy', unpublished PhD Dissertation, Department of Marketing, University of Utah, Salt Lake City, UT.

Levy, Sidney (1950) 'Figure Drawing as a Projective Technique', in Lawrence E. Abt and Leopold Bellak (eds), *Projective Psychology: Clinical Approaches to the Total Personality*, New York: Grove Press, pp. 257–297.

——— (1981), 'Interpreting Consumer Mythology: A Structural Approach to Consumer Behaviour,' *Journal of Marketing*, 45 (Summer), 49–61.

——— (2006) 'History of Qualitative Research Methods in Marketing', in Russell Belk (ed.), *Handbook of Qualitative Research in Methods Marketing and Consumer Research*, Cheltenham, UK: Edward Elgar, pp. 3–18.

Lincoln, Sian (2004) 'Teenage Girls' "Bedroom Culture": Codes versus Zones', in Andy Bennett and Keith Kahn Harris (eds), *After Subculture: Critical Studies in Contemporary Youth Culture*, Houndsmills, UK: Palgrave Macmillan, pp. 94–106.

——— (2005) 'Feeling the Noise: Teenagers, Bedrooms and Music', *Leisure Studies*, 24 (October), 299–314.

Lincoln, Yvonna and Egon G. Guba (1985), *Naturalistic Inquiry*, Beverly Hills, CA: Sage.

Lofland, John and Lyn Lofland (1995) *Analysing Social Settings: A Guide to Qualitative Observation and Analysis*, New York: Wadsworth.

Liu, Bing (2008) *Web Data Mining: Exploring Hyperlinks, Contents, and Usage Data*, New York: Springer.

Loisos, Peter (2000) 'Video, Film and Photographs as Research Documents', in Martin W. Bauer and George Gaskell (eds), *Qualitative Researching with Text, Image and Sound*, London: Sage, pp. 93–107.

Lowrey, Tina, Cele Otnes, and Mary Ann McGrath (1998) 'Shopping with Consumers: Reflections and Innovations', *Qualitative Market Research*, 8 (2), 176–188.

Lutz, Catherine A. and Jane L. Collins (1993) *Reading National Geographic*, Chicago: University of Chicago Press.

MacDougall, David and Judith MacDougall (1997) 'Photo Wallahs: An Encounter with Photography in Mussoorie, A North Indian Hill Station', 60:00 minutes, Canberra: Ronin Films.

MacInnis, Deborah and Valerie Folkes (2010), 'The Disciplinary Status of Consumer Behavior: A Sociology of Science Perspective on Key Controversies', *Journal of Consumer Research*, 36 (6), 899–914.

Maharidge, Dale and Michael Williamson (1989) *And Their Children After Them: The Legacy of Let Us Now Praise Famous Men: James Agee, Walker Evans, and the Rise and Fall of Cotton in the South*, New York: Pantheon.

Marcus George (1998) *Ethnography Through Thick and Thin*, Princeton, NJ: Princeton University Press.

Marcoux, Jean-Sebastien and Renauld Legoux (2005) 'Ground Zero: A Contested Market', 27:00 minutes, in special 2-DVD issue of *Consumption Markets and Culture*, 8 (3).

Mariampolski, Hy (2006) *Ethnography for Marketers: A Guide to Consumer Immersion*, Thousand Oaks, CA: Sage.

Markham, Annette N. (1998) *Life Online: Researching Real Experience in Virtual Space*, Walnut Creek, CA: Altamira.

Marschan-Piekkari, Rebecca, Catherine Welch, Heli Penttinen, and Marja Tahvanainen (2004) 'Interviewing in the Multinational Corporation: Challenges of the Organisational Context', in Rebecca Marschan-Piekkari and Catherine Welch (eds), *Handbook of Qualitative Research Methods for International Business*, Cheltenham, UK: Edward Elgar, pp. 244–263.

Marshall, Catherine and Gretchen Rossman (2011) *Designing Qualitative Research*, 5th edn, Thousand Oaks, CA: Sage.

Martin, Diane, John Schouten, and James McAlexander (2006) 'Reporting Ethnographic Research: Bringing Segments to Life Through Movie Making and Metaphor', in Russell Belk (ed.), *Handbook of Qualitative Research in Marketing*, Cheltenham, UK: Edward Elgar, pp. 361–370.

Marvin, Carolyn (1988) *When Old Technologies Were New: Thinking About Electric Communication in the Late Nineteenth Century*, New York: Oxford University Press.

Maulana, Amalia and Giana M. Eckhardt (2007) 'Just Friends, Good Acquaintances or Soul Mates? An Exploration of Website Connectedness', *Qualitative Market Research: An International Journal*, 10 (3), 227–242.

McCahill, Michael and Clive Norris (2002) 'CCTV in London', Working Paper 6, Centre from Criminology and Criminal Justice, University of Hull, Hull, United Kingdom. Available online at http://www.urbaneye.net/results/ue_wp6.pdf

McCann-Erickson (1988) 'The Mind of a Roach Killer', *The Wall Street Journal*, May 14 (3), Colonial Contest, London: Routledge.

McCracken, Grant (1988) *The Long Interview*, Newbury Park, CA: Sage.

———— (2009) *Chief Culture Officer: How to Create a Living, Breathing Corporation*, Philadelphia, PA: Perseus.

McCreadie, Marsha (2008) *Documentary Superstars: How Today's Filmmakers Are Reinventing the Form*, New York: Allsworth Press.

McGrath, Mary Ann, John F. Sherry, Jr., and Sidney J. Levy (1993) 'Giving Voice to the Gift: The Use of Projective Techniques to Recover Lost Meanings', *Journal of Consumer Psychology*, 2 (2), 171–191.

McQuarrie, Edward and David Mick (1992) 'On Resonance: A Critical Pluralistic Inquiry into Advertising Rhetoric', *Journal of Consumer Research*, 19 (September), 180–197.

Menzel, Peter (1994a) *Material World: A Global Family Portrait*, San Francisco: Sierra Club Books.

Menzel, Peter (1994b) *Material World: A Global Family Portrait* (CD-ROM), San Francisco: StarPress Multimedia.

Merton, Robert (1987) 'Three Fragments From a Sociologist's Notebooks: Establishing the Phenomenon, Specified Ignorance, and Strategic Research Materials', *Annual Review of Sociology*, 13 (August): 1–29.

Merton, Robert and Patricia Kendall (1946) 'The Focused Interview,' *American Journal of Sociology*, 51, 541–557.

Mick, David Glen (1986) 'Consumer Research and Semiotics: Exploring the Morphology of Signs, Symbols, and Significance', *Journal of Consumer Research*, 13 (2), 196–213.

Mick, David and Laura Oswald (2006) 'The Semiotic Paradigm on Meaning in the Marketplace', in Russell Belk (ed.), *Handbook of Qualitative Research Methods in Marketing*, Cheltenham, UK: Edward Elgar, pp. 31–45.

Miles, Matthew B., and A. Michael Huberman (1994) *Qualitative Data Analysis: An Expanded Sourcebook*, 2nd edn, Thousand Oaks, CA: Sage.

Miller, Daniel (2008) *The Comfort of Things*, Cambridge: Polity.

——— (2011) *Tales from Facebook*, Cambridge: Polity Press.

Miller, Daniel and Don Slater (2000), *The Internet: An Ethnographic Approach*, Oxford, UK: Berg.

Miner, Horace (1956) 'Body Ritual among the Nacirema', *American Anthropologist*, 58 (June), 503–507.

Moisander, Johana, Anu Valtonen, and Heidi Hirsto (2009) 'Personal Interviews in Cultural Consumer Research: Post-structuralist Challenges', 12 (4), 329–348.

Moore, Elizabeth and Richard Lutz (2000) 'Children, Advertising, and Product Experiences: A Multimethod Inquiry', *Journal of Consumer Research*, 27 (June), 31–48.

Moore, Karl and Susan Reid (2008) 'The Birth of the Brand: 4,000 Years of Branding', *Business History*, 50 (July), 419–432.

Moore, Michael (1989) 'Roger and Me', 91:00 minutes, Hollywood, CA: Warner Brothers.

Moore, Michael (2002) 'Bowling for Columbine', 120:00 minutes, Alliance Atlantic.

Moore, Michael (2007) 'Sicko', 123:00 minutes, Dog Eat Dog Films.

Morgan, Christiana D. and Henry A. Murray (1935) 'A Method Investigating Phantasies, the Thematic Apperception Test', *Archives of Neurological Psychology*, 35, 261–287.

Morgan, David and Richard Krueger (1993) 'When to Use Focus Groups and Why', in David Morgan (ed.), *Successful Focus Groups: Advancing the State of the Art*, Newbury Park, CA: Sage, pp. 3–19.

Morris, Desmond, Peter Collett, Peter Marsh, and M.O'Shaughnessy (1979) *Gestures: Their Origins and Distribution*, London: Jonathan Cape.

Mosco, Vincent (2004) *The Digital Sublime*, Cambridge, MA: MIT Press.

Muñiz, Albert M. and Thomas C. O'Guinn (2001) 'Brand Community', *Journal of Consumer Research*, 27 (March), 412–432.

Muñiz, Albert M. Jr. and Hope Jensen Schau (2005) 'Religiosity in the Abandoned Apple Newton Brand Community', *Journal of Consumer Research*, 31 (March), 737–747.

Murchison, Julian (2010) *Ethnography Essentials: Designing, Conducting, and Presenting Your Research*, San Francisco, CA: Jossey-Bass.

Murray, Jeff B. and Julie L. Ozanne (1991) 'The Critical Imagination: Emancipatory Interests in Consumer Research', *Journal of Consumer Research*, 18 (September), 129–144.

Nguyen, Thuc Doan and Russell Belk (2007) 'This We Remember: Consuming Representation in Remembering', *Consumption, Markets and Culture*, 10 (September) 251–291.

Nichols, Bill (2001) *Introduction to Documentary*, Bloomington, IN: Indiana University Press.

Nunes, Michael, Saul Greenberg, and Carman Neustaedter (2009) 'Using Physical Memorabilia as Opportunities to Move into Collocated Digital Photo-Sharing', *International Journal of Human-Computer Studies*, 67, 1087–1111.

Nye, David E. (1994) *American Technological Sublime*, Cambridge, MA: MIT Press.

O'Barr, William (1994) *Culture and the Ad: Exploring Otherness in the World of Advertising*, Boulder, CO: Westview Press.

O'Connor, John E. (1988) 'History in Images/Images in History: Reflections on the Importance of Film and Television Study for an Understanding of the Past', *American Historical Review*, 93 (December),1200–1207.

Odom, William, John Zimmerman, and Jodi Forlizzi (2011) 'Teenagers and Their Virtual Possessions: Design Opportunities and Issues', *CHI 2011*, 1491–1500.

Olsen, Barbara (1995) 'Brand Loyalty and Consumption Patterns: The Lineage Factor', in John F. Sherry, Jr. (ed.), *Contemporary Marketing and Consumer Behavior: An Anthropological Sourcebook*, Thousand Oaks, CA: Sage, pp. 245–281.

Otnes, Cele, Tina Lowrey, and Young Chan Kim (1993) 'Gift Selection for Easy and Difficult Recipients: A Social Roles Interpretation', *Journal of Consumer Research*, 20 (September), 229–244.

Otnes, Cele and Mary Ann McGrath (2001) 'Perceptions and Realities of Male Shopping Behavior', *Journal of Retailing*, 77, 111–137.

Ozanne, Julie and Bige Saatcioglu (2008) 'Participatory Action Research', *Journal of Consumer Research*, 35 (October), 423–439.

Pace, Stephano (2008) 'YouTube: An Opportunity for Consumer Narrative Analysis?', *Qualitative Market Research*, 11 (2), 213–226.

Page, Edwin R. (2001) 'Social Change at Bike Week', *Visual Sociology*, 16 (1), 7–35.

Page, H. (1988) 'Dialogic Principles of Interactive Learning in the Ethnographic Relationship', *Journal of Anthropological Research*, 44 (2), 163–181.

Papacharissi, Zizi (ed.) (2011) *A Networked Self: Identity, Community, and Culture on Social Network Sites*, London: Routledge.

Parkin, Katherine (2004) 'The Sex of Food and Ernest Dichter: The Illusion of Inevitability', *Advertising and Society Review*, 5 (2), online, npn.

Patterson, Anthony (2005) 'Processes, Relationships, Settings, Products and Consumers: The Case for Qualitative Diary Research', *Qualitative Market Research*, 8 (2), 152–156.

Peñaloza, Lisa (1994) 'Atravesando Fronteras/Border Crossings: A Critical Ethnographic Exploration of the Consumer Acculturation of Mexican Immigrants', *Journal of Consumer Research*, 21 (June), 32–54.

Pettigrew, Simone (2011) 'Hearts and Minds: Children's Experiences of Disney World', *Consumption, Markets and Culture*, 14 (June), 145–161.

Pfeiffer, John (1982) *The Creative Explosion: An Inquiry into the Origins of Art and Religion*, Cambridge: Harper & Row.

Pink, Sarah (2001) *Doing Visual Ethnography*, London: Sage.

Pinney, Christopher (1997) *Camera Indica: The Social Life of Indian Photographs*, Chicago: University of Chicago Press.

Prasad, Pushkala (2005) *Crafting Qualitative Research: Working in the Postpositivist Traditions*, Armonk, NY: M.E. Sharpe.

Pratt, Mary Louise (1986) 'Fieldwork in Common Places', in James Clifford and George E. Marcus (eds), *Writing Culture: The Poetics and Politics of Ethnography*, Berkeley, CA: University of California Press, pp. 27–50.

Prelinger, Rick (1996) *Our Secret Century*, Irvington, NY: Voyager (12 volumes of varying lengths).

——— (2010) 'The Appearance of Archives', in Pelle Snickars and Patrick Vonderau (eds), *The YouTube Reader*, Stockholm: National Library of Sweden, pp. 268–274.

Prosser, Jon (1998) *Image-Based Research*, London: RoutledgeFalmer.

Quart, Alissa (2003) *Branded: The Buying and Selling of Teenagers*, New York: Basic Books.

Rabiger, Michael (2009) *Directing the Documentary*, 5th edn, Stoneham, MA: Butterworth.

Rapaille, Clotaire (2006) *The Culture Code*, New York: Broadway Books.

Rathje, William and Cullen Murphy (1992) *Rubbish! The Archaeology of Garbage: What Our Garbage Tells Us About Ourselves*, New York: Harper Collins.

Reckwitz, Andreas (2005) 'Toward a Theory of Social Practices: A Development in Culturalist Theorizing', *European Journal of Social Theory*, 5 (May), 243–263.

Richards, Lyn (2005) *Handling Qualitative Data: A Practical Guide*, London: Sage.

Riis, Jacob A. (1973) *How the Other Half Lives: Studies Among the Tenements of New York*, New York: Dover.

Robson, S. and A. Foster (1989) *Qualitative Research in Action*, London: Edward Arnold.

Rook, Dennis (1988) 'Researching Consumer Fantasy', *Research in Consumer Behavior*, 3, Greenwich, CT: JAI Press, pp. 247–270.

Rook, Dennis (2006) 'Let's Pretend: Projective Methods Reconsidered', in Russell Belk (ed.), *Handbook of Qualitative Research Methods in Marketing*, Cheltenham, UK: Edward Elgar, 143–155.

Rose, Diana (2000) 'Analysis of Moving Images', in Martin Bauer and George Gaskell (eds), *Qualitative Researching with Text, Image and Sound*, Los Angeles: Sage, pp. 246–262.

Rossell, Daniela (2002) *Ricas y Famosas*, New York: Art Publishers.

Rowe, John Howland (1965) 'The Renaissance Foundations of Anthropology', *American Anthropologist*, 67, 1–20.

Salinger, Adrienne (1995) *In My Room: Teenagers in their Bedrooms*, San Francisco, CA: Chronicle Books.

Sandikci, Özlem and Güliz Ger (2010) 'Veiling in Style: How Does a Stigmatized Practice Become Fashionable?', *Journal of Consumer Research*, 37 (June), 15–36.

Sanjek, Roger (1990) 'On Ethnographic Validity', in R. Sanjek (ed.), *Fieldnotes*, Ithaca, NY: Cornell University Press, pp. 385–418.

Saunders, Dave (2010) *Documentary*, London: Routledge.

Sayre, Shay (2006) 'Using Video-Elicitation to Research Sensitive Topics: Understanding the Purchase Process Following Natural Disaster', in Russell Belk (ed.), *Handbook of Qualitative Research Methods in Marketing*, Cheltenham, UK: Edward Elgar, 230–243.

Scaraboto, Daiane and Eileen Fischer (2013), 'Frustrated Fatshionistas: An Institutional Theory Perspective on Consumer Quests for Greater Choice in Mainstream Markets,' *Journal of Consumer Research*, April, forthcoming.

Schatzki, Theodore R. (1996) *Social Practices: A Wittgensteinian Approach to Human Activity and the Social*, Cambridge: Cambridge University.

Schau, Hope Jensen, Albert M. Muñiz Jr., and Eric J. Arnould (2009) 'How Brand Community Practices Create Value', *Journal of Marketing*, 73 (September), 30–51.

Schouten, John (1991a) 'Land of the Winnebago', in Russell W. Belk (ed.), *Highways and Buyways: Naturalistic Research from the Consumer Behavior Odyssey*, Provo, UT: Association for Consumer Research, p. 13.

—— (1991b) 'Sorting', in Russell W. Belk (ed.), *Highways and Buyways: Naturalistic Research from the Consumer Behavior Odyssey*, Provo, UT: Association for Consumer Research, pp. 112–113.

—— (1993) 'Recommended Daily Allowance', *Journal of Advertising*, 22 (1), 24.

Schouten, John W. and James H. McAlexander (1995) 'Subcultures of Consumption: An Ethnography of the New Bikers', *Journal of Consumer Research*, 22 (June), 43–61.

Schutz, Alfred (1962), *The Problem of Social Reality*, The Hague: Martinus Nijhoff.

Schwandt, Thomas A. (2001) *Dictionary of Qualitative Inquiry*, Thousand Oaks, CA: Sage.

Sherman, Sharon R. (1998) *Documenting Ourselves: Film, Video, and Culture*, Lexington, KY: University of Kentucky Press.

Sherry, John (1991a) 'Postmodern Alternatives: The Interpretive Turn in Consumer Research', in Thomas Robertson and Harold Kassarjian (eds), *Handbook of Consumer Research*, Englewood Cliffs, NJ: Prentice-Hall, pp. 548–591.

Sherry, John F., Jr. (1991b) 'Trivium Siam', *Consumption, Markets and Culture*, 1 (January), 90–95.

Sherry, John F., Jr. (1995a) *Contemporary Marketing and Consumer Behavior: An Anthropological Sourcebook*, Thousand Oaks, CA: Sage.

Sherry, John F., Jr. (1995b) 'Bottomless Cup, Plug-in Drug: A Telethnography of Coffee', *Visual Anthropology*, 7, 351–370.

Sherry, John F., Jr. (1998) 'Three Poems', in Barbara Stern (ed.), *Representing Consumption: Voices, Views, and Visions*, London: Routledge, pp. 303–305.

Sherry, John F., Jr. (2008) 'Three Poems on Marketing and Consumption', *Consumption, Markets and Culture*, 11 (September), 203–206.

Sherry, John F., Jr. and Robert Kozinets (2001) 'Qualitative Inquiry in Marketing and Consumer Research', in Dawn Iacobucci (ed.), *Kellogg on Marketing*, New York: Wiley, pp. 165–194.

Shove, Elizabeth (2003) *Comfort, Cleanliness and Convenience*, Oxford: Berg.

Sieber, Joan E. (ed.) (1991) *Sharing Social Science Data: Advantages and Challenges*, Newbury Park, CA: Sage.

Silverman, David (2011) *Interpreting Qualitative Data: A Guide to the Principles of Qualitative Research*, Los Angeles, CA: Sage.

Sinclair, Upton (2003) *The Jungle*, Tucson, AZ: Sharp Press.

Singh, Sachil and David Lyon (forthcoming) 'Surveilling consumers: the social consequences of data processing on Amazon.com', in Russell Belk and Rosa Llamas (eds), *The Digital Consumer*, London: Routledge.

Sirsi, Ajay, James Ward, and Peter Reingen (1996) 'Microcultural Analysis of Variation in Sharing of Causal Reasoning about Behavior', *Journal of Consumer Research*, 22 (March), 345–372.

Sivilich, Daniel M. (1996) 'Analysing Musket Balls to Interpret a Revolutionary War Site', *Historical Archaeology*, 30 (2), 101–109.

Sivulka, Juliann (1998) *Soap, Sex, and Cigarettes: A Cultural History of American Advertising*, Belmont, CA: Wadsworth.

Skeggs, B. 1994. 'Situating the Production of Feminist Ethnography' in M. Maynard and J. Purvis (eds), *Researching Women's Lives from a Feminist Perspective*, London: Taylor and Francis.

Smith, Andrea, Yionjan Chen, and Eileen Fischer (2012) 'How Does Brand-Related User-Generated Content Differ Across YouTube, Facebook, and Twitter?', *Journal of Interactive Marketing*, 26 (2), 101–113.

Snickars, Pella and Patrick Vonderau (ed.) (2010) *YouTube Reader*, Stockholm: National Library of Sweden.

Sobh, Rana and Russell Belk (2010) 'Domains of Privacy in Arab Gulf Homes', 16:11 minutes, Toronto: Odyssey Films.

———— and ———— (2011a) 'Gender Privacy in Arab Gulf States: Implications for Consumption and Marketing', in Özlem Sandicki and Gillian Rice (eds), *Handbook of Islamic Marketing*, Cheltenham, UK: Edward Elgar, pp. 73–96.

———— and ———— (2011b) 'Privacy and Gendered Spaces in Arab Gulf Homes', *Home Cultures*, 8 (3), 317–340.

———— and ———— (2012) 'Domains of Privacy and Hospitality in Arab Gulf Homes', *Journal of Islamic Marketing*, 2 (2), 125–137.

Sobh, Rana, Russell Belk, and Justin Gressel (2010) 'The Scented Winds of Change: Conflicting Notions of Modesty and Vanity among Young Qatari and Emirati Women', *Advances in Consumer Research*, 37, 905–907.

Spaarman, Anna (2007) 'Up the Walls! Children Talk about Visuality in Their Own Rooms', in Karin M. Ekström and Birgitte Tufte (eds), *Children, Media and Consumption: On the Front Edge*, Göteborg: Nordicom, pp. 301–318.

Spencer-Wood, Suzanne M. (ed.) (1987) *Consumer Choice in Historical Archaeology*, New York: Plenum Press.

Spiggle, Susan (1998) 'Creating the Frame and Narrative: From Text to Hypertext', in Barbara B. Stern (ed.), *Representing Consumers: Voices, Views, and Visions*, London: Routledge, pp. 156–190.

Spurlock, Morgan (2004) 'Supersize Me', 100:00 minutes, Roadside Attractions, Samuel Goldwyn Films, and Showtime Independent Films.

Standage, Tom (1998) *The Victorian Internet: The Remarkable Story of the Telegraph and the Nineteenth Century's On-line Pioneers*, New York: Walker.

Steele, Jeanne R. and Jane D. Browne (1995) 'Adolescent Room Culture: Studying Media in the Context of Everyday Life', *Journal of Youth and Adolescence*, 24 (October), 551–575.

Stern, Barbara (1989) 'Literary Criticism and Consumer Research: Overview and Illustrative Analysis', *Journal of Consumer Research*, 16 (3), 322–334.

———— (1993) 'Poetry and Representation in Consumer Research: The Art of Science', in Barbara B. Stern (ed.), *Representing Consumers: Voices, Views, and Visions*, London: Routledge, pp. 290–307.

———— (2004) 'The Importance of Being Ernest: Commemorating Dichter's Contribution to Advertising Research', *Journal of Advertising Research*, 44, 165–169.

Stewart, David W. (2010) 'The Evolution of Market Research', in Pauline McLaren, Michael Saren, Barbara Stern, and Mark Tadajewski (eds), *The Sage Handbook of Marketing Theory* Los Angeles, CA: Sage, pp. 74–88.

Stewart, David, Prem Shamdasani and Dennis Rook (2007) *Focus Groups*, 2nd edn, Thousand Oaks CA: Sage.

Strauss, A. (1987) *Qualitative Analysis for Social Scientists*, Cambridge: Cambridge University Press.

Strauss, Anselm and Juliet Corbin (1998) *Basics of Qualitative Research: Techniques and Procedures for Developing Grounded Theory*, Thousand Oaks, CA: Sage.

Sunderland, Patricia L. and Rita M. Denny (2007) *Doing Anthropology in Consumer Research*, Walnut Creek, CA: Left Coast Press.

Szykman, Lisa and Ronald Hill (1993) 'A Consumer-Behavior Investigation of a Prison Economy', in Janeen A. Costa and Russell Belk (eds), *Research in Consumer Behavior*, 6, Greenwich, CT: JAI Press, pp. 231–260.

Thomas, Tandy Chalmers , Linda L. Price, Hope Jensen Schau (forthcoming), 'When Differences Unite: Resource Dependence in Heterogeneous Consumption Communities', *Journal of Consumer Research*, published online June 29, 2012.

Thompson, Alex (2011) 'Videography and the Production of Commercial Ethnographic Practice', presented at Consumer Culture Theory Conference VI, July, Evanston, Illinois.

Thompson, Craig (1990) 'Eureka! and Other Tests of Significance: A New Look at Evaluating Interpretive Research', *Advances in Consumer Research*, 17, 25–30.

Thompson, Craig, Willian Locander, and Howard Pollio (1989) 'Putting Consumer Experience Back into Consumer Research: The Philosophy and Method of Existential Phenomenology', *Journal of Consumer Research*, 16 (2), 133–146.

————, ————, and ———— (1990) 'The Lived Meaning of Free Choice: An Existential-Phenomenological Description of Everyday Consumer Experiences of Contemporary Married Women', *Journal of Consumer Research*, 17 (December), 346–361.

Tian, Kelly and Russell Belk (2005) 'Extended Self and Possessions in the Workplace', *Journal of Consumer Research*, 32 (September), 297–310.

———— and ———— (2006) 'Consumption and the Meaning of Life,' *Research in Consumer Behavior*, 10, 249–274.

Turkle, Sherry (1995) *Life on the Screen: Identity in the Age of the Internet*, New York: Simon & Schuster.

Underhill, Paco (1999) *Why We Buy: The Science of Shopping*, New York: Simon & Schuster.

Üstüner, Tuba and Douglas Holt (2010) 'Toward a Theory of Status Consumption in Less Industrialized Countries', *Journal of Consumer Research*, 37 (June), 37–56.

Vanden Bergh, Bruce G. (1992) 'Volkswagen as Little Man', *Advances in Consumer Research*, 19, 174.

Van House, Nancy (2009) 'Collocated Photo Sharing, Story-Telling, and the Performance of Self', *International Journal of Human-Computer Studies*, 67, 1073–1086.

Van Maanen, John (1988), *Tales of the Field: On Writing Ethnography*, Chicago: University of Chicago Press.

Van Ness, Elizabeth (2005) 'Is Cinema Studies Degree the New MBA?', *New York Times*, 6 March, online edition.

Venkatesh, Alladi, Annamma Joy, John F. Sherry, Jr., and Jonathan Deschenes (2010) 'The Aesthetics of Luxury Fashion, Body and Identity Formation', *Journal of Consumer Psychology*, 20 (4), 459–470.

Vidich, Arthur J. and Stanford M. Lyman (1994), 'Qualitative Methods: Their History in Sociology and Anthropology,' in Norman K. Denzin and Yvonna S. Lincoln eds, *Handbook of Qualitative Research*, Thousand Oaks, CA: Sage, 23–59.

Von Hippel, Eric (1986) 'Lead Users: A Source of Novel Product Concepts', *Management Science*, 32, 791–805.

Wagner, Jon (2007) 'Observing Culture and Social Life: Documentary Photography, Fieldwork, and Social Research', in Gregory C. Stanczak (ed.), *Visual Research Methods: Image, Society, and Representation*, Thousand Oaks, CA: Sage, pp. 23–59.

Wallendorf, Melanie and Eric Arnould (1991) 'We Gather Together: The Consumption Rituals of Thanksgiving Day', *Journal of Consumer Research*, 18 (1), 13–31.

_____ and _____ (1988) '"My Favorite Things": A Cross-Cultural Inquiry in Object Attachment, Possessiveness, and Social Linkage', *Journal of Consumer Research*, 14 (4), 531–547.

Wallendorf, Melanie and Russell Belk (1987) 'Deep Meaning in Possessions: Qualitative Research from the Consumer Behavior Odyssey', 46-minute video, Cambridge, MA: Marketing Science Institute.

Wallendorf, Melanie and Russell Belk (1989) 'Assessing Trustworthiness in Naturalistic Consumer Research', in Elizabeth Hirschman (ed.) *Interpretive Consumer Research*, Provo: Association for Consumer Research, pp. 69–84.

Wallendorf, Melanie and Michael Reilly (1983) 'Ethnic Migration, Assimilation, and Consumption', *Journal of Consumer Research*, 10 (December), 292–302.

Walsh, David. (2000) 'Doing Ethnography', in Clive Seale (ed.), *Researching Society and Culture*, 2nd edn. London: Sage.

Warren, Carol A.B. (1988) *Gender Issues in Field Research*, Newbury Park, CA: Sage.

Webb, Eugene, Donald T. Campbell, R.D. Schwartz and L. Sechrest (1966) *Unobtrusive Measures*, Chicago: Rand McNally.

Weinberg, Bruce D. (2001) 'Research in Exploring the Online Consumer Experience', in Mary C. Gilly and Joan Meyers-Levy (eds), *Advances in Consumer Research* Volume 28, Valdosta, GA: Association for Consumer Research, pp. 227–232.

Wellman, Barry (1988) 'Structural Analysis: from Method and Metaphor to Theory and Substance', in B. Wellman and S.D. Berkowitz (ed.), *Social Structures: A Network Approach*, Cambridge: Cambridge University Press, pp. 19–61.

Wesch, Michael (2008) 'An Anthropological Introduction to You Tube', presented at the Library of Congress, 23 June. Avaiable online at http://www.youtube.com/watch?v=TPAO-lZ4_hU.

Whyte, William Foote (1955), *Street Corner Society*, Chicago: University of Chicago Press.

Wijland, Roel, John Schouten, and John F. Sherry, Jr. (2010) *Canaries Coalmines Thunderstones*, St. Barhans, New Zealand: University of St. Bathans Press.

Wilson, William A. (1986), 'Documenting Folklore', in Elliot Oring, (ed.), *Folk Groups and Folklore Genres: An Introduction*, Logan: Utah State University Press, pp. 225–254.

Witkowski, Terrence (1989) 'Colonial Consumers in Revolt: Buyer Values and Behavior During the Nonimportation Movement, 1764–1776', *Journal of Consumer Research*, 16 (2), 216–226.

Wolcott, Harry (1992) 'Posturing in Qualitative Inquiry', in M.D. LeCompte, W.L. Millroy, and J. Preissle (eds), *The Handbook of Qualitative Research in Education*, New York: Academic Press, pp. 3–52.

_____ (1994) *Transforming Qualitative Data*, Thousand Oaks, CA: Sage.

_____ (2001) *Writing Up Qualitative Research*, Thousand Oaks, CA: Sage.

_____ (2008) *Ethnography: A Way of Seeing*, Lanham, MD: AltaMira Press.

Wolfinger, Nicholas H. (2002) 'On Writing Fieldnotes: Collection Strategies and Background Expectancies', *Qualitative Research*, 2 (1), 85–95.

Wood, Natalie T. and Michael R. Solomon (eds) (2009) *Virtual Social Identity and Consumer Behavior*, Armonk, NY: M.E. Sharpe.

Workman, John, Jr. (1993) 'Marketing's Limited Role in New Product Development in One Computer Systems Firm', *Journal of Marketing Research*, 30 (November), 405–421.

Wright, Terence (1999) *The Photography Handbook*, London: Routledge.

Yablonsky, Lewis (1976) *Psychodrama: Resolving Emotional Problems through Role-Playing*, New York: Basic Books.

Young, Rick (2004) 'Is Wal-Mart Good for America?', 60:00 minutes, Boston, MA: WGBH and Public Broadcasting Service,.

Zaltman, Gerald (2003) *How Consumers Think: Essential Insights into the Mind of the Market*, Boston, MA: Harvard Business School Press.

Zaltman, Gerald, Karen LeMasters, and Michael Heffring (1982) *Theory Construction in Marketing: Some Thoughts on Thinking*, New York: John Wiley & Sons.

Zaltman, Gerald and Lindsay Zaltman (2008) *Marketing Metaphoria: What Deep Metaphors Reveal About the Minds of Consumers*, Boston, MA: Harvard Business School Press.

Zhao, Xin and Russell Belk (2008) 'Politicizing Consumer Culture: Advertising's Appropriation of Political Ideology in China's Social Transition', *Journal of Consumer Research*, 35, (August), 231–244.

Ziller, Robert C. (1990) *Photographing the Self: Methods for Observing Personal Orientations*, Newbury Park, CA: Sage.

Ziller, Robert C. and Douglas Lewis (1981) 'Orientation: Self, Social, and Environmental Percepts Through Auto-Photography', *Personality and Social Psychology Bulletin*, 7 (2), 626–639.

Zinkhan, George M. (1998) 'Time and Timelessness Through Consumption: A Reflection on the Social Meaning of Things', in Barbara Stern (ed.), *Representing Consumption: Voices, Views, and Visions*, London: Routledge, pp. 299–302.

Zwick, Detlev and Nikhilesh Dholakia (2006) 'Bringing the Market to Life: Screen Aesthetics and the Epistemic Consumption Object', *Marketing Theory*, 6 (1), 41–62.

Index

coding, 93, 125, 139–55; definition of, 139; of metaphors, 141; *open* and *axial*, 149–50; and prior literature, 144–5; relationships between codes, 149–55; and research traditions, 145–7; of sound and video, 208
collage construction, 51
Collett, Peter, 85
Communispace, 83
comparative mining, 98
computer programs, use of, 207–8
conditions that give rise to a phenomenon, 152–3
conference attendance, 208–9
conference papers, 194, 196
confidentiality of data, 193
consent forms, 129
consequences precipitated by a phenomenon, 152–3
consumer behaviour studies, 63–4, 131
consumer culture theory (CCT), 12, 204
consumer desire, 148, 150–2
consumer needs and preferences, 171–6
consumer sovereignty, 145, 156
consumption connections, 163
consumption stereotypes, 47
content analysis, 108–9
content mining, 95, 97, 113
contextualised research, 3–4, 73, 91, 177, 188
contradictions in data, 142, 178–9
Cooper, Charlotte, 145–6
coping strategies, 143–4
Corbin, Juliet, 149–50
Costa, Janeen, 32
Cote, Joseph A., 87
Coulter, Robin, 51
Coupland, Jennifer Chang, 75
Cresswell, John, 139
critical research traditions, 23–4, 146
cultural differences, 6, 51

Danes, Jeffrey E., 45
'dashboards', 83
data analysis, 138–43; borderline with data collection, 168
data collection: aids to, 120–37; informal, 168; *manual* and *automated*, 112–13; in netnography, 108–10, 113–16
data mining, 93–105, 114; applications of, 94; definitions of, 95; example of, 101–3
data sharing, 193–4
Davis, Murray, 189
debriefing meetings, 168–9
decision graphing, 164
Denny, Rita, 66, 79, 133–4, 160
Denzin, Norman K., 186
depth interviews, 31–40, 55, 75, 119, 128; as conversations, 35–40; preparation for, 33–4
De Valck, Kristine, 153–4
Dichter, Ernst, 8
digital single-lens reflex (DSLR) cameras, 130

disclosures by research participants, 77
discovery-oriented research, 188–9
documentary films, 85, 130, 184–5
Douglas, Jack, 32
doxic reality, 68
dream exercises, 54
Duhacek, Adam, 144
Duncan, Isadora, 191
Durgee, Jeffrey, 51

Earley, Mandy, 4
elicited data, 112; *see also* visual elicitation
Emerson, Robert M., 71
emic codes, 140, 146
Emmison, Michael, 127–8
emotional involvement of researchers with informants, 207
emotional understanding, 186
emotions: aroused by ethnographic writing, 185; expressed in data, 141
empirical phenomena, 17–18, 27
Enron, 184–5
Envirosell, 165–6
equipment failure, 206
ESP Zone, 161
ethical issues, 129, 136
ethics committees, 82
ethnographic interviews, 117
ethnographic quality, assessment of, 176
ethnographic skills and training, 204–5
'ethnographic year', 70, 74
ethnography, 20–1, 36, 60–74, 82, 89–91, 185; *academic* and *practitioner* types of, 74; definitions of, 63, 74; illustrative case of, 68–74; key characteristics of, 65, 67–8; marketing-oriented, 64; *see also* netnography; participant-observation; video ethnography; virtual ethnography
etic codes, 141
eureka moments, 148, 178
Evans, Walker, 184
existential phenomenology, 21–2
experience-close and *experience-distant* observational methods, 82
experiential knowledge, 186
extreme cases in data, treatment of, 209

Facebook, 81, 83, 94, 99, 104, 107, 114, 134, 202–3
fan communities, 69–70
Farnell, Brenda, 193
Fernandez, James, 178
Fernback, Jan, 106
fieldnotes, 67, 70–3, 80, 112, 116–17, 121–4, 131, 165; what to include in, 122
fieldwork, 65, 68, 73
film festivals, 194–5
films, analysis of, 85–6
Films by Consumer Researchers (website), 131, 195
Fischer, Eileen (co-author), 4, 7–8, 22–3, 151, 197, 209–10

FLAG (Fits-Like-a-Glove) framework (Allen), 156–7
Flickr, 134
focus groups, 9–10, 40–56, 204; analysis of data from, 43; appropriate and in-appropriate use of, 42–3; preparation for and running of, 42; recruitment of members, 41–2
Folkes, Valerie, 12
'force-fitting' data, 144
'forensic' consumer research, 84–5
Fournier, Susan, 25
'front porch' ethnography, 65
'funnel' approach to interviewing, 37

Galton, Sir Francis, 44
gaps in the market, 163
garbology, 87–8
Geertz, Clifford, 71, 185–6
General Motors, 184
generalisability of research findings, 90
Ger, Güliz, 85, 129, 148, 150–2
gestures, recording and study of, 85, 124
Giesler, Markus, 19, 152, 156, 195, 209–10
Glaser, Barney, 10, 143, 150
Goffman, Erving, 68, 144
Goldberg, Jim, 184
'Goldilocks' principle or theory-practice combination, 179
Google, 81, 107, 134
Gordon, Wendy, 44, 51
Gore, Al, 185
Gould, Leroy C., 127
Goulding, Christina, 68
Grayson, Mark, 10
Greimas, Algirdas, 155–6
grounded theory, 21, 143, 149–50, 170
group dynamics and group interaction, 41–3
group interviews, 118–19, 125
group-think, 42–3
Guba, Egon G., 63

habitus concept, 156–7
Haire, Mason, 48–9
Haythornthwaite, Caroline, 104
Henry, Paul, 156, 185
hermeneutics, 22–3, 27, 145, 170
Herodotus, 59, 201
Hill, Carole, 160
Hill, Ronald, 64, 70, 185
Hine, Lewis, 106, 184
Hirschman, Elizabeth, 11, 86
Holbrook, Morris, 10, 61, 86
Holt, Douglas, 23, 64, 156–7, 161
Homer, 85
Hotspex (company), 82
Huberman, A.M., 111
Humphreys, Ashlee, 157
Hunt, Shelby, 11
Huntley, Joan, 193
hyperreality, 69
Hyve (company), 174

immersion: in data, 140; in field phenomena, 63–4, 70, 74, 91
An Inconvenient Truth, 185
infographics, 170, 181
informed consent, 33, 35, 79
innovative theory, 157–8
insights, 7, 169–71, 177–8, 181
in situ research, 4, 73, 91
'interestingness' of research, 189–90
internet resources, 202
interpretation of data, 138–9, 154, 168–9, 186–97; and theory building, 147–8
interpretive nature of research, 2, 185–6
interpretivism, 20
interviews: transcription of, 124–5; videotaping of, 78; see also depth interviews; observational interviewing; online interviews
introspection as part of research, 26, 111
inventories of possessions, 86

Jackson, Janet, 81
Jayashinghe, Laknath, 78
Jones, Robert, 150
jottings: in ethnography, 71–2; in netnography, 117
Journal of Consumer Research, 12, 195
Journal of Marketing, 195
Journal of Marketing Research, 11–12, 195
journals see academic journals; reflexive journals
jurying, 194–5

Kärreman, Dan, 155
Kassarjian, Hal, 206
ketchup bottles, 172
Kozinets, Robert V. (co-author), 7–8, 20, 24, 58, 69–73, 106–7, 115–16, 130, 153–4, 156, 161, 190–1, 196–7, 209–10
Krueger, Richard, 10

Langer, Roy, 109
Langer, Suzanne K., 186
Langley, Anne, 151
Langmaid, Roy, 44, 51
language, consumers' use of, 172, 178–9; compared with what they actually do, 179
language of research, 208–9
Lazarsfeld, Paul, 8–9
learning, supervised, partially-supervised and unsupervised, 97–8
Levi jeans, 161
Lévi-Strauss, Claude, 63
Levy, S., 9, 63
Lewin, Kurt, 160
Lewis, Douglas, 133
Library of Congress, 108
'life-world' concept, 22, 26
Lincoln, Yvonne, 63
Listerine, 175

perspectives in action and *perspectives of action*, 131–2
Pettigrew, Simone, 135–6
Pfeiffer, John, 84–5
phenomenology, 21–2, 26–7, 68, 145
philosophical assumptions underlying research, 21
photographs, use of, 85, 126–9, 133
picture drawing, 49–54
Pittsburgh Children's Hospital, 161
poetry, 190–1
Polo, Marco, 59
postmodern research tradition, 23, 27, 145–6
PowerPoint presentations, 180, 192
Practica (marketing research agency), 134
practical purpose of theory, 160–2, 166, 179
'practice theory' orientation, 59
pre-existing theoretical perspectives, 155–7; *see also* prior research
presentations of research findings, 179–94; *academic* and *managerial*, 192; interactive, 193; what to include, 192–4
Price, Linda L., 64, 69, 79, 190
prior research, 17–20, 188; and coding, 144–5; *see also* pre-existing theoretical perspectives
probes used in interviewing, 38
process theory, 151–2
Procter & Gamble, 174
projective methods, 36, 42, 44–55, 75–6
'prolonged engagement', 70
propositions included in research, 154
protocols: for focus groups or interviews, 35, 39, 42; for qualitative research generally, 167
pseudonyms, use of, 107, 129
psychodrama, 54
public relations films, 85–6
publication outlets for research findings, 7, 158, 194–9

qualitative data analysis (QDA) software, 72, 117, 169–70
qualitative research: beginning a project of, 16–29; credibility and legitimacy of, 9–10; criticisms of and bias against, 11–12; distinguishing characteristics of, 3–4; goals of, 184–5; in marketing, 8–12; quantitative methods used in, 203; time needed for, 204–5; value and importance of, 5–8, 177
qualitative researchers: choices made by, 16–17, 57; education of, 12, 205; as instruments of data collection, 4, 57–8, 66, 120, 137, 206; prior knowledge about the subject of research, 32–3; skills needed by, 6–7, 204–5
quality of analysis, 176–9
quantitative research: attitudes to, 10–11; as distinct from qualitative, 2–3, 93, 203–5

Rapaille, Clotaire, 161
recording of interviews and field experiences, 33, 71–2, 75, 121–6; *see also* audio recording; audio-visual material

recruitment: of focus group members, 41–2; of interviewees, 34
reflexive journals, 71
reflexivity of researchers, 187
Reilly, Michael, 87
research questions, 17–21, 23, 26, 114, 143–4, 165
research traditions, 20–1, 25–9; and coding, 145–7; data collection plans matched to, 26–9
reviews and revision of research reports, 196–9
'rich' data, 3, 93, 113
Richards, Lyn, 117
A Right to Life, 185
'risky shift', 41
Ritson, Mark, 78
Rook, Dennis, 44, 54, 173
Rossell, Daniela, 184

Saatcioglu, Bige, 24
SAMDOK software, 135
Sandikci, Özlem, 129
Sanjek, Roger, 176
Scaraboto, Daiane, 140
Schau, Hope Jensen, 114
Schouten, John W., 64, 69–70
search engines, 99, 114, 169
Second Life, 118
segmentation of consumers, 163–4, 171
self-discovery through qualitative research, 209
self-publication, 196
'semiotic square', 155–6
semiotics, 24, 28, 146
sentence completion, 45–6
sentiment classification, 99
shampoo, protein-based, 174–5
Shaw, George Bernard, 200
Sherry, John, 11, 55–6, 58, 66, 86, 93, 206
shop-alongs, 76–7, 164–6
shopping list studies, 48–9
'sidetrips' in the course of interviews, 39–40
silence used as a probe, 38–9
Sinclair, Upton, 185
Skype, 118
Slater, Don, 106
small samples, use of, 89–90
smartphones, 80, 130, 208
Smith, Philip, 127–8
'snowballing', 34
Sobh, Rana, 31, 58, 128–9, 132–5
social construction, 23–4, 157–8
social engagement as part of qualitative research, 207
social interactions, *face-to-face* and *online*, 106–7
social media, definition of, 106
social mention software, 100–1

social network analysis (SNA), 93, 99, 103–5, 109, 113
social networks, 83
Social Research Inc. (SRI), 8–9
Spencer-Wood, Suzanne M., 86
Spiggle, Susan, 187
Stamey, Mark, 64, 70
Star Trek, 69–73
Statnet software, 104
Stern, Barbara, 11
Stewart, David, 42
story-telling, 190
Strauss, Anselm, 10, 143, 149–50
Sunderland, Patricia L., 66, 79, 133–4, 160
symbol matching, 46–7

taken-for-granted understandings, 23–4, 27, 68, 81, 156–7
target markets, 164
Tate Modern gallery, 136
team research, 76, 168, 206
technological innovation, 202–3
television programmes, analysis of, 85–6
television viewing habits, 81–2, 89
'temporal bracketing' (Langley), 151
textual data, 27–8
thematic stories and thematic apperception tests (TATs), 52–4, 93
theoretical saturation, 70
theory: definition of, 139, 147–8, 160; relevance to management, 164; *see also* practical purpose of theory
theory building, 24, 138–9, 147–8, 154–5
'thick' description, 64, 163, 185–6, 196
Thompson, Alex, 131
Thompson, Craig, 11, 19, 21–2, 156, 204
Tian, Kelly, 34, 127, 133
Titicut Follies, 184
TiVo (company), 81
To Sir with Love, 187
'trackers', 165
transcription of interviews, 124–5
translation (of languages), 31–2, 124
trendspotting, 82–3
triangulation, 28, 127, 186–7
tripods, use of, 130
trust in researchers, 75
Tumbat, Gülnur, 205–6
Tuncay, Linda, 22–3
Twitter, 4, 83, 93–4, 101, 104, 108, 114
Tybout, Alice, 11

Underhill, Paco, 165
understanding, creation of, 185–8; *see also* emotional understanding; taken-for-granted understandings
Üstüner, Tuba, 157

Van Maanen, John, 10, 65, 72, 190
vanitas art, 85
VapoRub, 177–8
variation in data, 148–9
video, use of, 188–91, 194–5; in presentations, 180–1
video diaries, 79–80
video ethnography, 130–1
videography, 77–80, 130, 180
virtual ethnography, 106; *see also* netnography
visual elicitation, 55, 127, 135
voice recognition software, 124, 162–3, 208
Volkswagen cars, 47
Von Hippel, Eric, 174

Wallendorf, Melanie, 11, 64, 69–70, 87, 123, 126, 128, 149, 178, 206
Wal-Mart, 184–5
Walsh, David, 65
Warhol, Andy, 132
Watson, Stephen, 185
web mining, 95, 97
Wesch, Michael, 130
'why?' questions, 37, 153
Williamson, Michael, 184
Wilner, Sarah, 153–4
Wiseman, Frederick, 184
Witkowski, Terrence, 11
Wittgenstein, Ludwig, 208
Wojnicki, Andrea, 153–4
Wolcott, Henry, 111, 138, 187, 192
word association, 44–5
Workman, John Jr, 64

'yes/no' questions, 37–8
YouTube, 80, 83, 86, 134

Zaltman, Gerald, 161, 189
Zaltman, Lindsay, 161
Zaltman Metaphor Elicitation Technique (ZMET), 51, 53, 161, 178
Zhao, Xin, 24–5
Zhou, Nan, 34
Ziller, Robert C., 133
Zwick, Detlev, 209–10

Printed in Great Britain
by Amazon